Conscious Divorce

CONSCIOUS
DIVORCE

Ending a Marriage with Integrity:
A Practical and Spiritual Guide
for Moving On

Susan Allison

THREE RIVERS PRESS
NEW YORK

Published by Three Rivers Press, New York, New York. Member of the Crown Publishing Group.

Random House, Inc. New York, Toronto, London, Sydney, Auckland
www.randomhouse.com

Three Rivers Press is a registered trademark and the Three Rivers Press colophon is a trademark of Random House, Inc.

Printed in the United States of America

Design by Susan Hood

Library of Congress Cataloging-in-Publication Data
Allison, Susan.
    Conscious divorce / Susan Allison.
    1. Divorce. I. Title.
HQ814 .A45 2001
306.89—dc21   00-059735

ISBN 0-609-80808-7

10   9   8   7   6   5   4   3   2   1

First Edition

In memory of my mother, Kay,
whose love continues to heal me

Contents

Give me at our parting
No flowers that fade
Give me no keepsake
Another's hands have made,
Nor the singing silence
Of a final kiss;
Give me for remembrance
Nothing less than this—
To know your heart more swift to feel,
Your eyes more clear to see,
Your hands more strong to serve earth's need
Because of me.

Author unknown

Introduction

I believe in marriage. This is why I remained in my relationship for nearly thirty years. This is also why I encourage my clients, colleagues, and friends to do everything to preserve their marriages. In my case, my husband and I continually worked on our union, and saved our marriage several times. We had regular therapy, went to weekend workshops, took romantic vacations, and did everything else we could think of. And, still, my husband and I divorced. This happened because we didn't know how to express our anger or sadness; we spent too much time working and too much time apart. Finally, we left one another emotionally, and all that remained was to divorce legally. In retrospect, the two of us would have been better friends than lovers and mates, but as twenty-year-olds in college, we did the best we could, eventually raising two wonderful children, and remaining friends to this day.

I am still a proponent of marriage, and, also, I know how important it is to realize when it's time to separate. This doesn't mean I handled my divorce perfectly. I made many mistakes, mostly out of inexperience and fear. At the same time, I feel good about the way my husband and I treated one another. I've also learned about divorce from my clients, colleagues, other professionals, and friends, whom I've interviewed for *Conscious Divorce*. I hope our views and experiences will be of benefit during your own process. The first chapter will guide you in making a decision whether or not to separate. The rest of the text will assist you to lessen your stress and anxiety as you plan your divorce, interact with loved ones and professionals, and negotiate an equitable settlement. *Conscious*

Divorce will help you to feel less guilt and anger as you move confidently into the future, knowing you've done all you can to create the most loving and peaceful divorce possible.

To be conscious means to be perceptive, to act with critical awareness, to show concern and deep feelings of compassion and love. A conscious sense of personal responsibility is needed when deciding whether or not to divorce, because divorce is an act of great magnitude that demands awareness of its potential impact.

One definition of *divorce,* originating from the Latin *divertere,* means "to divert, to change course." This phrase indicates that divorce is about normal change between two people who need to move in new directions. The above definition is without the negative connotations that often accompany the word today. As my colleague Kathy Beckerman, a psychotherapist, says, "It's terrible that it's called divorce. It's sad that our culture doesn't recognize the positive aspects of this life change, such as blended families. It should be called renegotiation." The concept of renegotiation, in which couples jointly redefine their relationship, is at the heart of this book. With the help of this text, which includes the advice of professionals and couples, you can create a conscious divorce, a critically aware dissolution of one stage of your relationship. The connection between you is not severed, just altered.

Initially, the title *Conscious Divorce* may seem paradoxical. How can divorce, which is literally an act of separation and dissolution, also be an act of awareness, unity, compassion, and love? Love, in this context, is not romantic love but deep integrity and respect, a sense of honoring and caring for yourself and others. It is a love that is all-embracing, filled with benevolence and charity. This is the definition of love I use throughout the book, each chapter suggesting how to remain loving to yourself, your partner, and your family, even during the most challenging moments.

This philosophy is built on the Hierarchy of Love, formulated by my colleague and friend, therapist Halimah Ashley. In order of importance, the hierarchy is:

1. The connection to God/Great Spirit/Higher Power/ Highest Consciousness
2. The love of self, gained through listening to intuition/ inner wisdom and taking action
3. The caring for family and friends
4. The love of work and service
5. The love of the rest of humanity
6. The appreciation of other aspects of life

Ashley sees her hierarchy as essential to one's focus and happiness. As she explains it, "If we find ourselves out of balance, sick or unhappy or both, then surely our priorities are out of line, too. If, for instance, love of work is the number-one focus, as it is for millions of Americans, then there is too little connection to God, to our own inner needs, and to the needs of our loved ones. Our life feels more harmonious and we feel healthier when we can balance these priorities."

The most important focus, according to the above hierarchy, is our connection to and respect for the Creative Force in the Universe, which we may call different names. In this text, the "God-Force" mostly will be referred to as Highest Consciousness; please use whatever term you wish. Part of creating a conscious divorce is realizing that we cannot have all the answers. We alone do not have ultimate wisdom or ultimate power. When we need guidance, we can turn to Highest Consciousness, which may be defined as Power, Energy, Love, Spirit, or Source. It is my belief that all creation is "plugged into" this Highest Consciousness; all of us have Spirit or Source within us, this Energy of Love inside. When we turn to Highest Consciousness for help, we may receive it as a feeling of comfort, or if we've asked a question, we receive a sign or answer that feels right. Throughout the text, you will be asked to do exercises in your journal, some of which involve turning to Highest Consciousness. Also, a few of the rituals at the end of chapters ask that you connect with your own Source. This process can help you to feel less alone and more supported during your divorce.

Ashley's hierarchy relates directly to the book's theme and title. As expressed in chapter 1, Careful Choice, if you can ask for guidance about your relationship from Highest Consciousness, then you can love yourself by following intuition and acting with awareness. Then, as presented in chapter 2, Clear Communication, the most respectful thing you can do is to share your realizations with your mate and listen to his or her response. There is no guarantee you'll be heard in the way you desire, but you will have acted consciously. Attempting to be love-centered and aware of your actions, using this hierarchy, is the central principle in the rest of the chapters as well. Caring for yourself and loved ones means handling all financial, legal, familial, and personal needs as presented in chapters 3 through 8. By acting from a compassionate and forgiving perspective, you can heal the issues in your relationship, even as you are leaving it. If, however, you intuitively know you need to divorce, but instead stay with your partner to "love" him or her and be loved, then you are lying to Highest Consciousness, to yourself, *and* to your spouse. You are not acting out of love at all, but out of fear.

Life is richer and more fulfilling when we act out of love instead of fear. As children, we are openly loving and trusting, but after many disappointments while growing up, we hold back and hoard our love, hoping that our ego defenses can protect us. Unfortunately, in the process, we miss many opportunities to be loved and loving. And so, the challenge while going through a divorce is to recognize that the ego wants to be right and safe from fear and pain. If you can recognize and quiet the ego voice, which seeks to defend you and hurt anything threatening its power, then you can listen to the voice of love during the divorcing process. Every time you become angry, resentful, jealous, or spiteful, the ego-self is in charge. The key to handling these negative feelings and reactions is to be aware of the emotions when they surface, to release them appropriately, and to return to whatever thoughts or actions create inner peace. This means acknowledging hateful or blaming thoughts and the desire for revenge, and then focusing instead on your own character and behavior, and what ultimately returns you to harmony.

Seeing a therapist during the divorcing process can help you discover the thoughts and behaviors that are causing unhappiness and distress. Then, you can work on changing your thinking to change your experience. This doesn't mean that you stay in a marriage that no longer works or supports you, nor that you whitewash your spouse's actions, but it means that you honestly acknowledge your own part, as well as the good in the marriage and in your partner. This is best done as a couple, with a neutral therapist helping you to communicate honestly and openly, as you work toward closure in your relationship. If your spouse refuses to go to therapy, as is sometimes the case, then go on your own. To seek help in healing yourself is an act of self-love.

It is also helpful to see a mediator together, rather than hiring separate attorneys, in order to deal with issues that affect you both. The legal system wants you to believe that you need your own attorney to protect you and make sure you win financially. On the contrary, according to those interviewed, hiring separate attorneys actually increases the paranoia and the stress for couples, and escalates the animosity in the process. You also end up spending thousands of dollars on two attorneys, and have a smaller settlement to divide with one another. Instead, you could hire one mediator to meet with you as a couple and help you organize and share all vital financial information. Best of all, a mediator can train you to become better communicators during the divorce and beyond. This is especially important if children are involved, because you will be co-parents who will be discussing the needs of your family. Even if you don't have children, it is less traumatic and more fulfilling to negotiate a fair divorce, and to remain acquaintances, than to battle like enemies over spoils and eventually become strangers. Although you may think you hate your partner at times during the divorce, he or she has been a vital part of your history and your life. Several chapters in this book will emphasize the importance of this partnership and the value of a respectful and cooperative divorce. Good therapists and mediators help you realize you can change your relationship without diminishing its meaning in your life.

You may think your marriage is over from the moment of separation, but it really just takes a different form, and the relationship continues to evolve. This is why it's important to be careful of your words and actions, to realize that this person will still be part of your life, especially if you have children to co-parent. All the past experience and energy between the two of you—the celebrations; the difficulties; home and children; being friends, lovers, and parents, feeling joy and sadness—*everything* still exists and represents this life together. Nothing is wasted. The years are not meaningless, to be erased by a divorce decree. The energy in relationships does not end. It can be transformed. All it takes is consciousness, a decision to love, and time.

Critics of divorce say that our era has given rise to a society of uncommitted, immoral citizens, and the high number of divorces is corroding our world. I believe this is a reactionary view, but I agree with the need for caution, the need to assess our relationships carefully before taking action. We owe ourselves, our partners, our children, and, in a sense, our world, this kind of critical approach. *Conscious Divorce* may not be for newly-weds in their first quarrel. It is for those of you who have done all you can to preserve your marriage, and now realize you must separate. Divorce, according to those interviewed, is not taken lightly, and it affects everyone deeply, whether or not they admit it. Divorce is not the first choice. It is the final solution.

We know from studying statistics on life changes that divorce is second only to the death of a loved one in terms of stress. In my experience, divorce can be even more challenging. When someone dies, there is always cause and even logic; if the illness is prolonged, we have time to prepare emotionally for the person's death. Afterward, established rituals and ceremonies help us to mourn our loved one. In divorce, however, the reasons for leaving are often emotional and subjective, and society has no standard rituals or ceremonies to ease the mourning process. In America, we are told in childhood, from fairy tales, movies, and parents' stories, that people marry for love based on physical attraction and romantic ideals. This search for love and home is lifelong, and the number of relationship books illustrates this focus on romance, on finding a soul mate, on reaching a safe, blissful haven. And so, after finally finding a mate, marrying in a symbolic ceremony, and settling down for life, we are shocked to discover we aren't happy and do not want to be in this relationship, or our partner confronts us with this realization. Divorce, then, is not just the tremendous loss of another person; it is the loss of the dream you have believed since childhood. And it doesn't seem to matter whether you are leaving or being left, have been married half a lifetime or three months (as the interviews will illustrate)—the stages of loss, in varying degrees, will visit you at some point in the divorcing process.

We experience loss on many levels, from denial and confusion to fear and anger, from guilt to sadness, grief, and final acceptance. In order to help you understand your feelings and behavior, the stages and emotions associated with loss will be presented in detail in the chapters that follow.

Each of the eight chapters of *Conscious Divorce* presents a chronological stage in the dissolution process:

Careful Choice
Clear Communication
Practical Planning
Separation
The Divorcing Process
Loved Ones
Self-Care
Healing the Heart

Each chapter contains suggested plans of action, journaling exercises, and optional rituals to perform. *Conscious Divorce* has been written from research and from interviews with clients, colleagues, and friends. It has also been formed by my own experience of separation and divorce, taken from personal journals, therapy sessions, and workshops. My purpose in writing *Conscious Divorce* is to help you feel less anxious and more hopeful while going through your divorce, to encourage you to be honest with yourself and your partner, to be respectful and honorable, in order to create a fair and amicable divorce. My hope is that this book will help you through each day and will encourage you to remain loving and peaceful, to know that for every stage, every week, every month, divorce is a teacher, the lessons are internalized, the awareness is great. Acceptance will come.

1

Careful Choice

A white crescent
moon
pales to silver
as the sun rises—
    whispers:
"Listen
to
your heart's voice."
       Genesis

Making the decision whether or not to leave a relationship may be the most daunting part of the divorcing process; at least it is the one filled with the most anxiety. This is partly because divorce is a choice made of our own free will, and we sense the enormity of this responsibility. Also, confusion and indecision are uncomfortable for most of us. We want this initial stage to be over, so we can move on. At the same time, we realize that our choice will affect our partners, our families, and our friends; it will be a decision we must live with all our lives. We want to choose carefully.

This chapter and book are for those of you contemplating a separation and divorce. If you feel you are not the one choosing to end your marriage but your partner is, this section and text can still be of great value. It can offer an explanation of the stages and process of divorce, an understanding of your feelings, and a possible course of action. The exercises can help any of you questioning whether or not to stay in a relationship, no matter who initiated the process. Making the initial decision can be challenging, and the purpose of this chapter is to make your process easier and less stressful.

One of my workshop participants, Marion, whose husband initiated their divorce, comments, "At first, I didn't want the divorce, mostly because of the children, and my fear of being on my own. But with therapy, I realized I hadn't been happy for years. Deep down I knew I needed to leave, but I just couldn't do it myself." And so, when contemplating a divorce, intuition and intellect can help us make a decision. If we feel unsure about our choice, we need to trust that the answer is already inside us. All we have to do is listen to our intuition, think about our choices and their consequences, and decide the next course of action.

EARLY INKLINGS

The choice to stay or leave begins in "the gut." Eileen, a former client, points to her stomach when she says, "I knew something was wrong months and even years before I left each of my relationships; I felt it in my gut. I didn't always take action as soon as I should have, but my body knew." I, too, felt the misgivings about my marriage in my body. These first warnings came on my wedding day, but I didn't heed them. Standing in the shower, the ceremony an hour away, my heart pounded and my head hurt. My body knew I felt unsure, but it was too terrifying to bring to consciousness. He was my dear friend, and I respected and trusted him. Our guests waited at the church; a white satin dress and gossamer veil hung in the closet, and bridesmaids laughed in the next room. But I ignored my inner voice that knew I was uncertain, and, instead, I married for security and companionship. My body knew the truth but swallowed its secret for more than twenty years.

When my husband was away for three months and I had the space and silence to breathe, I finally allowed this realization to surface. I wrote in my journal, "I'm glad he's away. I'm free to eat and sleep when I want, to write all night, to completely be myself for the first time." In trying to be the perfect wife, I adapted so thoroughly to my husband that I lost my own artistic nature. Guiltily, I dreaded his homecoming and going back to a false life, but this time I couldn't return. Like Pandora, I had removed the lid, releasing the honest feelings inside my body. Finally, after two decades, my real self was out, and not only did she not fit in the box, she was unwilling to go back.

During this period of discovery, I attended personal-growth workshops and spent time alone thinking about my life and writing in my journal. These experiences helped fine-tune my intuition, which had been dormant since childhood. As children, our intuition is very present. If we don't want a certain food, we refuse to eat it; our bodies and minds know instinctively if we're hungry and what it is we want. We say exactly what we think. We know if we like the color red, if a shirt is scratchy, and we won't wear it even if Grandma gave it to us. Children listen to their inner voices on a moment-to-moment basis, unlike adults, who eat by the clock, wear fashionable, uncomfortable clothes, and say the right thing in order to please other people. As adults leading busy lives, we get caught up in what we *should* be doing to be successful, and don't always stop to listen to our intuition. This may continue until a crisis occurs in our life: a family member dies, we are injured or seriously ill, or problems occur in a relationship. Then we are forced to pay attention to our true feelings.

ACCESSING THE INTUITION

Intuition comes from the Latin verb *intueri,* which means "to look or to know from within." It is immediate insight or awareness of what is true that comes as an inner voice. No one knows exactly where intuition resides, but it seems to come first from the body and then from the mind. For centuries people have said, "Follow your heart; listen to your gut," and have used expressions such as "heartfelt" and "gut reaction." In my experience, I first feel a knowing in my stomach, a hunch or hint about an issue, and then a word or phrase comes into my mind; it is instantaneous, and at times defies precise tracking. Remembering Ashley's Hierarchy of Love, from the introduction, listening to the intuition is about loving yourself. It's about trusting the voice of deepest truth and wisdom within you, first asking for guidance from Highest Consciousness, then lovingly following the voice and message you hear. Even if your intuition is dormant, it can be awakened with practice, trusted, and heeded. More specifically, accessing the intuition can help you decide whether or not to divorce.

The following intuition exercises can be written in a notebook or journal. I suggest keeping a journal during the decision-making process and for all the chapters in this book. It might seem unnatural at first if you've never written in a notebook or diary. Trust me. Writing in your journal will be a creative and emotional outlet. It will be your friend. It can save you thousands of dollars in therapy bills. Please, just do it. Before beginning the exercises, you may want to turn to the last section of chapter 1, entitled Optional Rituals. If you wish, you can perform a ritual before the intuition exercises, as preparation, and then afterward as a form of closure.

When you are ready to begin, use a stream-of-consciousness approach: try not to think too long, and instead, write quickly what comes to mind. First thoughts or feelings are often the deepest, most truthful ones. If you spend several minutes going back and forth, trying to decide what to write, you might record what *should* be believed or done, perhaps from society's perspective, rather than what your own true feelings tell you to do. It is important to be alone and have plenty of time to do these exercises. Once you're settled comfortably, take one or more deep breaths. Imagine inhaling positive energy, especially love, and exhaling all negative energy, especially fear.

Close your eyes and relax. Sit a few moments in silence, listening to your breath, quieting your mind and body. This is the process in Zen Buddhism called *beginner's mind,* in which the mind is like an empty rice bowl. When it is truly empty, it is open to be filled with insight by unconscious knowing. If you meditate or pray in a specific way, do so before beginning to write. The point is to clear your mind of all distractions, to feel relaxed and open to all possibilities.

Intuition Exercises

These questions begin generally, and in the next section, progress to specific queries about your relationship. The only guideline is to tell the truth by quickly writing down the first response that comes to mind. There is no right answer, only what is true for you. Open your journal and write "Intuition Exercises," then the number, and your answer.

1. What is your favorite color?
2. During what part of the day is your energy highest?
3. What is your least favorite food?
4. Which season do you like best?
5. What makes you happy?
6. How does rain make you feel?
7. Which holiday was your favorite as a child?
8. Where have you traveled that you've enjoyed?

9. What is one word that describes you?
10. Do you dream in color?
11. What is your happiest childhood memory?
12. What room in your house is your favorite?
13. What do you like most about your body?
14. Who is your best friend?
15. When was the last time you felt joy?
16. What would you grab first from your burning house?
17. What two possessions would you want to have with you on a deserted island?
18. For which parent do you feel the most love?
19. What is the deepest regret of your life?
20. What is it you have always wanted to do?

Now, look at your answers, and don't change any. Just read them over. Do any surprise you? Write down which ones, and your feelings about these answers. Perhaps elaborate on your initial answers. For instance, if you wrote "mother" for number eighteen, what else comes up for you regarding your answer? Why didn't you write "father"? Do you have any feelings about this? Keep journaling until you feel complete. Do this for every answer that makes you think or question something. Overall, write down what you learned from this exercise. Finally, can you hear your inner voice or intuition? Let's proceed to questions about your relationship.

Again, answer the following questions quickly in your journal, recording your first thought or reaction. Some answers may require more than a one-word response. Write the truth. Trust the process. Take a deep breath and begin.

1. Did you love your partner when you were first married?
2. Why did you get married?
3. Do you love your spouse now?
4. Why are you still married?

5. How do you and your partner get along?

6. What do you and your spouse have in common?

7. What do you like most about your partner?

8. What do you like least about him or her?

9. How does your spouse treat you?

10. How would you like to be treated?

11. How do you treat him or her?

12. When were you happiest in this marriage, and why?

13. Are you happy in this relationship right now?

14. What would you like to change or improve in this marriage?

15. Do you think it's possible to improve your marriage? Why or why not?

16. What have you done personally to make your relationship better?

17. What are your greatest fears about staying married?

18. What are your greatest fears about divorcing?

19. Do you have children? What role do they play in your choice?

20. Overall, what does your gut, or intuition, tell you to do about your marriage?

Which of these answers surprises you? Write these reactions in your journal. What are the emotions coming up right now? Feel them. Write about these feelings in your notebook. Do this for every question that seems to require more response. Take all the time you need. What is your overall realization? Write one sentence to express this truth.

When facing a confusing or challenging issue, it helps to write down feelings and ideas quickly without stopping to edit or question. This keeps the unconscious mind moving and your beliefs surfacing. Use this technique in the following exercises to discover your deepest thoughts and feelings. Write the question and answer in your journal, including everything that surfaces, both positive and negative. Begin with the expression "I feel . . . ," and if you get stuck, write "I feel . . ." again and keep writing. Don't censor yourself or edit your work. Just be totally honest. Stop when you feel complete or emptied of this issue.

1. What do I feel about my current relationship and partner?

In questions two and three, begin with the words "I want" and write fast. If you pause or get stuck, just write "I want" and begin again. Don't worry about practicality or reality. Imagine that you have all the choices and resources you need. Just write your heart's desire about the relationship and the life you want. When I did this exercise, it came out as a poem, but the form is immaterial. The most important thing is to honestly realize your deepest truth and write it down. End when it feels complete.

2. What do I want in a relationship?
3. Ideally, what kind of life do I want to be living?

The journal becomes a way to process and record what may have been stored inside you for many years. Reading your words becomes a concrete confirmation that you are beginning to make a decision that is completely your own. This discovery can be exhilarating, and at the same time, frightening. Everything you have thought to be true may now be in question. Allow these feelings to surface before, during, and after writing in your journal. Notice if your existing marriage has the qualities you listed for an ideal relationship, or if it does not. Take in this realization.

Finally, is it possible for you and your partner to change, for the relationship to come closer to what you want? Write your immediate response of "yes" or "no" in your notebook. Then write quickly how this can or cannot happen.

When finished, reread your response. How are you doing emotionally? Be aware of your feelings. Perhaps take a break. Lie down, have some tea, go for a walk, do whatever would be supportive right now. Let the realizations come and go. It may help to say phrases such as, "Everything I'm discovering is creating my greatest good. I trust my inner voice and know all is well."

If your answers to these questions indicate there are problems in your marriage, and even that you want a separation or divorce, you may not want to take immediate action. It isn't rational to initiate a divorce based on one questionnaire. What you can do, however, is think about your responses, keep writing in your journal, take the survey again, and see how you feel in a week or two. In the meantime, you can also talk with a therapist, a friend, or colleague, someone who is going to listen attentively to you. It helps to process all your realizations in writing or verbally, and fully express your truthful feelings. It is also important to take care of your health, focusing on proper rest, exercise, and nutrition. If you need specific suggestions about personal health, turn to chapter 7, Self-Care. Remember to treat yourself as you would a loved one or best friend, with kind and gentle nurturing.

If your partner is aware of the issues in your marriage, and would be open to talking about them with you alone or with a therapist, this would be a good time. If you are already in couples' counseling, and it feels safe, discuss your answers to the above intuition exercises with your partner, having him or her take the questionnaire, too. Part of creating a conscious relationship is to share your feelings with your spouse when you sense it's the right time. The point is, be careful of your actions. Don't act rashly, but don't discount your intuitive responses either. Let your answers and feelings settle for a while. Let yourself daydream about the choices you have, the options and their consequences.

OPTION ONE: DO NOTHING

After hearing the messages of the intuition, you have many options. One choice is not to choose at all but to put away your journal and do nothing. Be aware that this decision may come from fear. Our realizations are so scary, so revolutionary that we cannot face them. We consciously choose homeostasis, to have stability and normalcy. Our marriage may not be ideal or even good, but it is familiar and we are used to it. This is one reason people stay in relationships, even abusive ones, longer than they should. What is known is somehow comforting, and the unknown can seem terrifying. Don't forget, however, that you chose to read this book for a reason. If you sense that there are problems in your marriage, or you feel unhappy in some way, these initial feelings will not disappear. In taking the intuition survey, perhaps you've realized you want changes in your marriage or your spouse. Unless you act on this discovery, your relationship will continue as it is, and you will still have misgivings even if you try not to.

In my own marriage, I stayed for twenty-six years. I wasn't physically abused, but I was neglected. My husband traveled three months a year, while I cared for our children and juggled home and career. When he didn't travel, he worked six days a week as well as evenings, while the children and I spent time together. As I became aware of my own needs as a woman and parent, I realized I no longer wanted to be married to someone who was physically and emotionally absent. But it took me a quarter of a century to act on this realization. One woman, Jade, was married for forty-six years and lived with an alcoholic all this time. Her own children, other family, and friends told her she deserved more, but she wasn't ready to leave her husband. It took a trip with a friend to help her gain the perspective and the courage to leave, which she did upon returning home.

Lana is still with her husband of eighteen years, but she is talking to friends and family about leaving. She has known for at least ten years that she needs to leave, but it is only now that she feels the courage and the support to do so. Constance was married to her first husband for twenty-two years and says she stayed twenty years too long. Finally, she left when their two children were grown, and she has been in a fulfilling second marriage for the past twelve years. If you are choosing to stay and do nothing at this point, it is understandable. However, inaction can be a kind of death. The longer we remain in rigid roles and patterns that no longer have meaning, the more depressed and powerless we feel. To choose, to act, to change, is to feel alive.

OPTION TWO: STAY AND CHANGE

Another choice is to stay and recommit to the relationship. After doing the exercises, you realize there is hope for your marriage. You do not want to separate or divorce. What you want is change. Perhaps you hoped that thinking about divorce and even discussing it with your spouse would bring about the improvement you want. Be careful not to threaten your partner with something you don't really want to do. This could backfire and cause you tremendous unhappiness. Attorney Laika Grant Mann advises, "If you don't really want a divorce, but what you want is change, then don't threaten your partner with divorce so he or she will shape up. I've seen so many clients, mostly women, who tell their husbands they want them to change or they're getting a divorce, and the men say, 'fine.' They move out, find someone else very quickly, and the wives are crying in my office about not really getting what they wanted." It would be wiser to talk to your spouse about how you're feeling, ask him or her to go to therapy, and work on your marriage. For those of you who wish to stay in an existing marriage, thousands of books and clinicians exist to help you. Briefly, I am including some suggestions here.

At this point, relief may be the prominent emotion, relief that the marriage is not ending, the relationship is not dead but only in need of revitalization. Be careful not to be lulled into false optimism. The reasons that first drove you to read this book, to do these exercises, still exist and must be addressed if change and progress are to occur. Furthermore, you have been reading, writing, and feeling deep feelings about your marriage and partner while reading this book. Perhaps you have been trying to decide whether to stay in your relationship for many weeks, months, or years. Has your spouse been doing the same? If he or she has been on a similar course, including sharing these insights with you, then the prognosis is good. Talk to one another; share these realizations; compare notes on what you want in a relationship. Perhaps go to a therapist or continue to see one, and talk about these issues.

Overall, what is important is communication, lots of it. Chapter 2, Clear Communication, presents ways to talk to one another and get results. You can agree to spend more time together, plan a trip, make love in new places, and whatever else works. The keys are willingness, determination, and action. A marriage and family therapist agrees: "Whatever you first loved in your partner is still there, still exists. All you need to do is rediscover it."

If, however, one partner has not been exploring his or her feelings about the marriage, then more work must be done. It is usually the case that one spouse initiates the process of questioning the relationship and sharing these realizations with the other partner. This process can be mutual; ideally, both partners will want to make an effort to change the marriage for the better. If one spouse sees nothing wrong with the relationship and likes things the way they are, it can be more difficult. Laika Grant Mann says that in her experience one spouse is nearly always in denial, saying he or she is shocked at the partner's unhappiness or desire to change things. This spouse must be willing to listen, look at his or her behavior, and choose to work on the marriage, if progress is to be made.

Once we realize that we're not completely happy in our relationship and we know what we want, it's hard to go back, to pretend we are satisfied, to pretend we haven't been enlightened. In fact, I think it's nearly impossible to suppress this truth. If this is the case for you, it's important to say something to your spouse such as, "I'd like some things to change in our relationship. I hope we can work together to create an even better marriage." Rachel, married for seventeen years, said something similar to her husband Bill. Unfortunately, he denied that anything needed changing, and he refused to go to therapy. Over several years, she did everything she could to preserve their marriage, but she could not do it alone. All you can do is ask for what you want with love and honesty, knowing that you cannot direct what your spouse decides.

Once again, the next step is honest dialogue with or without a therapist, and the sometimes lengthy process of renegotiating the marriage contract. By this I mean potentially changing much of the relationship, from the way you communicate, to the quality of time spent together. Everything may come into question. Everything may need to change. Sometimes the process can save a marriage, as John, a former client, married for thirty years, expresses. "Fifteen years ago I had an affair. My wife discovered it and confronted me. I realized I hadn't been happy for years, and, in a sense, wanted her to catch me. I wanted her to realize that her withdrawal had hurt me deeply, and I wanted to punish her. After many sessions with our therapist, and plenty of tears, I realized I still loved her very much and wanted to stay." If you want to work on your marriage, don't wait. Begin right now.

OPTION THREE: PREPARE TO LEAVE

If you have decided to leave your relationship, it usually doesn't mean you pack your bags and move out. However, if you are in an abusive marriage, especially a physically violent one, you need to leave immediately. This book does not address the issues of abusive relationships, except to advise action. One of my clients, Jeri, married four years, whose husband tried to strangle her, says, "Get out. Get out now. It's not going to improve permanently. Sure he may apologize each time, beg forgiveness and even cry, but when the stress builds, he's going to do it again. Save yourself and your kids." A word of caution. Call a local women's crisis agency or family therapy center while your partner is away from home. Get the address of the local shelter, pack whatever is necessary, and leave before he returns.

Some of you, who intuitively know you want to separate, may decide to wait a while before taking any action. This becomes a time for careful thought and planning. Many of those interviewed stayed a year or more after their first thoughts of leaving. The reasons for this are diverse. Joshua, married for eight years, felt that he needed this time to be with his children because they were so young. Leaving his wife meant leaving the children he loved so much. It took him ten months to finally tell his partner he wanted a divorce, and another four months before he actually moved out. Michael stayed three years after he first felt the misgivings and sensed he wanted to leave. Financial problems, and a fear of being alone, caused him to stay longer than he wished. He shared his feelings in a recent workshop. "I knew I no longer loved Patty, but I didn't think I could make it on my own. She had a better job and brought in twice the salary I did. I felt the stress of starting my own business, and it took three years to begin seeing a profit. Then I could leave."

Part of creating a conscious divorce involves carefully planning a course of action. A few months before my husband and I separated, I researched the housing market and knew exactly where I wanted to live and what I could afford. I knew what I wanted to take from our house, such as my computer and mountain bike. I opened my own bank account and stopped sleeping in the same bed before we discussed a separation. In some ways, I wish I had talked with my husband before taking these steps, but I feared I would hurt him, or he would convince me to stay. Now I realize it would have hurt him less, and improved our communication, if I had told him sooner. Attorney and divorce mediator Chip Rose suggests telling your partner how you're feeling as early as possible. He says that, otherwise, feelings of anger and betrayal will escalate, and the chance of being able to communicate calmly and practically will lessen. You can plan whatever is necessary for your own survival, but don't take any action that will be seen as a threat to your mate. Remember, the two of you are still married, and perhaps parenting together as well. Potentially, you may always have a relationship with one another, divorced or not. It is essential that you do nothing to cause a bigger tear in the fabric of your marriage.

OPTION FOUR: SEPARATE AT HOME

Peter and Jennifer, married for six years, found that they could not reconcile their differences, but could not afford to live apart. Their choice: live separately in the same house. This option is not ideal, in that if a decision has been made to sever the relationship, the tension can be palpable. Peter made these comments in a couples' session: "I don't want this divorce. I don't want to sleep separately. I feel pissed off every time she walks by. But I guess we need to save money and have to live under one roof." Jennifer adds, "We have no choice but to live together. It's hard, but in some ways it's a good transition to living apart. Finally after years of begging him, Peter's coming to therapy and we're resolving some stuff. Not enough to stay married, but it's helping us move on." For most couples, living in separate parts of the house is not a permanent arrangement, but a stopgap, usually needed for financial reasons. Terry, married nearly nine years, slept on the couch for a year because his wife was ill, and his young children needed him there full-time. This was not ideal, but it was a necessary part of their process. When his wife healed, and after many counseling sessions, they separated.

OPTION FIVE: SEPARATE AND DIVORCE

If you have decided to separate and file for divorce, or your partner has made this decision, then you can begin to take action. The rest of this book gives the specific stages and tools.

THE EMOTIONS DURING
THE STAGE OF CAREFUL CHOICE

During the decision-making stage, the most important thing to realize is that having emotions is completely natural; whatever you're feeling at any time is perfect. No emotions are *wrong,* even though you may have been told this by others. Janice, a middle child in a family of six, was told by her parents not to get angry or cry in public; so she learned to yell or cry alone in the bathroom. This early experience made it difficult for her to be emotional as an adult going through a separation and divorce. Having feelings is the healthiest thing you can do anytime, especially when going through a stressful period.

It's a good idea to set aside the necessary time to feel your feelings. When I first began the process of leaving my husband, my emotions constantly surfaced, but I couldn't burst into tears or go into a rage while at work or at the grocery store. So I had to schedule time alone in nature or at home. When I tried to hide my emotions, I got headaches and stomachaches, or suffered from insomnia or depression. Also, at times, I took out my unresolved feelings on my children, colleagues, or friends. This is why it is helpful to allow your emotions to surface, and to express them. Your own health, and your ability to function normally and interact with others, depend on it.

If you're in therapy, continue to share your feelings with your counselor. If you're not in counseling, I suggest finding someone soon. It's a good idea to interview potential therapists. One of the most important criteria in choosing a therapist is your intuition. Choose the individual with whom you have the most rapport and connection, someone who listens and is supportive. Then, you can freely share your emotions, and feel better in the process.

Denial

When a situation is too difficult, too stressful, too unbelievable, the mind blocks the reality. If you are unable to absorb the fact that your relationship may be ending, you experience the symptoms of shock, termed "denial" in the grieving process. Denial is the mind's way of dealing with such overwhelming reality. In order to cope, you may feel numb and distant from all that is happening, drifting through your days feeling empty and unfocused. This is a normal reaction to stress, and you need to be gentle and compassionate with yourself. If you are in shock, you may tire quickly or not feel like doing much at all. Your body might feel heavy, your speech might be slower than usual, your mind dazed. It is vital to listen to your mind and body, to rest, work sensibly, exercise moderately, eat balanced meals, and be patient. I talk more about denial in chapter 4, Separation.

In time, as you adjust, the numbness lifts, and a new set of emotions will surface.

Confusion

While in the process of making a decision, you may feel confused. One moment you may want to leave, and the next, to stay. Confusion has been the uncomfortable emotion prompting you to find clarity and make a choice. By using the intuition exercises and writing down your answers, you become clearer. Any time you feel confused, it is wise to open your journal and write, "I feel confused about . . ." "What I'm really feeling is . . ." "What I truly want is . . ." If you hate to write, do it anyway, or talk into a tape recorder, to a therapist, or perhaps to a friend. Friends are not always the best choice because they want to give advice, but all we usually want is someone to listen. If you are talking to a friend, set the ground rules first: No advice. No interrupting. Little self-disclosure about their own issues. Friends have had their own relationships, and they may project on us these positive or negative experiences.

A social worker and former client, Sandra, found herself getting angry with her best friend, Cynthia, who was leaving her husband. Upon reflection, and after discussing this with her friend, Sandra realized that because her own husband had left her, she was projecting the rage she never had directed at her mate. Several of my friends wanted to give me advice, especially the ones who were divorced. Most of them told me not to leave my marriage, and even became upset with me when I decided to divorce. Over time, these relationships healed, but I took care of myself by not calling or seeing two friends for several months after my separation. In order to love and support yourself, be careful how and with whom you share your confused feelings. Unless you have an extraordinary friend, I recommend writing in your journal and talking with your therapist.

Guilt

Guilt occurs when we blame ourselves for what is happening. Often the person initiating the process of a possible separation and divorce feels the most guilt, and the other partner feels the most self-righteous anger. Of course, individuals feel the entire gamut of emotions from moment to moment, but guilt often has a link to some form of real or imagined wrongdoing. For those of us raised in religious households, especially ones in which the words *sin, shame, damnation, hell,* and *repentance* have been commonly used, guilt may be deeply embedded.

Even for those of us raised in nonreligious homes, guilt exists in some form. Perhaps we had a parent, peer, or teacher who shamed us at one time, helping us to layer these guilty feelings until we created an inner core of shame. As a child, I received many shaming messages. One was from my fifth-grade teacher, who announced to the class that my mother had written my poem for me, and she threw it in the trash. Not only did I hide my poetry until a few years ago, but for many years I felt guilty for being successful. Some writers speak of "healthy shame" or "healthy guilt," referring to the importance of conscience and responsibility for one's actions. For the purpose of this book, guilt will not be referred to as healthy.

In fact, as a friend and colleague of mine has stated, "Guilt is a useless emotion, causing much more harm than good." She sees guilt as part of the core of shame created since childhood, a core that burdens the individual and causes low self-esteem, depression, and immobility. On the other hand, guilt lets us know we have a conscience; we have a responsibility to ourselves and to others, and when we have hurt someone, we can make amends. Guilt, however, should not be the reason to stay with partners, becoming martyrs on the crosses we build.

If, during the process of decision making, you are feeling guilt, that nagging sense of wrongdoing, then use it as a "feeling barometer," helping you to discover your inner atmosphere. Again, it helps to write in your journal, beginning with "old guilt" from childhood and working up to the present and any "new guilt" related to your relationship.

Old and New Guilt

In your journal, title the page "Old Guilt" and write down as quickly as possible what you have felt guilty about in your life. Some of these guilty feelings may be resolved and some may not. Begin each sentence with "I feel guilty about . . ." and don't stop to judge or debate the reasons. Just write in a stream of consciousness fashion to empty all the guilt. As you write, your feelings might range from anger to resentment to sadness. This is perfectly natural. Just let the feelings surface and let them out. When you feel complete with this exercise (no other examples are coming to you), then review what you have written. From which part of your life have you absorbed the most guilt? From family, school, church, sports, in friendships, and so on? Write a sentence or two about this. Notice the guilt that has been resolved or forgiven and the guilt that is still with you. Star the numbers or statements that you still feel guilty about. Next, you can forgive yourself and others in order to "clean the slate," to release the guilt and no longer feel burdened. Write the sentence, "I forgive myself (or a person's name) for (state what happened)." You can write this phrase as many times as you wish, until you release the past and feel a sense of peace and acceptance.

Next, title your journal page "New Guilt," and write as quickly as you can all the things you feel guilty about in your current relationship, beginning with the phrase "I feel guilty about. . . ." Write fast, and squelch the critic and editor. When you are finished and the exercise feels complete, look over your answers. Which statements are purely about you? Which did your spouse have a part in, too? For example, I chose to leave my husband, and I felt enormous guilt because I abandoned him. However, upon reflection, he had abandoned me years earlier, choosing to work twelve-hour days and travel extensively. We were both responsible for our choice to divorce. It takes two. This is a time of honesty and fairness, not self-mutilation. You can choose to let the guilt go, to forgive yourself and your spouse by using the technique illustrated in the section on old guilt, writing forgiveness statements until you feel a sense of completion and relief.

As a point of reference, the following statements from my clients express the most common feelings of guilt.

1. If we split up, it's all my fault because I first brought it up. If I hadn't said anything, things would still be okay.
2. How can I be thinking of leaving? My partner can't survive without me. Maybe he or she will completely fall apart or die.
3. How can I possibly think of leaving my children? I'm destroying my family. I'm destroying my kids' lives.
4. What will people think of me, wanting to get a divorce? I'll lose everyone's respect. I'll lose my parents, my in-laws, and our friends.
5. I've had doubts for a while. How could I be such a liar, and not tell the truth sooner?
6. How can I be so selfish? All I want is my own way.

7. I should have done more to keep this marriage together. How could I be so irresponsible?
8. If only I had been better in bed, a better provider, a better cook, a better organizer, etc., then this wouldn't be happening.
9. What am I doing thinking of my own happiness? What about the happiness of my family?
10. I'm horrible to be sexually attracted to other people, and not to my husband or wife.
11. My marriage isn't that bad. What am I thinking?

Perhaps you can relate to some of the feelings of guilt expressed above, and can also recognize the overgeneralization in each statement. This comes about because guilt is a grandiose emotion. We think we are solely responsible for the problems in our relationship, and perhaps for world hunger and the international debt as well. Looking clearly and honestly at your own journal exercise should illustrate the point that both of you *share* the success or failure of your marriage. It is a dance between two people, not a solo ballet performance. Yes, you may have lied or said something that hurt your spouse; you may have left in the middle of an argument or used the silent treatment for days. However, why did you do these things? You're not acting in a vacuum. You are responding to many other factors, including your partner's behavior.

This doesn't mean that if you've done something hurtful, you shouldn't apologize. One of the most healing phrases to use in a relationship is, "I'm sorry." This isn't to be done so you can feel even more guilt. Nor are you telling your partner that he or she is right, and you are completely wrong. All you are doing is making amends for your part. That's all. This act of apologizing also can eliminate the guilt and allow for self-forgiveness. It can diminish the ego and help the two of you open your hearts. It can create a climate for honest communication. At this stage, you may not feel ready to make amends, but perhaps you will later. Two other chapters—Clear Communication and Healing the Heart—offer chances to forgive and make amends. You will know when it's time.

Fear

Fear, according to my friend and mentor Judy Wardell-Halliday, stands for "feeling ego as real." In other words, fear comes from thoughts in the mind that originate from the ego's projections. When life seems uncertain, the outcome unknown, our minds play with possible scenes to make the situation less formidable. Sometimes our minds run ahead, creating horrific pictures of what could happen to us. Fear, then, is not real, but the ego would like us to think it is. Our focus, then, is on eliminating fearful thoughts and beliefs as they arise, replacing them with a sense of trust and feelings of love. In this way, life can be lived more peacefully in the present moment. While making a decision about your relationship, it may seem difficult to stay in the present. You may be thinking either of what occurred in the past or what might occur in the future. Often, we are powerless to do anything about what happened or will happen, yet the tapes in our minds keep rewinding and fast-forwarding. Fear thrives in this focus on the past and future. If you want to feel a sense of peace instead of fear, it's helpful to stay in the present moment, focusing on what you can change and letting go of what you can't.

At the same time, it is a normal human reaction to feel afraid during the decision-making process. You are deciding whether or not to end your marriage. What, except for death, is potentially more upsetting? Don't discount your feelings. Feel them, and realize that fear is energy; reframed, it is excitement, the thrill of newness and of great adventure. At first, though, fear is just plain fear. You may be afraid of being left or of being alone. You may fear you will never love again or be loved. In itself, the prospect of all that lies ahead, including the possible emotional pain, can cause you to fear this change. This reaction is natural, but how will you cope with your anxiety?

The first step is to acknowledge and feel the fear. Then, journaling can help to make the intangible, fearful thoughts more understandable. First, write what you fear in general, beginning with, "I'm afraid. . . ." Write down each of your fears, until the list feels complete. Then, go back and write options or solutions for the fears that are realistic. This will dispel the fear by making the issue more concrete, and it will help you take action. Next, answer the question, "What do I fear most?" I did this exercise in my journal while camping alone in the California desert. I wrote, "My greatest fear is living alone without love." During the three days of solitude, I discovered we are never alone; we are surrounded by the natural world, its sounds, its silence, and its beauty. By the end of my stay, I realized I had never felt more secure and loved in my life. Our greatest fears usually involve the ultimate terror that we will be abandoned in the universe. Steve, who divorced at forty-eight, spoke of his fear. "My health hasn't been so good. I had a melanoma removed a year ago, and then my wife left. I found myself waking up in the middle of the night and thinking, 'I don't want to die alone.' "

In conducting interviews I have found that the major fears that arise during the decision-making process are about others' judgments, finances, the children, being alone, and facing the unknown. You will be doing exercises in the next few sections to help you identify and release your fears.

Fear of Others' Judgments

During the several months before I left my marriage, I felt incredibly vulnerable to others' opinions, especially those of people closest to me. My husband's parents were dead, but I still worried about his brother's response and the reaction of my mother. My brother-in-law had been divorced three times and lived out of state, and was not involved closely in our lives. My mother, on the other hand, had lost my father recently and lived alone, and I was her only child. I felt terrified she would disown me or somehow love or respect me less for even considering a separation. But I underestimated her. My mother's only words during this stage were, "All I want is your happiness; I know you will make the right decision." A tremendous weight lifted from me in that moment.

My friends, however, told me I was crazy to leave such a wonderful man, to leave my home and security. In each case, my friends projected on me what had happened in their own lives and gave advice based on these experiences. I know this now, but at the time I felt desperate and depended on them to tell me what to do. The best thing is to listen to others objectively, realizing that they, too, have made mistakes and are likely not experts either when it comes to relationships.

Wanting the approval of everyone is unrealistic; we've never had it before and will not have it now. Generally, it's best to say very little at first except to your spouse and therapist. Telling too many people just complicates the issues and causes unnecessary worry and confusion. Once a decision has been reached, it isn't wise to share it with someone who is critical and judgmental; that type of person can make the situation more difficult and increase your level of stress. Choose which family members and friends you can trust, and tell them what you've decided. The people who honestly love you, who know the inner you, will continue to support you no matter what.

Financial Fears

One reason people stay in a relationship is because of economic worries. A couple used to two incomes, to sharing expenses for their home and family, are naturally afraid of the financial difficulties associated with divorce. Rightly so. Two people living together can live more cheaply than two people living separately. Where there was one mortgage or rental payment, one electric bill, one phone bill, and so on, there will be twice the bills if one partner moves out.

At this point, to help you alleviate any concerns, open your journal and list all of your financial fears, beginning with the words, "I'm concerned/scared/nervous about . . ." When you're finished, look over the unrealistic fears and acknowledge their lack of substance. You can erase them, cross them out, burn them, or just picture them dissolving or floating away. Next, put stars by the statements that are realistic and need solutions. Then, write one or more possible solution for the starred fears. Now think back to before you met your current partner. How did you support yourself? Where did you live? What bills did you have? Write down these answers, and as you do so, realize that most likely you have supported yourself before, and can do it again. Facing your financial fears and then taking action will lessen your stress and increase your confidence.

Also, no-fault divorce and community property laws in many states make it mandatory to divide all assets fifty–fifty. Both parties begin a new life with an equal portion. In my divorce, my husband kept the house, refinanced it, and gave me half of its value, which I used to buy my own home. If you were living with your parents as I was, or being supported by someone else prior to your marriage, the situation can feel challenging. Even though I had my own career, I still questioned leaving a financially secure marriage for an unknown future, and I feared I couldn't survive on my own. You may wonder how you will manage, especially if you believe you have few employment skills for today's market. In reading chapters 3 and 4 on the finances and laws of divorce, be assured that you can receive spousal support in order to return to school, upgrade your skills, and make yourself employable. You can succeed. It just takes faith in your intuition, determination, and the courage to take action.

Fear for Your Children

If you have children, their welfare is probably foremost in your mind. No one wants to destroy a nuclear family or harm children in any way. Thus, in this decision-making stage, you may be worried about the effect of your choice on your children. It is wise to be cautious and conscious about your decision, to do everything you can to ensure your happiness, and to protect your kids in the process. First, however, you must realize your fears and deal with them before a decision can even be reached.

Open your journal and write down your fears concerning your children, beginning with "I'm afraid that . . ." Then reread the list, noticing which statements seem to be realistic fears that need solutions. Star these. Below your list of fears, write possible solutions for the logical ones. For instance, if you write that your children will not have a father, put down the ways that their father can be in their lives through joint custody and visitation, or who in their life could be a surrogate father. If a fear is that your children will be emotionally scarred, write down ways to help them, such as open communication with you, family meetings with both parents, alerting teachers, seeing therapists, and so on. Dispel your fears by writing down logical solutions. The rest of the fears on your list may be unrealistic, the result of panic and an overactive imagination. Take each unrealistic fear, imagine it in a bubble, and picture it disappearing from view. Ask that it be permanently removed from you.

Be assured that if you are acting from a place of honesty and love, your children know this. Most parents who divorce do so with a great deal of conscious thought and careful action. Sarah, a colleague and a mother of four boys, was married for nineteen years to a drug addict. She knew for two years that she needed to leave, but she put it off because of her children. "Nick was only four when I left and the divorce was very hard on him; the other boys were older and it affected each one differently. Today, they are well adjusted and they understand why I left their father because they still see him stoned. I couldn't live with a man who was an addict, but because of my kids, it was hard to leave our family."

If, during this stage of making a choice, you are fearful for your children, it is understandable. You may wonder if your decision will ruin their lives or at least alter them irrevocably. You may ask if it is better for children to be in a two-parent dysfunctional home or two separate, healthier homes. Most of those interviewed, both colleagues and clients, believe that as challenging as divorce is for everyone, it is less harmful to couples and children than staying in a marriage that is intolerable. A childhood friend, Rob, told me recently, "My mother stayed with my father until my sister, brother, and I were grown. We knew she was miserable. We could hear them fighting constantly. For some reason she thought it was best to keep the family together, but I don't think so. We lived with a mother who cried a lot and was often sick. After they divorced, she met and married her high-school sweetheart. Finally, we saw our mother laughing and lighthearted. I just wish she had found happiness sooner." Rob's own first marriage ended in divorce; he feels his mother modeled behavior that said, "Stay in an unhappy marriage without options," but Rob rebelled and has found great happiness and longevity (twenty years) in his second marriage. On the other hand, Elena has chosen to stay with her alcoholic husband of eighteen years because of her two daughters. She feels it is better for them to have a father full-time rather than part-time, even though he has a drinking problem that isn't improving. When both daughters are on their own, Elena says, she may leave.

The decision whether or not to divorce when children are involved is heart-wrenching. Even though my son and daughter were nearly grown, our divorce was very hard on them. Recently, while doing research, I learned that divorce is hardest on teenage boys when their mothers leave. In that moment, I re-experienced guilt and sadness for my son's pain. At the same time, I know I made the right choice, and now my children agree. It has taken time, but everyone in our family is happier. Initially, a divorce will be an adjustment for everyone, including children, but there is help for you and for them, including the information in chapter 6, Loved Ones.

Fear of Being Alone

Of all the fears, this one seems to be the most common, at least among those I've interviewed. People are afraid they will be alone for the rest of their lives, and so they decide to stay in unhappy marriages. Jackie, a former client, married for four years, says of this, "I stayed a year longer than I should have, all because I couldn't face being alone. Now I've left, I still get scared; I sleep with my cat and stuffed bunny." Jeff, a construction worker, married for six years, adds: "The idea of splitting up and being alone in that huge house, in that bed, was the worst part for me. I'm from a big family and used to having lots of people around. I've never been by myself much, and I didn't want to be." Not only do individuals fear the space, the silence of a home without their spouse, but they fear being alone socially. Bill, married for eight years and thinking about divorce, comments, "My best friend's divorced and used to go out on Friday night alone; I'd see him hanging out in a coffee house talking on his cell phone, looking busy, but really avoiding contact with women. Then eventually he'd go next door to listen to the band and have a beer, but all he did was lean on the wall. I don't want to be like that."

At this point, open your journal and answer the question, "How do I feel about being alone?" Write until you feel complete, then reread your answer. If you wrote that you're afraid of being alone, then list what you can do to ease this feeling. Then take action.

What those interviewed seemed to fear was not being alone, but being lonely. Often being alone is therapeutic, exactly what each partner needs, at least for a while. It is the loneliness, however, the deep feeling that we will be isolated, abandoned, and unloved forever, that causes the terror. Julie, separated from her husband of two years, expressed in a recent workshop, "I'm going to be forty-nine on my next birthday; I look in the mirror and panic. Will anyone else ever want me? Will I end up like my mom, living in a tiny apartment watching TV on weekends? I know this sounds pathetic, but I'm really serious." Julie's fears are valid. It is scary to leave a relationship and be single in midlife. I left my marriage at forty-eight, but I had spent so many years alone emotionally. Being married to someone who was always working or traveling had hurt me deeply. Living alone in a marriage was much worse than being on my own. Even though I moved to a small cottage, leaving a beautiful home and financial security, I realized the truth. I was alone, but no longer lonely.

Being single doesn't have to be so frightening. For some of us, it's the first time we've had our own lives and our own space, "a room of one's own" as Virginia Woolf called it. It doesn't mean we're entirely alone, either. Many of us have families, friends, and colleagues, as many people as we want at a given time. We can join support groups or clubs, or take up a sport or hobby. Most cities and towns offer more activities than one person has time for. Ultimately, we can choose to be solitary or social. Either way, solitude can be beneficial and loneliness can be managed.

Fear of the Unknown

Before leaving her husband, a friend consulted an astrologer who looked at both their charts, gave an opinion, and helped her make a decision. It can be terrifying to contemplate the end of a relationship. We don't know the future; we cannot guarantee that our decision will be the right one, that we will be happier, that our lives will, indeed, be better. This is why so many people consult psychics, palm readers, astrologers, and others in order to make concrete something that is so abstract. We want to know the outcome, the end result, in order to prepare, and in order to feel safer. This is human nature. I can recall asking friends and family their opinions before deciding to leave my husband; I talked to a therapist regularly, read my horoscope, wrote in my journal, and continually wanted to know exactly what would happen "if." Ultimately, I was the only one who could make the decision, and finally I had to trust and follow my intuition. This didn't mean I was exempt from fear of the unknown. It is normal to feel fear; it is a reaction to the threat of harm. In this case, the threat feels like annihilation, at least the destruction of all we've known, all we've been, all we've believed would be our future.

While deciding whether or not to leave my marriage, I felt moments of panic. For half my life I had lived with one person; my world was settled, predictable, and safe. Our children were adults, the house and cars were paid off, and everything was secure and known. Until I thought about leaving. Then my mind filled with unanswerable questions, my heart began to pound, and I had trouble breathing. For someone who had married in part for security, for protection from the world, the thought of leaving this womb caused anxiety. I finally realized that I had no control over the unknown future. Being absolutely certain of my destiny, of the outcome of my decision, was impossible. All I could do was follow my intuition and trust that I would be guided to make the best choice.

In order to better understand your personal fear of the unknown, it may help to write in your journal, answering questions as you have earlier in this chapter. Write quickly and honestly the first responses that come to you.

1. What frightens me most about the unknown future?
2. What do I fear could happen if I decide to stay in my relationship?
3. What do I fear could happen if I leave my relationship?

Reread your answers without judgment. Then, answer this final question as truthfully as possible: Overall, what is my greatest future fear about my marriage? Write this realization in one sentence. Sit back for a moment and take in this discovery.

We can turn over our fear. We can replace it with trust that the highest good is unfolding, not just for us, but for everyone involved. During moments of doubt when the unknown loomed threateningly, I took a deep breath and asked for help from Highest Consciousness and my inner guidance. Using the teachings of various spiritual practices, I found several sayings to help me, changing the phrasing to assist me most. During my divorce, I said the Serenity Prayer daily, sometimes dozens of times, asking God for help in releasing my control, and receiving inner peace. This prayer helped me believe that I could turn over my fears and trust that all would be well. I even wrote down the things I couldn't control and imagined letting go of them. Then I focused on what I could change, especially myself, and began to take action. If, while deciding whether or not to divorce, you ever feel unstable or scared, you can do whatever will stop the downward spiral. You can say, "I need help"; "I release all fear"; or "I focus on what I can change, and release what I can't"; "I want peace in my life." Listen to your intuition, and then use whatever words or actions contribute most to your sanity and well-being.

After studying the beliefs and practices of the Huichol Indians from Mexico, I have learned to pray in the Huichol way. I say this prayer every morning, focusing on gratitude and asking for protection for my loved ones and myself. The exact words are less important than the sincere plea for help. I pray aloud, letting the words come quickly from my heart:

Great Spirit. Thank you for this day. Thank you for my life. Thank you for my mate, for my children, and my children's children. Please put white light around us and keep us safe. Thank you for my home and for my many blessings. Oh, Spirit, free me from fear. Fill me with love.

From here, I ask spontaneously for whatever is needed at the time, and express more appreciation.

I've found that recounting all my blessings allows me to feel accepting of what I have, and ready to attract more happiness and abundance. The following prayer helps me feel less powerless and alone, and more willing to trust in the future.

I ask to be of service to the Great Spirit and my fellow creatures. May I bless, love, and forgive all I meet, including myself. I accept with gratitude my life as it is. I welcome the blessings and bounties, the abundance of a life dedicated to service and to love.

Praying is my personal way of coping. To lessen your fear of the unknown, you can use your own belief system in whatever way benefits you most.

Another helpful tool is a "let-go box." I made mine from a shoe box and covered it with pictures of nature and sayings to inspire me. Then I placed small pieces of paper and a pen next to the container. During my divorce, when I felt fearful about the future or about any person or situation, I wrote my fear on the slip of paper and put it in the box. I envisioned myself letting go of my anxiety, the issue, or the person, and could feel the fear and tension evaporate.

At this point, it may help to write affirmations to keep you out of fear, and in faith. An affirmation is a statement that "makes firm" a positive attitude about an issue in your life. Writing affirmations can dispel negativity and replace it with a belief that all is well. Affirmations are always written in the present tense, as if the belief is already true for us, and recorded in a positive way, that is, not mentioning the word fear but reinforcing an affirming truth. You can write the following up to ten times each, or until they feel anchored or believable for you.

1. I, (your name), trust that my highest good is unfolding.
2. I, _____, am filled with love.
3. I, _____, faithfully follow the wisdom of my intuition.
4. I, _____, accept what I cannot change.
5. I, _____, have courage to change what I can.
6. I, _____, live in the present moment and accept what is.
7. I, _____, am filled with calmness and peace.

You can write your own affirmations, taking the fearful statements you have written previously and changing them with positive language. The goal is to replace anxious thoughts with hopeful ones, in order to reduce stress and improve the quality of your life.

This chapter has helped you consciously make the initial decision whether or not to divorce. You have learned how to access your intuition, and now you can listen to this inner voice at any time. In addition, you have experienced many emotions and are learning how to deal with them when they arise. You have practiced treating yourself with love and compassion and have been encouraged to extend the same gifts to your partner. Finally, you have begun to write your thoughts, beliefs, and feelings in your journal in order to record all you are going through. Contemplating a separation and divorce is a complex process. Now you have a framework of stages, suggestions, and exercises to help you.

In a recent workshop, Jane said, "Twenty years ago when I divorced, we didn't do it consciously at all. I'm afraid we just muddled through, shouting in front of the children and generally making a mess of everything. But we were so young, and we just didn't know how to do it any better. We didn't have the tools. I wish we had." Unlike Jane, you do have the tools you need. Congratulations. You've begun.

OPTIONAL RITUALS FOR CAREFUL CHOICE

In deciding whether or not to remain in your relationship, you may wish to perform simple rituals to help with your clarity, confidence, and acceptance. A ritual is a rite or ceremony, a symbolic, meaningful act performed to celebrate or support an event or phase of our lives.

Beginning Rituals of Clarity

Before doing the intuition exercises in the beginning of this chapter, you can use one or more of the following rituals to attain clarity. Do these in a quiet, private, and supportive place.

1. Write a loving letter of personal support to yourself.
2. Say a prayer, or ask for assistance from Highest Consciousness, or whatever you call your source of help.

3. While you work on the journal exercises, play soft music or light a candle to relax you and symbolize your quest for truth.
4. Wear or hold a special piece of jewelry, stone, or whatever has meaning, that helps you feel secure and protected.
5. Design your own ritual or means of support. This is your process. Do whatever works for you.

Rituals of Acceptance and Closure

After doing the intuition exercises, or after reading this chapter, you may wish to perform one or more of these rituals of acceptance and closure, to bring meaning to the experience and anchor your choice.

1. Write a letter to your spouse, saying everything you feel about him or her and the relationship. Write your decision in the letter and then when you feel complete, tear or burn the letter.
2. Go to a place in nature and write or "speak" your decision onto a piece of wood or a stone, and throw it into a sea or river, in order to let go of the outcome. You could also hold a feather that represents your relationship or partner; if you can let it fly away, then you can release your relationship. If you can't let it go, then you're not ready to release your spouse, or you've not truly decided yet.
3. Continue to write affirmations in your journal and say them aloud, phrases of your own or like the ones in this chapter. Ritualizing your decision with affirmations can help you to feel a sense of confidence and, ultimately, a sense of peaceful acceptance.

2

Clear Communication

Truth sits
in a high-backed chair
at the walnut table
nibbling toast
and waiting
to be asked
to speak.
                        Fantasy's Not
                        an Option

On the way to the airport, I rehearsed what to say to my husband, who had been away on business for several months. I could tell him the truth, that I couldn't live together any longer, that I needed to move out as soon as possible. It seemed fairly easy to think these words, and I felt confident . . . until I saw him standing in front of the baggage claim area, smiling and waving to me. Taking a deep breath, I realized I couldn't tell him how I felt, at least not yet. How could I hurt him? How could I do something I might regret forever? All I could do was park the car and wave back.

It took me two more months to finally say the words, "I need to leave." During those weeks, we spent hours alone and with therapists talking about the past and the present, trying to sort out what had happened to our marriage. Eventually, during a session with our counselor, I realized it was too late for me. I couldn't go back. I had to tell my husband I wanted to separate. This was the most difficult moment of my life, and I needed help in knowing how to communicate my feelings.

At this point, you are deciding whether or not to leave your marriage, or you have already made a decision. Is there a way to tell your partner the truth that is less hurtful, and less likely to cause permanent estrangement? Is there an easier and less stressful way for your spouse to listen to your words? The answer is yes, to both questions. The main goal of this chapter is to help you learn to speak clearly and listen openly, while facilitating necessary changes in your relationship.

As couples trying to talk to each other about change, it's often difficult to know how to express ourselves effectively and how to hear our spouses without becoming defensive. I have heard many clients and friends say about their partners: "He just doesn't understand me," or "She never listens," or "I can't talk to him." These words may mean, "I'm frustrated that I can't say what I really feel or be listened to; I'm afraid she doesn't even know who I am." This chapter can help you to feel more understood by your partner, by training you to speak tactfully yet truthfully, and to listen intently and patiently. More specifically, this chapter is about how to tell your spouse what you've decided, how to discuss these changes, and how to listen to one another in the process. These skills can help both of you learn to share what you're feeling and what you want.

According to my research, and observations of clients and workshop participants, women and men often communicate differently. Women tend to communicate more frequently and directly than their husbands, both in conversation and during arguments. Women give positive and negative messages verbally and nonverbally, while men tend to give neutral messages or remain silent. Females tend to initiate conflict, escalate it, and at the same time, try to resolve the dispute. My women clients are often more emotional, at times more threatening verbally, while as a rule, their male partners tend to use logic or, if this tack fails, try to postpone or end the conflict altogether. Many of my colleagues agree that women are external processors and most men are internal ones. Women need to say how they're feeling out loud and don't want advice or someone to fix their problem; all they want is to vent, to get the words and feelings out, and then they feel better. Men often don't want to talk, but want to have some quiet time alone to mull things over. At times, we may wonder how people manage to have relationships at all.

Generally, the clients, colleagues, and other professionals I've interviewed believe that communication may be more difficult for the person being "left." The individual talking about leaving may have had weeks or months to think about this change, whereas the other partner may feel unprepared for and even shocked by the news. It certainly can be an adjustment for the person left, but talking about ending one's marriage is challenging for both spouses. I initiated the change in my relationship and eventually moved out, but there were weeks and months of worrying about what to do and at least a year of fearing I had made the wrong decision. It can be a stressful time for both of you, and learning to communicate clearly can help the process immensely.

BODY LANGUAGE, SPEAKING SKILLS, AND LISTENING TECHNIQUES

Before talking with your partner about your marriage, it would be helpful to learn or review basic verbal and listening skills and positive body language. Most of us assume that we know these techniques, but in a stressful situation, we don't always remember to use them.

We are constantly communicating, if not with words, then with body language. Think for a moment about your partner. What does he do to convey certain feelings or thoughts without uttering a word? How does she look when happy? playful?

loving? angry? hurt? or in disagreement? The eye contact or lack of it, the turn of a shoulder, the drop or rise of the head, the gestures or lack thereof, the proximity or distance from you, all tell a story about what your spouse is feeling and thinking at the time. Words, of course, are less subtle and tell you what your partner is feeling or thinking, at least on the surface. Speech can also be deceiving or incongruent. It's important to notice if the words expressed match the body language. For instance, if your spouse says, "I'm fine," when asked, but says it with lips and teeth clenched, arms crossed, and voice strained, it might be good to probe further. You can tell a great deal from the tone of voice being used—whether it's high or low, whether the words seem to flow smoothly or are bitten off sharply. You can learn to "tune in" to your partner and to speak up when something in his or her body or voice seems amiss. Also, it helps to use a neutral "I" message rather than a confrontational "you" message when communicating with your mate.

"YOU" AND "I" MESSAGES

Many of us have used "you" statements, especially when feeling threatened or defensive. During a conflict or in a tense or stressful situation with our spouses, we may make statements to them that are blaming, such as

"You make me sick."
"You always ignore me."
"You're never here for me."
"You don't really love me."
"All you care about is yourself."

"You" messages judge or label our partners and cause them to say something judgmental in return in order to defend themselves and their pride. This escalates the conflict because neither of us is really taking responsibility for our true feelings. We may fear rejection if we're vulnerable and tell the truth: "I feel so alone in this big house and wish we could spend more quality time together." Instead, out of fear, the ego creates a shield or defense mechanism, and we say, "All you do is work; you're married to your job." Such a remark only serves to separate us further.

The other danger in "you" messages is that they are often accompanied by the words "always" or "never." Whenever we're in an argument or conflict with our partners, we may use these words for emphasis, to make our position stronger, to make us right and them wrong. Such overstatement is guaranteed to provoke a reaction in our spouses, to push their buttons and to further escalate the dispute. If you truly want to improve communication, to create peace and not war in your relationship, then these words must go. The key is consciousness, paying close attention to what you say and how you say it, and being willing to change your patterns when you become aware of them.

If you learn to use "I" messages, your partner will become less defensive. If you swallow your pride and become vulnerable, telling the real truth, your partner will be encouraged to listen more openly and reply from an equally honest level. Then, both of you are taking responsibility for your feelings and behavior. Instead of saying, "You make me mad," which is a perfect example of not taking responsibility, you could say, "I feel angry when . . ." You might try the following formula while communicating.

1. I feel . . .   (*Admit your honest feelings.*)
2. When you . . .   (*Cite a specific act or statement that bothers you.*)
3. I'd like you to . . . (*Name a specific action that you want.*)
4. Because . . .   (*Give your reasons.*)

For example: "I feel angry and hurt when you don't call when you're going to be late for dinner. Please call me next time you're late so I won't worry or feel resentful." Of course, you need to experiment to find just the right order and wording that works for you. These are the general techniques to use when you're the speaker, but what do you do as the listener?

Listening skills may seem harder to learn and practice, especially with our spouses. This is because we have so much to say, and, again, because we want to be heard and we want to be right. If, for one moment, you can see that what you want is what your partner also wants, you have taken the first step. You must show him or her the same courtesy that you would like to receive. You must listen without interrupting. Try this technique: choose a small object to pass between you, and take turns speaking. Only the person holding the object may talk. In therapy sessions, I give the speaker a red glass heart and ask him or her to speak the truth from the heart. Use any object, but one that has meaning for you both is preferable. If you have a pattern as an interrupter, then you may need to bite your tongue, sit on your hands, and have the masking tape ready for your mouth. The point is to be quiet unless it is your turn to speak. The "listening half" of the above four-part speaking model is as follows:

1. Pause and breathe . . .   *(Wait for your partner to deliver all four parts before saying anything.)*

2. Paraphrase . . .   *(Repeat in your own words what your partner has just said, even if you disagree. You're showing you are listening.)*

3. Empathize . . .   *("I can see how you might . . ." See your partner's words as part of his or her experience and not the*

entire truth. You are trying to understand his or her view.)

4. Look for the grain of truth . . .

(There is some validity to what your partner is saying. If you can acknowledge any part, it will help ease tension and create the possibility of agreement.)

The following listening skills, including appropriate body language, have been adapted from the work of therapist Carl Rogers. They have evolved over the years in my work leading communication workshops. First of all, you should strive to convey respect, empathy, and genuineness when speaking or listening. Respect can be expressed by showing courtesy and attentiveness, making direct eye contact, and using open body language. Do not cross your arms or legs or sit sideways or with a shoulder to the other person, but sit in a relaxed and receptive manner. Respect also means not passing judgment, and remembering the information shared. Show empathy by nodding as the person speaks, using direct eye contact and similar facial expressions as the person talking. We are empathetic when we use active listening, giving responses such as, "That must have been really hard to do," or "I can understand why you feel that way."

These reflective expressions show that you are concerned and listening closely. When you are the speaker, these expressions help you continue because you are being heard. Genuineness is conveyed by warmth, including smiling, nodding, and using eye contact, which expresses that you care, that you are being honest. Make sure that your nonverbal behavior matches what you are saying. If you express that you are concerned, but you are looking at a fly buzzing around the room, then your words will seem false. If your partner is crying while talking but you begin to smile or laugh, you will seem insensitive, and your actions could cause a deeper rift. Some general guidelines for listeners that summarize the above qualities are:

1. Focus on your partner by looking only at him as he speaks. Clear the room or space of all distractions or find a space that is clear. No phones, no TV, no radio, no music.
2. Listen for the content and feelings of her words.
3. Show that you understand what is being said through your eye contact, open body stance, and facial expressions.
4. Summarize or feed back his main points, ideas, and feelings: what you hear, see, and sense. Do this only when he has completed what he is saying. Use a pencil or other object to pass from speaker to speaker. If you are not the one holding the object, you may only nod or give brief feedback on what your partner is saying. The focus is not on you until you hold the object.
5. Avoid labeling, judging, giving advice, or interrupting to tell your story or in any way minimizing what your partner is saying.

Overall, true listening means no fiddling with objects; no mumbling under your breath; no negative facial expressions such as raising eyes and eyebrows, frowning, or shaking your head sideways; no sighing to show boredom or condescension. In other words, let go of your ego and your agenda. Be there for your partner by listening from a place of love and respect. You will want the same courtesy.

For a more specific model of speaking and listening skills, use the Steps to Delivering Uncomfortable Communications, outlined below, created by my mentor, Judy Wardell-Halliday. I have used these steps successfully with everyone in my life, and I am confident that these skills will work for you, too.

STEPS TO DELIVERING UNCOMFORTABLE
COMMUNICATIONS

Purpose: To allow both parties to release past grievances and tell the truth, so that each is free to choose to have the relationship in the present form, or in a new form, or not at all. You may repeat steps if necessary to better facilitate the process.

Before Communication
1. Clean the emotional slate of feelings such as fear, pride, anger, judgment, and guilt.
   a. Responsibly express and release feelings with a confidant or in your journal before talking with the person.
   b. Write forgivenesses for the other person or for your own specific behavior. (Forgive whatever you are able to forgive at this time. The more you can forgive, the more the communication can be delivered from a loving, present-time place).
2. Review the above steps for communication.
3. Review what you want to communicate, and assess the time it may take for the process.

During Communication
1. Tell the person:
   a. You want to deliver a communication.
   b. How much time you desire.
   c. Ask: "Is this a good time?" If not, see "d."
   d. Set up mutually agreed upon time.
2. Tell him or her your greatest fears about delivering the communication.
3. Tell him or her what you want ideally *during* the communication.

4. Tell him or her the whole truth, and deliver your communication from a loving place until you feel complete.
5. Hear his response without interrupting. Acknowledge her position and whatever response she gives. It may not be your ideal, but it is his or her truth.
6. Repeat any of the above steps, as necessary.

SPECIFIC GUIDELINES FOR THESE STEPS

Before Communication: Acknowledging Feelings and Emotional Blocks

Creating readiness to communicate can begin within yourself, then with a therapist or trusted confidant, and finally with your partner. You can communicate more clearly with your spouse if you have made a decision or are close to deciding what to do. Second, it helps to know how to articulate your ideas before speaking with your spouse. This is not deceptive or manipulative. You are merely being careful and becoming conscious of your inner feelings and how to express them before speaking with your partner. At this point, you may wish to turn to the final section of this chapter and perform some of the optional rituals for clearer communication, to further support you.

Returning to Ashley's Hierarchy of Love presented in the introduction, first ask for help from Highest Consciousness or whatever you call God. Ask that it become clear to you what it is you need to communicate about your relationship. You can do this aloud, or silently in your mind. Then, write this question in your journal: "What do I need to say to my partner?" Let the answers come quickly from your intuition. Write uninterrupted until nothing else surfaces. Read back what you've written, and see if you've omitted anything. If so, add it now.

After you're clear about what you need to say, you may want to talk to someone neutral, such as a therapist, friend, or family member. If you choose to talk with a friend or relative, be sure the person can listen in a nonjudgmental way without interrupting or offering advice. All you need is an ear. After choosing a listener, ask for help concerning how and when to discuss your decision and feelings with your spouse. Saying how you feel out loud will clarify your position and give you confidence. When you finally talk to your partner, you'll be truly prepared.

To communicate effectively, you should eliminate as many blocks to the process as possible. These barriers are often emotions that could keep you from speaking and listening with a whole heart; they create veils that may seem to protect you, but actually keep you from acting from a place of love and truth. These emotional blocks can be seen clearly in the following diagram, which shows fear to be the usual catalyst for the resultant defense mechanisms.

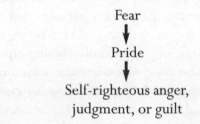

Fear
↓
Pride
↓
Self-righteous anger,
judgment, or guilt

As expressed in chapter 1, fear is often the cause of negative emotions that can hamper communication. Fear, according to many experts, is a product of the mind, at times fabricated yet driven by our insecurities, and in other instances, based on past negative experiences. In either case, the emotion is not based on what is really happening in the present moment. But during divorce discussions, when we're afraid of being hurt or fearful we'll lose something or have to change, we may react defensively to protect ourselves. For example, you might worry that your partner will yell at you, not listen, try to change your mind, or harm you in some way. These concerns could be based on normal fears of the unknown, or on prior experience with your spouse or another person.

During my marriage, I feared my husband's disapproval, partly because he had been judgmental in the past, partly due to my own low esteem, and also because my father had been highly critical and verbally abusive. All these elements caused me to feel uneasy about telling my former husband I wanted a divorce. In another instance, Ted, who was married for nine years, says he feared his wife's anger and did anything to appease her, including saying what she wanted to hear rather than how he truly felt. This continued until he finally told her his true feelings during a therapy session. Overall, fear is a powerful catalyst that can keep us in a defensive posture, unable to love ourselves enough to express the truth or to hear our spouse.

This would be a good time to open your journal and write: "What scares me about talking to my partner?" or "What do I fear about talking to him or her?" Then begin with "I'm afraid . . ." and list all your fears until nothing else surfaces. Finally, write: "What is my greatest fear about communicating with my wife or husband?" List quickly what comes. Take some time to reread your answers. What are some logical solutions to your fears? For instance, if you're afraid your spouse will no longer care about you, or you'll lose this friendship forever, then write about these fears, and perhaps talk with your partner about them. On another level, if you write that you're afraid your partner will yell or hit you, and this fear is founded in past history, then don't talk to him or her alone. It's preferable to go to a therapist, but if your spouse refuses, then you still need to take care of yourself. Some people write letters, tell the person over the phone, or do so in a public place. If the situation is this volatile, then my advice is to leave first. Then contact the person through a mediator or an attorney.

In addition, some people, because of problems with their pride, fear losing control, being dominated, or being wrong. They will do anything to "save face," including stubbornly arguing their position, judging, blaming, or being unwilling to admit their part. My mother used to say to me when I became defensive and argumentative, "Do you want to be right or do you want to be happy?" As a teenager, I ignored her words, but as an adult, I try to live by them, giving up my pride, owning my part in a conflict, making amends, and feeling happier as a person. Chad, married for fourteen years, doesn't like himself and frequently projects his negative self-image on his wife, Elizabeth, saying to her in front of dinner guests something like, "Where'd you get this wine? It tastes like vinegar! Jesus, can't you even buy a simple bottle of wine?" Elizabeth, my former client, shares that she is afraid of doing something wrong to incur her husband's wrath. She rarely says how she feels because she fears his judgment, anger, and, even more, that he will leave her and the children.

If you are with a spouse who is verbally abusive, or who squelches communication by being aggressive, it's important to talk to him or her with a therapist or mediator present. Do not try to talk alone. On the other hand, if you're the one with these negative behaviors, you can write about your issues in your journal, and preferably discuss how to change these tendencies with a therapist. If you can identify this pattern of self-righteous anger before talking with your spouse (either in your journal or with a counselor), the awareness can keep you from "acting out" while communicating.

Several persons interviewed said that their spouses stubbornly refused to go to counseling at all. This is an unfortunate situation, especially when one partner is willing but the other will not cooperate. Janice, a writer and editor, married three years, is now separated and soon to divorce her husband, Jeff. She says of his actions, "Jeff wouldn't go to therapy; he said he'd never pay a stranger to listen to our business. He told me if I couldn't accept him as he was, then we might as well forget it. I knew deep down he was sad, but his pride kept him from showing he cared."

Besides the barriers of fear, pride, and self-righteousness, you may be feeling judgment or guilt, which could also hamper communication. This is because you are carrying the baggage of these emotions into the dialogue. Judgment is blaming the other person, and guilt is blaming yourself. Refer to the section on guilt in chapter 1 for more detail. It's difficult to have an equitable and productive discussion if you feel blame or guilt, because these feelings are too one-sided and ignore each person's part in the situation. It's never the case that one spouse is completely to blame and the other is totally innocent, but some partners unfairly judge their mates.

For example, Denise, married for nine years with one child, complains bitterly that Lyle doesn't pay enough attention to her or their son, that he studies all the time as a graduate student and never interacts with her or helps with the house or childcare. After more discussion, it becomes clear that Denise has never told Lyle her feelings. She makes all his meals, including his lunch; does his laundry; makes love when he wants to; never complains that they don't go out or have friends over. She had silently and bitterly held in her feelings, until she finally exploded during a couple's session, swearing and blaming him for everything from the leak in the roof to her headaches. Denise is not yet able to see her part in the dilemma.

According to my research and work with clients, those who tend to be "blamers" hold their partners responsible for their own feelings and actions. They respond to inner tension by verbally and at times physically attacking their spouses. These fault-finders have low esteem, feel weak, and thus need to make their mates responsible for existing problems. If you are a "blamer," it's important to acknowledge this pattern. The way to break the cycle is first to realize it, and then to take action. When interacting with your spouse, be sure to own your part by using "I" statements and avoiding "you" phrases. It would be good to write in your journal, answering the question, "What is it that I do to help create problems in my relationship?" "What exactly is my part?" Then write a list quickly, acknowledging honestly what you've done. This will help as a preparation for dialogue, because if you can admit that you have been at fault at times, you won't have the tendency to blame your spouse while under stress.

Guilt-ridden individuals can also cause imbalance during communication by taking more responsibility for the problems in the relationship than they should. These persons are often passive, overly submissive, and willing to be scapegoats. If you have a sensitive "guilt alarm" that is easily triggered by your mate, remember: never take more than half of the responsibility for your relationship. During dialogue with your spouse, be sure to own your part in the conflict or situation, but only your part. Be clear what you did and did not do. Be strong and stand up for yourself. Lucy, a nurse in her thirties, married for seven years and now separated, says she felt responsible for every problem in her marriage. As she explains, "Josh would come home from work and I scurried around to have dinner on the table, our son in bed, and the lights low. He still complained that the food was lukewarm or the house was dirty, and I would apologize and try to fix everything before he got even more upset." After months of therapy, Lucy was able to stand up to Josh and tell him she was no longer afraid of him, and that she wanted a separation.

A current client, Gypsy, cries when she says, "Roger tells

me it's my fault he's got another girlfriend. I'm just not attractive anymore." Gypsy and Roger have been married for thirty years, and he has convinced her she is the cause of their problems. Now, Gypsy is seeing a mediator and planning her separation. Another woman, Kay, planned to leave many times but stayed in her marriage until her husband's death, rarely feeling free of guilt and anger. If her husband was unhappy or dissatisfied with her, or with work, she felt guilty. If only she had fixed a better dinner or lost another five pounds. If only she had kept the children quiet or the dog from digging up the lawn. Sadly, Kay did not get therapy, did not talk to her husband about her feelings, and did not divorce him. Like many women of her generation, Kay stayed in her marriage and felt guilty and overly responsible for its success or failure. I know because Kay is my mother. From personal experience, I feel very strongly about the harm of carrying excess guilt. If you recognize yourself in any of these stories, if you are submissive or guilt-ridden, then write about this issue in your journal, being willing to admit your part and no more.

Before Communication: Clearing the Emotional Slate of Anger, Resentment, and Unforgiveness

Before talking with your partner, you may feel anger, resentment, and unforgiveness. This doesn't mean you're a horrible person; it just means you are human. Basically, you're doing the best you can to deal with your spouse from a place of love rather than ego. You are trying to be conscious and create the best possible outcome for everyone. At the same time, you have a right to your feelings no matter what they are. You are not a bad person for hating your spouse at times, or for feeling enraged or vindictive. These emotions and many others are perfectly normal. The worst thing to do is to swallow the anger, swallow the hate, grit your teeth, and smile.

The emotions of anger and resentment let us know that

something is wrong in our life, that perhaps we're being hurt or neglected. If you feel angry or resentful toward your partner, it's good to write about your feelings before communicating them. As presented in the Steps to Delivering Uncomfortable Communications, it's vital to clear the emotional slate by journaling. Begin by writing this question: "What am I upset about?" Then write, "I am angry/resentful that my partner . . ." Then write quickly in stream of consciousness until nothing else comes to mind.

Notice what kinds of things disturb you. Do you feel irritated when you are ignored or unappreciated? Is your anger about being criticized or blamed by your mate? Do you feel angry when you're not being listened to or understood? Next, write this phrase: "I get angry/resentful because . . ." and then finish the line or lines it takes to explain the reasons you become upset. This will help you to better understand your patterns. It will also help you to clarify your issues and clearly communicate them to your spouse. You may want to express and discuss your anger with a therapist after writing in your journal, or you may be ready to talk to your mate. In chapter 8, Healing the Heart, you'll have another opportunity to uncover and release any remaining resentments as part of the forgiveness process.

The inability to forgive, as you may have realized, has resentment at its core. Oftentimes when we're furious with someone, it seems difficult to forgive them. We're still too angry, too hurt, too unhealed to do so. However, if we can forgive even one injury or transgression before communicating with our partner, we can be more centered in love when we hold a dialogue. Reread your list of anger and resentments to see if you can find anything to forgive, anything to let go of. Forgiveness doesn't mean that your partner is completely innocent; on the contrary, he or she contributed fifty percent to the difficulties in your marriage. Forgiveness is really about freeing *you* from the "weight of hate" that can be such a tremendous burden. When you forgive, it releases the tension, the heaviness that literally sits on your shoulders and in your heart. So if you can forgive something that your spouse has done, do so now. Write in your journal: "I forgive you for . . ." Write this phrase as many times as you need to, over and over, until it truly feels right. If, while writing, you feel resistant, then write the uncensored thoughts, too, such as, "I forgive you for forgetting our anniversary last year. No, I don't, you jerk; how could you be so cruel?"

If you find another layer of anger when you try to forgive, just write down what is really on your mind, and realize you aren't ready to absolve your partner. At this point, the main purpose of trying to forgive at least some of your spouse's behavior is to clear the air before you even talk to him or her. Otherwise, there are so many unresolved issues and feelings that it's difficult to achieve clarity and consensus on any point. Just do your best.

During Communication: Step One

Readiness to communicate has a lot to do with timing. It's essential to choose a time to talk that is mutually agreeable, that is private, as calm as possible, and in a neutral setting. I am speaking from experience when I emphasize these conditions. When I told my husband that I wanted a separation, we were on a family vacation with eight people in Lake Tahoe. This was not the ideal time or location; things were not peaceful, nor were they private. But I told him anyway. From my perspective, I couldn't stand it any longer; I couldn't keep my feelings stuffed down another moment. However, the damage was considerable. My husband got on his bike and rode off in a highly charged emotional state, in shock and disbelief. While riding, he had a terrible accident and came back to the house with his face and body scraped and bleeding. He could have been killed. I bathed his wounds, bandaged them, and felt both guilt and annoyance. My ego rather than my love was in charge. All I cared about were my needs and plans, the immediate, short-sighted solution. What I didn't value at the time were my spouse's feelings, and the effect of my words on him. Communicating about such a difficult issue requires conscious planning.

The first step is to suggest a date to talk, to say how much time you need, and ask if this suggestion is all right. If not, negotiate a time and place agreeable to both of you. Agree upon a neutral, private place that feels safe for each of you, and where you will not be interrupted. Taking the time to set this up shows respect for your spouse and shows that you truly want the best interaction and outcome for both of you.

During Communication: Step Two

Of all Wardell-Halliday's steps, number two—"Tell him or her your greatest fears about delivering the communication"—is the most important. It makes you more vulnerable, which can be frightening, but it also makes your partner relax and be less defensive. You each can drop your guard and become honest and willing to get to a heart level. This is how it works. The person speaking says something like, "I have something very important to share with you, and it's taken me some time to work up the courage. I've been afraid you might refuse to listen/judge me/yell at me/reject me/no longer care about me/use my vulnerability against me," or whatever it is that you fear might happen. When I used this technique with my father, I was terrified. I waited until he was visiting, and we were sitting at the kitchen table in the early morning. I remember every detail about that moment. I said, "Daddy, I really want to talk to you about our relationship. I've wanted to speak with you for a long time, but I've been afraid you wouldn't want to talk, or worse yet, you might not care." I went on to say, "My greatest fear is that you wouldn't want a relationship at all or you might not love me." There, I finally shared my worst fear, that I would lose his love. My father, a very stern, stoic man, had trouble sharing his feelings. I waited nervously to hear my father's reply, trying not to count on a certain response. Part of Wardell-Halliday's plan is a complete letting go of expectations. This is the ideal. Finally, my father said, "I will always love you. Don't you know that? Go ahead and talk to me." Tears came to my eyes in that instant. My willingness to admit my fears, my complete honesty and vulnerability, melted my dad's heart. To say the least, the entire interaction was a miracle. And the key was step two of Wardell-Halliday's list of what to do during communication. You might want to write down the phrases you plan to use in your journal before the actual interaction, as I did. This helped me become clear about the fears that had kept me from speaking sooner.

During Communication: Step Three

The third step is about what you ideally want from your spouse while you are communicating. This doesn't mean what you want ultimately, just during the moment you are conversing. You might say something like, "Ideally, I'd like you to listen respectfully while I speak, and I will do the same for you. I'd like you to let me finish my thought before interjecting. I'd like you to listen without judgment. I'd like you to be open to what I am saying and honest in response. I'd like you to be calm and not yell." Of course, this will vary depending on what you particularly want. The key, as always, is consciously and honestly sharing your deepest needs.

During Communication: Step Four

"Finally," you might be thinking, "I can say what I need to. Finally, it's time to share the decision I've reached." Wardell-Halliday advises, "Tell him or her the whole truth, and deliver your communication from a loving place until you feel complete." First, it's a good idea for the two of you to go over the Rules for Fair Fighting, used by Patrick Meyer, a licensed California social worker, during his course on relationships. After reviewing the following guidelines, decide what you'll say to your partner, then deliver the words calmly and respectfully.

RULES FOR FAIR FIGHTING

Fair Fighting	*Unfair Fighting*
1. Take turns speaking, and allow equal time.	1. Name-call, interrupt, and finish sentences.
2. Look for compromises.	2. Open up old wounds.
3. Try not to generalize.	3. Get off on tangents.
4. Allow for time-outs and breathers.	4. Intimidate or threaten.
5. Observe rules that you set.	5. Change rules abruptly.
6. No hitting, threats, or force.	6. Expect a winner/loser.
7. Show personal respect.	7. Save gripes to dump.
8. Be honest with yourself as well as with your partner.	8. Try to read partner's mind.
9. Give clear reasons.	9. Deny the facts.
10. Admit when you're wrong.	10. Gloat over victory.
11. For clarity, repeat partner's words.	11. Ignore your partner.
	12. Use sex for leverage

During Communication:
Steps Five and Six

The final steps of Wardell-Halliday's model involve listening to the other person's response and repeating any steps if necessary. After telling your partner your decision, it is time to acknowledge his or her feelings. Be sure to use the techniques related to summarizing or giving feedback, listening for content and feelings and using nonverbal skills such as good eye contact, nodding, and open posture. You want to be supportive of your spouse. What you have just shared may have come as a shock or it may have been expected. Ideally, you have been communicating before this. You have been honest and there have been no surprises. In any event, it is still hard to hear that your wife or husband is thinking of leaving, beginning a separation, or filing for divorce. Be prepared for anything. When former client Jordan, living with Mariah and unmarried, told her that he wanted to end their relationship, she began crying hysterically. She threw plates, kicked furniture, and physically attacked him. After a year of trying to get her to stop using cocaine, he asked her to move out of his house, and she refused. Two months later, she finally moved all her possessions, but he would come home and find her in his bed. No amount of talking worked, and so he finally changed his phone number and his locks.

If the situation becomes so highly charged that you can't talk to one another, then it might be more productive and safer to talk in the presence of a third party. One couple I counseled in England came in for their regular session after seeing me for several months. The husband, Robert, suddenly said, "I'm leaving you; that's why I wanted to come in separate cars. Mine is packed with all I need right now. I have a place to stay. I wanted to say this now so I can leave you with Susan and she can help you." With that, he got up from his chair, walked out, and closed the door. I found out later that he had been planning this scene for a month. His wife, on the other hand, was unprepared and shocked. He had said nothing about leaving, and she felt they were getting along better. From my perspective, this was not an ideal way to leave a relationship, but apparently it was the only way he could. Number five on Wardell-Halliday's outline is ultimately about accepting whatever happens; you cannot predict what your partner will say or do, and you cannot script it or control the outcome in any way.

Number six, "Repeat any of the above steps . . . ," can be used if necessary. For instance, if you want to share why you waited so long to say something, or what your greatest fears are, then this may come out in more detail as you talk. You might have more of your truth to express if you're encouraged by your spouse. On the other hand, if your partner can't hear what you're saying or keeps interrupting, yelling, or leaving the room, then you should end the dialogue. If possible, agree to meet again, perhaps with a therapist or mediator.

At this point, decide what you want that is similar. Focus on positive actions and state what these are and when you will begin to practice them. For instance, if you've decided you want to work together amicably with a mediator to create a divorce settlement, then make an appointment. It is possible that your mate doesn't want to compromise, perhaps doesn't want to consciously create change that is mutually agreeable. You can't make your partner join you in this process, even though it is your ideal. You can ask for what you want, but you can't guarantee you will get it. Remember that you've done all you can to peacefully communicate and negotiate. From a spiritual perspective, you have acted consciously, respectfully, and lovingly. The outcome, no matter how it looks now, is ultimately for your highest good. The more you can trust this belief, the more easily you can accept what has occurred and the more at peace you will feel.

A SPECIFIC COMMUNICATION PLAN
FOR EACH OPTION

If you selected option one after completing the exercises in chapter 1—that is, if you've decided to do nothing about your relationship, it is my guess you're actually buying time in order to make a decision. This is exactly what my former client, Nancy, is doing. She's been married for nineteen years and has grown children from a previous marriage. She and her husband, Johnny, have not slept together for the past eight months, but neither of them has discussed this change. She shares that she's been pretending everything is the same. It has been too scary to do anything. Her children and friends have commented that she doesn't seem happy, but choosing to do nothing means she is choosing to stay. Nancy comments, "I guess everyone else can see what's going on but me. I hate change. I just don't have the energy to do anything else right now. I did tell my daughter we'll probably divorce someday."

If you're choosing to leave things the way they are, you don't have to say anything to your spouse. However, once you've figured out how you feel, it might be good to share this with a neutral party and then with your partner, in order for you to feel better. You could say to your spouse, "I'm not sure what to do about it, but I'm not very happy with our marriage right now." Just seeing you read this book may make your husband or wife ask you questions. I remember spending several months "doing nothing," but in actuality, I was readying myself for change. I was preparing emotionally and practically. This option may be only temporary before you move on to one of the other five choices.

If you've chosen option two, to stay and change, you want to work on the marriage rather than leave it. Elena, who is mentioned in chapter 1, has chosen to stay and has told her husband how she feels. "I love you and the kids, and I want us all to be together, but I can't make things better by myself. You need to be willing to meet me halfway." They have been to therapy, but it was only moderately successful. She has asked him to stop drinking, but that has not occurred on a consistent basis. At this point, they are getting along better, talking about their feelings, and, as Elena states, "Things are much more pleasant. We're not as angry as we were and accept one another with more tolerance." In this case, communicating honestly and often has helped this couple remain together.

In choosing to work on your marriage, it is essential to talk about your feelings, preferably on a daily basis. Perhaps set a time aside each day to do this, whether early in the morning in bed, at lunch if you can meet, or in the evening at dinner or afterward. If you have children, it's crucial to find time alone, even for a few minutes, to talk without little ears nearby. It's recommended that you "schedule" time each day to communicate. It doesn't have to be rigid or unspontaneous, but with everyone's lives so busy, communicating with our partners can all too easily be put aside. If this happens regularly, feelings are squelched, issues loom larger, tension mounts, and arguments or hurt feelings ensue.

Those of you staying in your relationship can use the many communication techniques outlined in this chapter. After following Wardell-Halliday's steps up to number four, you might say something like this to your spouse: "I feel sad that we aren't spending as much time together anymore. It makes me think we aren't as close, that we're like roommates rather than lovers. What's happened to us?" This is just one script of thousands. The only requirement is that you deliver the truth from a place of love. As expressed in step five, however, you must accept whatever response is given. You can't guarantee that your partner feels the same way or wants the same things you do. You can't make your partner change or be someone he or she is not. All you can do is state your feelings and accept what comes in return. You have a better chance of improving your marriage just by clearly telling your spouse how you feel.

Option three is to separate at home. As outlined in chapter 1, this choice is for those who have made the decision to separate, but need to share the same house for the time being. For most, this is a temporary decision based upon financial needs. This option does not always have a clear, verbal component, but it is best if it does. Many couples just begin sleeping apart. Turner began sleeping on the couch nearly two years before he and his wife separated. He blames his overworking, their lack of communication, and differences in personality for their problems. In any case, they stopped having sex and began sleeping in separate rooms, yet they lived together for two more years. Now that they are divorced, Turner says, "We needed to talk about what was happening, but instead we pretended that it was normal and temporary. I wish I had said something like, 'It's obvious something's wrong here. You're in the bedroom and I'm on the couch night after night. We need to talk.' But I think it was too late by then. We probably needed counseling, but we didn't go until I was moving out."

If you're considering this arrangement, you might say to your wife or husband, "It's not feeling comfortable to sleep/be in each other's space while there's so much conflict and so many unresolved feelings. I think we should try living in separate parts of the house and see what happens." If this is combined with therapy, the couple can either work toward a reconciliation or work on the next phase, which is a trial separation or divorce. Some discussion of financial issues is needed if this latter option is chosen. How can you generate the money so one of you can move out? For Peter and Jane, separating at home was filled with tension at first, and then they learned to adapt and live with it for over a year. They agree, however, that it's not a long-term solution, and it is usually for those who eventually want to live apart.

The fourth option, to prepare to leave, and the fifth, to separate and file for divorce, are where the most challenging communications begin. Choosing to leave a marriage and saying these words are stressful for any couple. It's important to understand all the ramifications and consequences of such a decision. I did a great deal of thinking, writing, and talking to my therapist as well as planning before ever sharing with my husband. I would recommend reading chapter 3, Practical Planning, before telling your wife or husband that you're thinking about a separation or divorce.

Telling your mate you want a separation or divorce is the moment of truth, and every individual interviewed remembers precise details about this instant. In my case, as I mentioned earlier, we were vacationing in Lake Tahoe when I told my husband. We sat looking at clear blue water, at our kayak tied to the dock, with ducks bobbing on the surface. And then I broke the stillness by saying, "I think we should separate for a while and see what happens. I need my space to find out who I am and what I want. I need to leave when we get back home." I said a few other things, to make it sound less final, less threatening and hurtful. As I spoke, I felt strong and exhilarated to finally be saying these words. I felt terrified as well.

Candace, now divorced for seven years, says of her "leaving speech," "I felt mixed emotions when I said to Lenny, 'I'm leaving and taking the children with me,' because I still loved him; I still love him to this day. But for three years I tried to get him to come to therapy with me. I tried to get him into rehab for his addictions, but he wouldn't go. He wouldn't look at his part. I feel I did everything to try to make my marriage work. Finally, I had to get out of there. Right before I left I had a dream or vision that said I was going to die if I didn't leave. I left to save my life in a way." Ironically, Candace is now a therapist who works with people with addictions. She feels healed enough to help others and is grateful she had the courage to leave her husband. As a therapist, her advice to those who are preparing to leave a marriage is, "Be honest. Tell the truth as long as you are safe to do so. Say: 'I'm leaving. This is what I need to do for me. I think it is the best thing for both of us at this time.'"

Depending on whether you are preparing to leave, wanting a trial separation, or ready for a divorce, your choice dictates the degree of finality in your words. The following scripts make this progression clear.

1. *Prepare to leave:* "I've been thinking a great deal about our relationship and I think it might be best to separate for a while. I don't have any timeline in mind, but I'd like to talk about it." Or, "Our relationship doesn't seem to be improving. We've tried a lot of things, we have been talking more, and I'm not sure it's better. What do you think about a separation?" In an ideal situation, both parties are open and agreeable, very adult and willing to listen calmly. In a more realistic scene, one person is dissatisfied and the other thinks things are fine, or is less invested in change occurring. It can be scary to tell your husband or wife that you have been thinking about leaving. This is why it's good to write in your journal, talk with someone, and do some planning (as outlined in chapter 3) before communicating with your partner.

2. *Begin a trial separation:* "I need some time and space to sort out my feelings about our relationship. I can't seem to get this perspective while we're living together. I just feel more confused. Maybe if we live separately for a while, we can get centered, continue to go to therapy, and be able to sort things out." Or, "For now, I think the best thing is to separate. It's just not working while we live together. Maybe some time apart will help each of us sort out our feelings and what we want." Or, "Living together right now is just not working. We don't seem to have the perspective or ability to understand the

problem or each other. It might be best if we live separately right now." How you say this depends on the desired outcome. Do you want the separation in order to eventually reconcile, or is the separation a stepping stone to divorce? You may not know the answer at this point. Some couples begin a separation in order to gain useful tools to negotiate a reconciliation. Others buy time with a trial separation because it's too hard emotionally or financially to file for divorce immediately. They are taking the first step toward dissolution. Some couples who think they want to reconcile end up divorcing. Some that think they want to divorce end up reconciling. There are even those who divorce and find themselves remarrying. You just need to take one step at a time, consciously choosing from a place of inner truth.

3. *File for divorce:* "I want a divorce." This phrase has been used by millions of people, at times at the height of an argument, at others after months or even years of work on the marriage. In my experience and in the interviews I have conducted, this is not typically the first indication of a problem. Asking for a divorce usually comes after lengthy discussions and a separation; it comes during or after therapy and mediation or consultations with an attorney. Talk of divorce, in my opinion, should not come until all other options have been exhausted, until a trial separation has been in place for a minimum of three months. If you are being asked for a divorce, and the two of you have not communicated, have not talked with a counselor, have not tried some of the other options such as an in-house separation, then suggest to your husband or wife that it is premature. If your spouse will not negotiate and insists on leaving and filing for divorce, there isn't much you can do to change his or her mind. You can ask for a trial separation, for time to try to renegotiate, but you can't change anyone. Jessie, separated from her husband, Mel, after four years of marriage, is in this situation. Mel would not return her calls, and

when she finally reached him, he said, "I don't want to be with you. I want a divorce." If, on the other hand, you are the person who wants the divorce, and you are certain that this is what you need to do, then you can say something like: "We have exhausted every option. We have tried to make this marriage work, but I don't see any other choice but to divorce."

As a free individual, you have the option to do whatever you want. You don't have to be conscious. You don't have to explore all options. You can just say you want a divorce. I believe, however, that as humans we have a higher consciousness; we have choice, and every action has a corresponding reaction. If we want "right relations" with others, then we need to think carefully about our choices and strive to harm no one in the process. I believe we should attempt to be conscious every moment, for the choices we make in the present will affect our lives in the future.

Part of my reason for writing about "right relations" is that I didn't always behave responsibly during my divorce, and it has taken a few years to rectify my behavior. After making amends to my former husband at several junctures, showing kindness to him in words and deeds, our relationship is again based on trust and friendship. But to be honest, while leaving my marriage, I often deliberately hurt his feelings. I was not tactful when telling him I was leaving; I was greedy about what I wanted from the house; and I left him with the responsibility for our son and the upkeep of our large home. In other words, I behaved selfishly. This doesn't mean I should have taken full responsibility for our marital problems, nor that I should have stayed in the marriage. His treatment of me, especially his absence and neglect, in part, caused me to be cruel out of anger and retaliation. However, I wish I could have been more aware of the effect of my actions and words on everyone. You have the opportunity to learn from my behavior and can act consciously.

I hope the communication skills and personal testimonies in this chapter have helped you to express your feelings and listen to your partner while processing past issues and reaching a mutually agreeable decision.

OPTIONAL RITUALS
FOR CLEAR COMMUNICATION
Before Communicating

1. Ask that the Highest Consciousness within you connect with the Highest Consciousness of your partner while you talk. You might ask that the dialogue be clear and kind, of the greatest integrity, and that the outcome be the best for you both.

2. Ask for the ability to listen with patience and sincerity, and for your spouse to be able to do the same.

3. Write or say affirmations in order to create the desired outcome. Remember to use "I," present tense, and positive language. Use the following or create your own affirmations.

   • I speak clearly from a place of love.
   • I listen patiently and speak only when it is my turn.
   • I know that highest truth is in charge.
   • I trust that the best outcome is occurring right now.

4. In the place you communicate, do what you can to create a feeling of calm and unity. Make sure that the chairs are facing one another and are of equal height. Turn off the phone and eliminate any distractions.

After Communicating

1. Write in your journal, and perhaps talk with a friend or a counselor about what has occurred. Remind yourself that you're doing the very best you can.

2. You may want time alone or with a supportive friend to

let your emotions surface and feel them fully. Gently take care of yourself by resting and giving yourself nourishment.

3. Try to feel accepting of the outcome, and know that feeling open to change will bring in more positive energy. Trust that what is best for you and your partner is already unfolding.

3

Practical Planning

To think of leaving it all
finding a cottage at the beach
moving the few things I possess:
clothes
wicker chair
oak desk.

Mecca

Yesterday, while I was reading a favorite book, a slip of paper fell from its pages. On the yellowed surface, scribbled in green ink, were lists of items to take from my home. In a few seconds I returned to that time several years ago, seeing myself walk through my house, listing the belongings I most cherished. This was months before my former husband and I separated. Yet, I had begun the process of leaving by daydreaming and planning. Around the same time, I read the newspaper and circled places to live; I opened my own bank account and wished I had kept my family name. I called an attorney and asked questions about finances, including ones about joint property and the cost of divorce. In terms of employment, I increased my number of clients and taught more classes. In addition, my husband and I met weekly with our therapist in order to express our feelings, clarify remaining issues, and decide what action to take.

You and your partner can use the communication tools in chapter 2 to create an action plan for your separation. Communication and mutual planning are at the heart of a loving, conscious divorce. I'm sure you're doing everything in your power to include your spouse in the process. If, however, your mate is unwilling to talk with you, or uncooperative in other ways, or if you have evidence that he or she is hiding assets or is planning to "cheat" you during the divorce, then by all means, meet with a trained mediator and do the necessary work on your own. A committed mediator will involve your partner by phone, can give him or her audio- and videotapes, arrange for him or her to be in another room—whatever it takes to create potential dialogue. You can begin taking action alone, knowing your spouse will eventually realize the economic advantage of being present during negotiations. This would be a good time to recall Ashley's Hierarchy of Love from the introduction. Listen and follow Highest Consciousness and intuition as you take care of your needs, and try to work with your partner to plan an equitable settlement.

During the early stages of her divorce, my former colleague, Rachel, developed a list of actions to take as she planned her separation from her husband, Bill. These included buying a self-help divorce book; obtaining a petition of dissolution; writing a letter to her husband; meeting with him; and talking with family, friends, and colleagues. She explains why she wanted to plan carefully. "For years, I'd heard horror stories about women whose husbands left them. They were destitute, unemployed, and living in their cars, not knowing if they had insurance or assets because their husbands handled the money. Even though I left the marriage as a professional woman, I'd heard enough stories like this to make me wary and proactive." In my marriage, I paid all the bills and managed the money for the day-to-day necessities. My husband did the income tax and took care of our long-range investments. I wish I had done the taxes and handled our portfolio because I had to learn about these financial matters as a single woman.

This chapter is designed to help you become educated, organized, and able to handle your financial needs before and during your divorce.

PLANNING TO LEAVE: FANTASIES AND DREAMS

Lyla and Jim have been married for more than twenty years, raising their own children and a son and daughter from Lyla's first marriage. The problems between them began several years ago when Jim lost his job. It has been five years; he is still out of work and has not been actively looking for employment. They have filed for bankruptcy, they owe the IRS $10,000 in capital-gains taxes, and they are living in separate parts of their house. Jim comments, "The stress on both of us has been tremendous. We had problems in our marriage before, but now the tension is high. I've been depressed and can't seem to shake it. Lyla seems stressed all the time since she's the only one working. She tries not to act mad at me, but I know she is. Or she's mad at what's happening but it seems like it's me." Lyla adds, "Jim can't help that he lost his job, but I don't see him trying to find another one. I've tried to be patient for the past few years, but I come home and see him in his chair watching game shows, and sometimes I lose it. I'm so tired I can barely walk, and he's just loafing. We don't even talk anymore. We can't afford to separate, but something has to give and soon. I have serious health problems that aren't improving. Friends and family are worried, and have talked to me about leaving. Actually, I've been thinking about it for over a year."

This couple illustrates the fact that change takes time, that leaving a relationship usually does not happen quickly. Also, it's not unusual for at least one person to begin the process by fantasizing. Daydreams, visions, and sleeping dreams may be filled with literal and symbolic images of separation long before any action is taken. This is because the unconscious mind often knows the truth before the conscious mind is ready to admit it. The importance of listening to your inner voice is presented in detail in chapter 1, and accessing the intuition can be especially helpful at this stage of preparation. What are your waking and sleeping dreams telling you about leaving your spouse? About your life after you separate? Many of my colleagues and I use visualization to help clients discover deeply held desires and feelings. The following exercises using guided imagery can help you "see" what kind of life you want.

Visualization 1: Your Current House

This visualization exercise is for those of you who have begun to think about the separation process, and it is especially good if you feel indecisive about whether or not to move out. Read the following section at least once before beginning. Plan this trance for a day when you have enough time, when you are alone and will not be disturbed. Turn off the phone, the TV, the stereo, anything that might distract you. Choose a place in the house that feels safe and supportive. Have your journal and a pen next to you and a glass of water if you wish. Get comfortable and close your eyes. Take a few deep breaths and feel your body and mind slowing down and relaxing more fully.

Now with your eyes closed, and feeling more and more relaxed, imagine yourself in front of the home you've been sharing with your partner. Walk up to the door and go inside. No one else is there. You are free to walk through each room and truly see the contents. One at a time, stroll through the rooms of the house, noting in your mind if you would be able to leave your home when the time comes, and what you might like to take with you. If emotions come up for you, just let them, feeling each one pass through your body. When you have walked through the entire house, and are outside looking back at your home, remember your feelings about leaving, and which items you wish to keep.

If you plan to stay in your home and know that your spouse is leaving, look around at the possessions that are yours or are the most important to you. Notice which ones do not really belong to you either physically or spiritually. Using your mind, remove these items. When you are finished, look around once more, walk out, and close the door. View the outside and know in your heart if you want to stay or leave. Using visualization, you can return any time you want for another visit. Thank your house for the shelter it has provided. As you walk away, let the sounds get softer, your vision dimmer, until no sound remains and the images fade from your mind.

Begin to stir, move your feet, legs, and arms, and then slowly open your eyes. Take three deep breaths, adjust your eyes to your surroundings, and become aware of the space beneath and around you. If you are having trouble reorienting, drink the glass of water, and again move your feet in contact with the floor. Pick up your journal and write everything that you remember, as quickly as possible, until you have recorded your journey inside the house, listing the items you wish to keep and any feelings that came up. When you feel complete, reread what you have written. Is there anything that surprises you or brings up more emotion? If so, write about it. This first visualization should tell you whether you want to stay in the house or leave, what possessions you wish to keep, and how you feel about the process.

One client, Curtis, who was separated after eleven years of marriage, did the above exercise and was surprised by what he realized. "I really thought I wanted the house, that I'd fight for it if necessary, but during the visualization I couldn't believe what I saw. Every time I walked into a room, I didn't feel at home there; my wife's stuff was all over it and I didn't even like it. The only places I felt comfortable were in my office, in the garage, and in part of the living room. I can't believe how little of me lived there." After this experience, it was easier for Curtis to make the decision to move out, and now he is furnishing his own home.

An Alternative to Visualization 1

For those of you still living in the house you share with your husband or wife, it may not take a visualization to realize whether you want to stay or leave. As you walk around inside and out, notice how you feel. Are you attached to this house and its contents? Are you attached to the land around the home? You might wish to write about the feelings that come up as you ask yourself these questions. Then, jot down the items that are very special to you, perhaps beginning with the things you think you can't live without, then the items that were yours before you married, or were given to you as gifts. Another way to complete this process is to look around with as much detachment as possible, noticing what you care *least* about. I recommend this method because when it comes time to split the contents of your house with your mate, you can avoid endless arguments by being detached and altruistic. However, don't let your guilt keep you from taking an object that you deeply love. The one initiating the separation, whether staying in the house or leaving, often gives away too much because of guilt. Do what is fair. Don't forget that this is a love-centered process, not one mired in ego. Over the years, I've kept returning things to my former husband because they belonged to his family or were special to him in some way. The longer I'm divorced, the less essential these things are. What is truly important is the peace between us and an ever-deepening friendship.

Separating possessions may be easier than actually leaving your home, if this is your decision. For at least three years after

I left, I had dreams of our house and life there, and for the first year, my longing for "home" was palpable. My heart literally hurt during each season when the apples and plums were ripe, or red berries appeared on the holly, because I wasn't there to see them. From time to time I wished I had kept the house, but I felt guilty and didn't think I had the right to stay. My message to all of you who are contemplating a divorce is to be sure you want to move out. You have just as much right to stay there as your spouse does, maybe more. My children were born in our house, my son at home in the room that became his. I planted the gardens, weeded and watered them, and watched my children climb the trees and slide down the hills. Leaving my home was one of the hardest things I've ever done.

Rod and Toni, a couple now divorced for twenty years, owned a house they had lived in for five years with their three-year-old daughter, Marky. Toni loved her house, but after at least a year of fighting and confronting Rod, she decided to move out. She regretted this decision later, but she never fought to regain her home. Her guilt made her think she didn't deserve the house, and Rod did. In reality, Rod had caused at least fifty percent of the problems, refusing to talk to her and spending several nights a week at a popular bar. If Toni had talked to a therapist or family law mediator, she would have realized that she could keep her home, giving Rod his half of the investment.

Before making a decision about who is to leave and who is to keep the house, talk to an attorney or a mediator. It is best not to move out until this has been decided, even though you can still be awarded the house. If you have removed some of the possessions and have taken up residence elsewhere, it may appear that you don't want the house. Be cautious.

Visualization 2: Your New Home

In this second visualization, follow the guidelines from the first exercise in order to get ready, including reading the following section before beginning. When you are totally relaxed, close your eyes. First, envision where you would like to live. Is it in an urban or rural area? Imagine the perfect setting for your needs, and then notice what your new home looks like. If you can imagine the room, studio, apartment, or house in your chosen location, go ahead and walk in. What does the interior look like? Notice how this home ideally meets your needs at this time. Walk from room to room and mentally record what you see. Picture your belongings fitting perfectly in this new space. Look around one last time and then go out and close the door. As you walk away, turn and "sweep" the scene with your eyes and heart, noting how you feel about it overall. Let the scene fade more and more, as you slowly return to consciousness. Move your arms and legs, feel your feet on the floor, stretch, breathe deeply, and open your eyes. Drink a glass of water if needed. Then, pick up your journal and record everything you "saw." Reread what you've written, and add any realizations about your vision. What have you discovered?

At least three months before I left, I kept seeing myself in a little cottage with a small backyard and an apple tree. For some reason I really wanted an apple tree, probably because I was leaving a home on several acres with an orchard. Intuitively, I called about a studio near the ocean and asked to see it. It was behind a larger house, and as I opened the gate and walked down a cement walk, I saw a leafy green tree. It was an old apple tree covered in fruit. The yard was overgrown, the house small, but it was perfect for me. I told the owner a bit about my situation and then, without warning, I began to cry. He knew as I did that this was my home. I have always felt grateful for his compassion and for my intuition. You may not be at this stage yet, envisioning a new place to live, but when the time is right, be sure to listen to the voice inside that "knows."

Visualization 3: Your Ideal Lifestyle

How do you envision your life without your current partner? What would you like to be doing? I remember a few months before I moved out, my husband was away for three months on business and I had the whole house to myself. I could write poetry all night, sleep and eat when I pleased, talk on the phone at all hours, and be more social with my friends. I realized during this time that I had never truly lived alone, and I craved the space and freedom to do as I pleased. My fantasies were about living in solitude and enjoying more spontaneity.

For this next exercise, you can close your eyes and try another visualization, or just think about what you would be doing with your life if you separated from your spouse. For the moment, don't limit yourself by finances or by practicality. We'll be practical later. Just daydream, and then write about your ideal life. Do you want to be alone or with other people? Do you prefer an urban or rural area? What kind of lifestyle do you want? Personally, I valued a quiet, simple life with few possessions, and time to be outdoors. When I left, I took my computer, my bike, minimal furniture, linens, and clothes. This was my ideal. It may be different for you. What is it that you value most? Write these things in your journal, beginning with, "I value . . ." or "I want . . ." This daydream will tell you about the future you can create, first in your unconscious mind, and then in reality. As Henry David Thoreau said, "If you have built castles in the air, your work need not be lost; that is where they should be. Now put the foundations under them."

Sometimes, when planning and beginning a new life, the ego may be in charge and not our intuition. Be sure to notice if what you plan seems to be meeting with resistance or obstacles. Cora, recently separated from Dale after thirteen years, has wanted to move from the city to a specific rural community, but she says, "It's been like pushing the river upstream. I can't find a place to live, can't seem to get established financially, and just yesterday I realized I'm not ready to move yet." She is currently living with her sister and senses that the two siblings need to work on their relationship. And so, she's staying until this is completed. Also, very honestly, she admits she was willfully trying to return to the town nearest her former partner, but, "The universe doesn't want me to go back to the past; I'm to move on." Like Cora, if you can trust your inner wisdom and follow its guidance, your path and destination will become clear to you.

PLANNING TO LEAVE: TIMING

Unless you're being abused, it is best to take your time. Many take at least a year to leave. This may sound like a long time, especially when things seem intolerable; however, the organization necessary to dissolve a marriage is considerable. The fallout from bad planning could last a lifetime. Of those interviewed, most take between three and twenty-four months to begin a separation, from first thoughts to actually living separately. One woman, Lynn, a workshop participant, took thirty-five years to leave her marriage. She knew early on that she and her husband had problems, that he was an alcoholic, but she just couldn't take action. As a housewife with small children, dependent on her husband for support, she felt economically trapped. And so, she made the best of the situation. Lynn thought she'd leave when the children were grown, but by then she and her husband were so used to each other that she stayed out of habit. She admits she kept expecting him to stop drinking, but he never did. Finally, when Lynn began getting Social Security, she felt able to leave. She doesn't regret her decision to stay so long or to leave so late in life, adding, "It took the time it took."

Of course, some individuals leave within a few months. Margie lived with Phil in Hawaii for five years, but she left him and moved on her own to California a few months ago. Phil worked as a waiter at a large resort and liked to party after hours with the other staff. His drinking never seemed to be a problem, but using cocaine made him incredibly nervous and unpredictable. The violence slowly escalated from name calling, to shoving, to hitting. Margie kept thinking it would get better, that he would stop "using" and get help. It didn't happen. She swore she would never let someone hit her, that she would leave that day, but it took her a month to call her family and ask for a place to live, to quit her job, pack her things, and buy a ticket home. She says of that time, "I'm hard on myself when you ask me about leaving. I'd been telling my friends for years never to let someone hit them. But when it was me, I had a hard time. I loved him, and I guess I still do, but I did leave and I'm not going back."

Christy, twenty-two, married Jesse, twenty-five, because she was pregnant and because they were attracted to each other and wanted to do the right thing. After three months of being married, Jesse went home to his wealthy mother. Jesse's aunt says of the early days of their marriage, "My sister spoiled Jesse rotten and it's going to be difficult for Christy; we just hope she can straighten him out." Now, Christy, who lives in Arizona, admits, "I had a dream of what we could create, a family, but it was just a dream and not real. I still can't think about the wedding and his leaving without feeling angry or crying. I never even picked up the pictures."

Jason left quickly as well, but he did so because of solid finances and indifference. With a six-figure income in Silicon Valley, California, he had no problem separating bank accounts, credit cards, and cars; finding another place; having his things moved—and all without missing a day of work. He and his wife are separated, seeing a mediator and still dividing the assets, but he left two weeks after he first felt the inclination. I asked him if he had had doubts about the relationship previously, or if he had had any earlier feelings that they would separate. His answer surprised me. "No. I was pretty happy with Laura for the year or so we were together. This sounds weird, but I woke up one morning, looked over at her, and knew I didn't love her. I didn't know why we got married, and didn't want to be with her. Now, looking back, I know we married too quickly and not for the best reasons. She was pretty upset at first, but now I think she feels the same way I do."

These cases are unusual, however. Most of us spend months or years entering a relationship, and we need a similar amount of time to exit. This was true for me. For over twenty years, my former husband and I had developed a relationship that ran smoothly, that, in retrospect, was like a successful business with each person fulfilling roles and positions, interacting effortlessly, yet with little emotion. Toward the end of our marriage, he commented, "I expected to grow old with you and our children and grandchildren, and didn't think much about it being better or different; it just was all I could expect." Both of us realize now, several years later, that the time together was finished, that we each had given and received all we could in the union and needed to move on. I left within three months of realizing I had to go, but the seed of that departure had been germinating for many years. Trust your intuition and take whatever time you need.

PLANNING TO LEAVE: THE STAGES

Emotional Detachment

Stage one of leaving begins when one or both partners become more detached, less engaged, or connected. This lack of connection may begin years before the legal divorce, but often one partner is already beginning to create emotional distance.

Many of those interviewed began to leave one another emotionally by scheduling separate events in the evening, watching television while their partner went to bed, staying at work late, going on separate trips, or being "too tired" to talk or make love. This was true for a former client, Ursula, married for six years, who says, "When we were first together, I hated leaving on trips, and I even traded with people to be able to get shorter legs, but in the past year, I've asked for the longest trips. I tell my husband it's for the money, but really I don't want to be with him." Usually one partner in the relationship is more unhappy or dissatisfied. Initially, this spouse may keep these feelings quiet, turning inward for answers and eventually seeking happiness outside the marriage. In my relationship, my husband and I turned to our work for satisfaction. Unfortunately, our addiction to work, and our silence about how we felt about one another, masked the real issues in the relationship.

Next, while still in the phase of detachment, the dissatisfied spouse may begin complaining or voicing his or her unhappiness. In addition to expressing indifference or avoidance, as in Ursula's case, one person may begin to criticize or belittle the other partner. At times, tension escalates and then one or both individuals may busy themselves with work, the children, the mundane tasks, in order to hide what is really happening in the marriage. A distant relative, Jenn, married to Parker for eight years and now divorced, lived in a state of tension and verbal abuse for three years. As she explains, "Parker and I would go out to dinner, and sometimes eat in total silence. My neck was so tight, my shoulders like rocks, and I usually got a bad headache. Other times Parker would start about my dress being too tight, or ugly, and it would escalate to screaming and throwing things. I even spent the night in the bathroom with the door double-locked."

Eventually, the situation can become so frustrating that at least one spouse takes action, either by saying the relationship is over,

or by "acting out" and having an affair. Several of those interviewed say that falling in love with someone else was how they
"got out" of their unhappy marriages. They just couldn't seem to
leave on their own, could not say, "I'm leaving because I no
longer love you," or "I'm leaving because I'm unhappy and no
longer want to be with you." For some couples, it can take something drastic, something strong that shatters all societal rules.

One fifty-year-old woman, a former colleague, Arden, married for twenty-seven years, left her husband, Rick, for a man
she met in a training course in another city. Arden talked with
me before she moved out, and again after she was settled in
her own place. She spoke of her need to leave, of her concern
for her teenage daughter, of her love for Martin. "Frankly, I
didn't know what love was before. Rick is a good man who
gave me all he had to give, but it wasn't love. For years we
were like housemates, not lovers. Our sex life was dull and
unimaginative, if it happened at all. He was not my soul mate,
but Martin is. It took meeting someone else to make me realize what I had been missing most of my life."

Falling in love with someone else as a way to leave your
marriage may not be the best choice. A better way is to know
yourself well, follow your intuition, and tell your spouse the
truth. This is the ideal. But sometimes we feel stuck. Sometimes we find ourselves in intricate familial webs that seem
impossible to escape. We feel trapped. And so, it may take
something powerful and life-altering to create the catalyst for
change, to get us to take action. This may be an extramarital
affair, as in Arden's case, or another life-altering experience,
such as a parent dying, children going to college, returning to
school or the job market, or a spiritual transformation.

Within a two-year period before I left my marriage, my
father died, my mother became ill, one child left home, I
returned to school, I began another career, and I became
attracted to someone else. Apparently, I needed more than

one catalyst in order to leave what had become a rigid life. Early in my marriage, I completely changed myself in order to please my husband. I tried to be his ideal of the perfect wife, who could work all day, have the house cleaned and the children quiet, and give a dinner party for twenty of his colleagues. In the process, however, I ignored my own inner longings for solitude, creativity, and spirituality. The more I allowed myself to listen to an inner voice, the more I realized how unlike my husband I was, how caged I felt, and the more I knew I had to leave. And so, you are engaged in this stage of detachment when at least one of you directly or indirectly says, "I can't do this anymore," and begins to take action.

Handling Finances

A second stage while planning to separate is the financial one, in which partners list and then divide their joint property and settle their debts before reaching a final agreement. Attorney and mediator Chip Rose advises communicating with your spouse about your feelings first. Then, work together to gather and record all your financial information. Finally, make a series of appointments with a mediator to go over financial matters. In this way, you can build the most trust and reduce stress by talking openly and sharing information, instead of secretly plotting and hoarding assets, which could create or escalate conflict. Once again, a conscious divorce is about thoughtfully negotiating an equitable settlement.

It does help to have all the financial information organized to present to your mediator. In this chapter you will learn how to research, list, and organize your finances, doing as much planning and collecting as you can before actually negotiating a joint-property settlement. Such gathering will save time and money once you begin meeting with a mediator. This is the practical, realistic process, mentioned earlier, that comes after fantasizing or visualizing what you want. Now is the time for action. Such organization is truly a way to take care of yourself, to say, "I'm important and worth this effort. I deserve financial stability." You can begin by listing all properties and finances, those solely yours, and those mutually owned, so you know what assets you possess. After this, you can record expenses and debts to create a clear picture of your financial situation.

Assets and Income

Note the worth of each of the following categories. If an item is solely owned by you, put the amount in the "yours" column. If it is jointly owned, or held only by your spouse, list the amount in the second column.

Item	$ Yours	$ Jointly or Spouse's
1. Monthly take-home pay		
2. Checking account/s		
3. Savings account/s, including interest		
4. Property: land, houses, and businesses		
5. Rent or other monies paid to you		
6. Other property such as cars, boats, jewelry, hobby collections, computers,sports equipment, furniture, stereos, clothing. Other ———————————— ————————————		
7. Investments: stocks, bonds, mutual funds, etc., including interest or dividends paid		
8. Insurance policies		
9. Retirement funds: IRA's, 401k's, employment pension plans, etc.		
Total $	———	———

Notice overall what is owned by you alone, what is jointly held by the two of you, and what is solely owned by your spouse. Now that this accounting is complete, what do you realize about your assets? This exercise can tell you a great deal about how solid you are financially, how much you have personally accrued, and what you own as a couple. All this information will be invaluable as you move closer to negotiating a settlement and dividing up property.

In addition to tallying the worth of your assets, it is crucial to list your expenses and debts, which also must be divided at the time of negotiation. They can be categorized most clearly as current and future monthly expenses. Once you have your monthly income listed above, you can subtract the expenses below from this amount. Of course, if you are the one to move out, your rent, utilities, and other expenses will be different from the ones you have now. We will go over the costs of moving out and setting up a new household in the next section.

Current Monthly Expenses in Your Joint Household	*$ Amount*
1. Mortgage (including house insurance and property taxes divided monthly) or rent:	
2. Utilities (gas, electric, water, garbage):	
3. Food, including vitamins, toiletries, and sundries:	
4. Medical and life insurance:	
5. Medical and dental expenses:	
6. Car expenses, including gas, repairs, insurance, and license:	
7. Phone, including the Internet:	
8. Household cleaning and repairs, including appliances and computers:	

Current Monthly Expenses in Your Joint Household	$ Amount
9. Clothing:	
10. Recreation, vacations, and entertainment:	
11. Children's expenses: childcare, tuition, sports, etc.:	
12. Federal and state taxes (divided by twelve for a monthly amount):	
Total $	_____

It's a good idea to assess your credit card debt at this time, too. Even though the above expenses were probably gleaned in part from your credit card statement, most people have amassed debts on several credit cards and don't pay the whole amount monthly. If this is the case, list your credit cards below and how much is owed in total on each. Then, you need a payment plan to get yourself out of debt. When you and your spouse begin talking about your separation and joint property, encourage him or her to become debt-free as well. If not, you could be left with a bad credit rating as a result. If you have your own cards to pay off, list them separately from those jointly owned with your spouse.

Credit Card Names	$ Owed by You	$ Owed Jointly
1.		
2.		
3.		
4.		
5.		
6.		

If your credit cards are held jointly with your spouse, it's best to negotiate new credit terms with the company. They may not be willing to establish a new account in your name until the divorce is final and you've established your own separate credit rating. If you're in debt to creditors or are unsure of your credit status, you can request and receive a credit report from TRW, one of the nation's largest credit reporting agencies. (See address in Resources.) If you've never had your own credit cards, it would be good to get one or two, such as a gasoline or department store card. Make sure you understand the credit terms before signing, especially the percentage of interest charged to your account. Unfortunately, many scams exist to ensnare naive consumers. Always read the small print, *literally*. It's usually at the bottom and makes a qualifying statement that the bolder print omits.

It's essential to get out of debt, preferably before leaving your relationship, and to encourage your partner to pay all his or her bills as well. At the time of a separation and divorce, you could be responsible for half of the amassed debt, just as you are entitled to half of the accrued assets.

Legal Assistance and Terminology

It's a good idea to see a mediator or attorney to go over your income and assets. Then he or she can give you a general idea of what you'll be receiving in the settlement. An attorney can discuss the meaning of no-fault divorce and whether or not you can expect spousal and child support. These two amounts can also come to you as income, the spousal amount usually on a temporary basis only and the child support payments until the children are eighteen or twenty-one. The dollar amount for each of these payments varies case by case, depending on the need of the spouse requesting support and the custody agreement established for care of minor children.

How to Choose a Mediator or Family Law Attorney

It is prudent at this early stage to seek legal assistance from someone who can answer your questions and help allay any fears. The sooner you begin, at first with one hour, the more realistic you'll be about attorney fees and how to keep these costs to a minimum. If you have any friends who are lawyers, ask them to recommend a mediator or attorney who would work well with you. My friend suggested a woman who only handles divorces, and who thoroughly knows the law, especially as it applies to women. I only talked with her once, but the hour I spent was worth the $150 fee. My advice is to see a mediator or attorney who specializes in family law to answer your initial questions. Then, I recommend seeing a mediator as a couple to handle the rest of your divorce. Having separate attorneys is incredibly expensive and it causes more paranoia between you. It's best to continue to work on your relationship with a trained mediator who can not only help you divorce but also assist you to communicate clearly and more amicably. If you do not have a friend to refer someone, perhaps your therapist can give you a name or two. You can also obtain a list of attorneys in your area by writing or calling the Academy of Family Mediators or the American Bar Association. (Addresses and phone numbers are in Resources.)

Many mediators and attorneys will give clients a free consultation, often over the phone and sometimes in person. When calling them, ask about a complimentary consultation, and then set an appointment. This first contact helps you to choose someone who is knowledgeable as well as supportive. He or she should be experienced, clear about fees, able to explain legal terminology, and realistic and honest about possible outcomes. Such an attorney is familiar with mediation or other means to settle out of court and, ultimately, wants to help create the best outcome with the least amount of stress.

When meeting with a mediator or family law attorney, take

the lists of assets and expenses that you have completed in this chapter. He or she will be able to summarize your financial situation and let you know what to expect in a settlement. This will not be specific, but a general amount. Ask the lawyer to explain the concepts of no-fault divorce, joint property, and spousal and child support. Until then, here are some basic explanations of these terms.

No-Fault Divorce

Until 1970, the year of the first no-fault divorce law in California, all divorces were fault-based. This means that one spouse had to prove that the other partner was guilty of some infraction. In many states, such as New York, in the first half of the twentieth century, the only ground for divorce was adultery. Attorneys had to find or create evidence of guilt, often by hiring professional witnesses who made their living by testifying and in many cases committing perjury. Even though several states allowed divorce on the ground of mental cruelty, the concept of finding one person at fault caused incredible paranoia and encouraged dishonesty.

Today, all fifty states have adopted a no-fault divorce law, but in some states, misconduct can still affect the awarding of custody and maintenance payments. In the past, spousal support might be awarded only to the innocent party, and if guilty of adultery or cruelty, the person would not receive alimony. With no-fault divorce, people can cite irreconcilable differences as the cause and obtain a divorce based solely on this claim. This law potentially seeks to create equality between men and women rather than seeing one person as wrong and the other right. No-fault divorce focuses not on past misconduct; it focuses with neutrality on the present and future. This is the essence of a conscious divorce.

In actuality, several states still allow traditional grounds for divorce, such as adultery, desertion, or cruelty, to be stated, in addition to no-fault grounds of incompatibility. Also, fault can affect the awarding of spousal support in some states. Furthermore, in nearly every state, one partner can sue the other for harming the estate financially or for wrongful acts that cause injury. One spouse can also sue or find fault in child custody cases involving alleged abuse. Be sure to research the grounds for divorce in your state, and their effect on you, by contacting the agencies listed in Resources.

According to attorneys, no-fault divorce is designed to create less stress and tension between spouses. It is true that more and more couples are avoiding the courtroom altogether in favor of mediators and paralegals who complete and file their divorce papers. No-fault divorce, when combined with skillful mediation, moves the process forward with as little animosity as possible. A detailed discussion of mediation will appear in chapter 5, The Divorcing Process.

The no-fault divorce law was supposed to simplify the division of property, called marital or community property in most states, by dividing it equally between spouses. This belief is based on the view that each partner contributed equally to the marriage, though often differently. It was true in my California divorce that our community property was divided fairly. I credit our mediator for making sure I received my share of our property, such as part of my husband's retirement plan. This is why it is crucial to hire a mediator who can be unbiased, who sees that wife and husband are equal partners who do not have gender-based roles. According to many women clients and colleagues, as well as several attorneys, no-fault divorce is not uniformly beneficial financially for women and children. In general, upon divorce, women are discriminated against by their gender, ethnicity, and age. They still make about seventy-four percent of what men make in income, and they often need retraining in order to re-enter the job market.

During marriage, women often give up the chance for

careers to stay home as homemakers and mothers. While their husbands are increasing their income, the women are falling farther and farther behind in the job market. Mara, a university professor, now divorced for sixteen years, with two children, was nearly denied tenure. This was because she had a four- and six-year-old to care for while trying to teach and do research. She bitterly remembers, "I was a nationally recognized scholar with dozens of publications, and yet I did not have as many published articles as my male colleagues. This was because as a mother I worked less in order to care for my children, both before and after my divorce. I never had a 'wife' like my husband did."

In our divorce, when my former husband protested about giving me spousal support to allow me to return to school, the mediator asked, "Who took care of your children and ran your household the majority of the time while you were building your career?" He had to say, "My wife did." Our mediator negotiated spousal support for me for one year and child support when our son stayed at my home. After all, I had been a devoted wife and mother for twenty-six years, and the mediator saw that equity governed our no-fault divorce. Be sure to claim what you deserve.

Spousal Support

A brief discussion of spousal support will be included in this chapter so you can understand what your potential income might be. Otherwise, you can't begin to plan in other areas such as housing, further education, and career. It might seem that this presentation is only for women. However, this is an outdated concept. In the twenty-first century, more and more women will be in the workforce, while more men will have the choice to stay home or work part-time. By 2005, according to the 1996 U.S. Bureau of the Census, sixty-three percent of adult women and sixty-nine percent of adult men will be employed, a nearly equal rate. And so, when couples are separating and negotiating their divorce, either may be eligible for spousal support, depending on need and the other factors listed below. Be aware that laws regarding spousal support may vary from state to state.

At this time, it is mostly women who are receiving spousal support based on temporary and renegotiable need. This means that courts favor temporary support for spouses to upgrade skills and become completely self-sufficient. Recipients are mostly older homemakers who have been in long-term marriages, of at least twenty years, and mothers with preschool children. As a professional in my mid-forties, I received support to go back to school and begin a second career. One former client, Claire, divorced with four children, received enough spousal support to quit her job and finish graduate school, allowing her to be home more with the children. Unfortunately, her ex-husband, Larry, paid the minimal child support, and Claire had to use the money from the sale of their home just to get by. Now, she owes the IRS tens of thousands of dollars and is contemplating bankruptcy. She didn't want a protracted court battle with Larry, so she's tried to settle her financial problems alone. Don't try to do this yourself. Get legal counsel to ensure you receive the financial support you deserve for the length of time you need.

Although spousal support is mainly a temporary arrangement, it can be awarded even after the recipient remarries. As mentioned above, it is usually given to those in longer marriages who have a specific need for financial aid, and it can be awarded for half the length of the marriage and, in some cases, for life. Your mediator will look at both your incomes and standard of living, at your abilities to be self-supporting, at your ages, your health, and whether one of you has more ability to pay. As an example, my ex-husband made nearly three times my monthly salary and was required to give me spousal support. This monthly allotment, however, was only given for one year, even though I could have asked for support for thirteen years. Our mediator constantly referred to his desire to "even the playing field," making sure that each of us came as close as possible to our previous standard of living. One of my current clients, Yvonne, married for forty-six years and separated for two years, is afraid to file for divorce for fear her husband will leave the state with all their assets. Even with the facts in front of her, that she is entitled to half their joint property and twenty-three years of spousal support, she can't seem to act. It's a slow process after such a long marriage, but Yvonne is taking action by living separately, limiting contact with her husband, and taking classes at a local college. One hopes that, in time, she'll realize she deserves even more.

It is essential that women and men who need support, even temporarily, ask for it. If we truly want a conscious and loving divorce, we desire the best outcome for everyone, including ourselves. This means we will be honest and fair in our request for (or our granting of) financial support.

Child Support

Again, to be able to project a possible income after separating, it's helpful to understand how child support payments are awarded. Child support, unlike spousal support payments, is required by law until minor children reach the age of eighteen or twenty-one. Child support in California is determined under the statutory guideline; please check with your legal counsel to clarify the requirements in your state. This guideline is an algebraic formula, used by paralegals, mediators, and other attorneys, that considers the following factors in its calculation:

1. The number of minor children of this relationship.
2. The approximate percentage of time each parent has primary physical responsibility for each minor child.
3. The gross income as well as earning capacity of each parent.

4. Each parent's tax filing status, whether single, married, married and filing separately, head of household; the number of dependents claimed by each parent; and all available exclusions, deductions, and credits.

5. The deductions claimed can include union dues, retirement benefits, health insurance, child or spousal support actually paid, and any necessary job expenses.

6. Additional child support will be required by the court for childcare related to employment or retraining for employment, as will insurance costs for the children, any special needs of each child, and travel costs for visitation. This additional support may be divided equally between parents or prorated.

7. Financial hardship includes extraordinary health expenses, uninsured losses, as well as minimum living expenses for a parent's natural or adopted children from other marriages or relationships who reside with the parent.

Our mediator used the above information in the standard formula to establish the amount of child support for our one minor child. We varied the amount based upon time spent with each of us, as this fluctuated from month to month. We listed the types of expenses for the month, such as: school costs (books, photos, prep courses, proms, graduation, college application fees, etc.), food, clothing, sports costs, lessons, hobbies, and entertainment. Children are expensive. It's important that the expenses be shared fairly. In our case, I received money each month, based on a flexible, varied need. We did have a base amount, but my ex-husband was very fair and generous to give more if needed. You may or may not have a similar experience. I advise giving or asking for a fair yet generous amount, considering that the cost of living continues to rise. Again, negotiate with integrity and love—in this case, mutual love for your children.

Many custodial parents are protesting the ending of child support at the age of eighteen, before the finishing of college. One recipient of support for several years, an adolescent client, Janis, says of her experience, "My dad has suddenly cut me off during my senior year and before I leave for college. I have a basketball scholarship but it's still not enough to pay all the expenses. It's like my dad is relieved that he's done with me and done with being a father. But doesn't he realize it isn't that simple?" Janis speaks for individual citizens and lawmakers, many of whom want the age for child support to extend at least until the completion of college. It is my recommendation that couples filing for divorce write an agreement to support the college educations of their children. In my case, we had been saving for college expenses since the birth of each child; we agreed to leave the money in the respective accounts and decided that my ex-husband would manage and disperse these funds to our children.

According to attorneys, the problems with "deadbeat parents" has caused a change in the 1988 Family Support Act, or rather an addition. As of January 1, 1994, in many states those paying child support automatically have the money deducted from their pay by employers and sent to the custodial parent. If a parent is a month or more late in payments, an employer is required to deduct the amount from the payroll check. A court order can require that other monies be withheld and sent to the custodial parent, such as from Social Security checks. Even though this sounds effective as a method to ensure support of children, it doesn't often work. Sadly, many parents still move, lie, or have family members lie about their whereabouts to avoid paying child support. Christy, mentioned previously, has filed for child support with her local District Attorney's office after repeated attempts to contact Jesse have failed. The D.A.'s office sent an undercover officer to watch the residence where Jesse had last been seen, but he never appeared. Now it is rumored he has moved to another state. In the meantime, the District Attorney's office has been alerted, and they will continue an attempt to find him and demand back and current support payments.

Several states are becoming tougher in their approach to child support, even threatening jail time if the parent does not get a job and make regular payments. In addition, federal agencies as well as parent locator groups are using every method available, from IRS records and Social Security records to motor vehicle statistics, to locate parents delinquent in their support payments. Sadly, it is the children who suffer.

Immediate Economic Goals

The following advice is based on my own experience and the experience of clients. It would be helpful to complete these tasks as part of practical planning, before or during discussion of a separation. More specific information on divorce finances and property issues, child custody, and support is presented in chapter 5. At that stage, the two of you will be discussing divorce and negotiating a settlement. So, for now:

1. Pay off your bills and set up a payment plan for your debts.
2. Set up a budget to help you accomplish number 1. If you need help making a budget, read the book *Divorce and Money* by Woodhouse and Felton-Collins, which has charts, checklists, and worksheets.
3. Open your own checking and savings accounts; if possible, have your paycheck automatically deposited. Establish your own credit, if you do not have credit cards now. Be careful. This isn't a license to spend. It's a way to establish good credit.
4. Put as much as you can into your savings account beginning today. You can have the bank take a certain amount out of your paycheck each month and put it in savings. If

you are the one leaving, you may need several thousand dollars to do it.

5. If you have a few thousand dollars in savings, look into putting it in a money market account with better interest, but make sure that you can withdraw money and write checks.

6. Make sure your car is in good condition; if not, schedule repairs or look into buying another car.

7. Increase your income at work or begin looking for another job. Remember, it will cost you more to live in two separate households. You will have half the money you are used to if you both have worked.

8. Learn everything you can about your investments, insurance, taxes, and the value of your current home. Make copies of all documents and take them with you to your hour-long appointment with an attorney. It might be good to talk with a financial consultant, too, if your joint property is considerable or confusing (or both).

9. If you need counseling, medical attention, dental work, or anything else, see professionals right away. Your mental, emotional, and physical health are very important. Do this while you still have two incomes.

10. As mentioned in the first section of this chapter, begin investigating the housing market if you are the one leaving. Depending on where you live, it could be challenging to find just what you want. Begin looking today.

Future Economic Goals

1. Look at the list of assets above. Write down the amount you estimate to be yours, that you can count on each month. If you have been to an attorney, then list what you have found to be your spousal and child support (if applicable). Otherwise, put down your monthly salary and any other income coming only to you.

2. Look at the list of monthly expenses above. Now, determine how much you would spend just on yourself, for instance, for food, clothing, and housing. Make a new list of expenses that can become a basis for a monthly budget.

3. From creating the above lists of income and expenses, you can more easily tell how much you can pay for housing. Write that amount here: _____. As you continue to look in the local paper for places to live, keep in mind what you can afford. Begin to match your earlier visualization with the reality. It can be done.

4. Make a decision about your current job, whether or not you want to remain there. If not, begin thinking about and researching a future career. This change may necessitate a return to school. If you know this by the time you see a mediator, you can get spousal support to help pay for your education in order to improve your employment status.

MORE ABOUT CAREER

If you're happy with your current job, both in terms of satisfaction and economics, then skip this section. Actually, don't skip it. You never know when you might want to change careers. Most of us work at several jobs over a lifetime, and some of us hold more than one at the same time. I've always had two or more careers at once, or have been in school while working. Think about your current career. To help this process, open your journal and write the answers to the following questions. Do you love getting up in the morning to go to work? In other words, do you look forward to your job on a daily basis? What do you like most about your career? What do you like least? If you could change anything about your job, what would it be? You can list more than one thing. Is it actually possible to change these aspects? Have you ever wanted to leave this job? What were the reasons? If you could have any career you want, or could do anything you want for a salary, what would it be? Don't laugh. Write down what popped into your mind.

Remember, you can access your intuition, your inner voice. Listen to it now. If this is truly what you would like to be doing, what has stopped you in the past? What is stopping you now? If you wrote the name of your current job, great. You are already set. If anything needs changing at this existing job in order for it to become more ideal, list it now. Also, note how these aspects can be changed and by when. Assigning a date can encourage you to take action and achieve your goals.

If you do not work at this time, but know you will need to find a job once you and your partner separate, read on. I still recommend writing down your ideal job from your intuition, perhaps answering the question, "What would I like to be doing that would be rewarding and profitable?" You may have tapped into this idea when doing the visualization at the beginning of the chapter concerning your ideal lifestyle. The reason I suggest starting with your unconscious mind is that it truly knows more than—or at least as much as —any test given to you in a career center. Of course, going to a local college career center or hiring a career counselor is a good idea, too. Just start with your inner self first.

For several years I've encouraged adolescent clients to do visualizations on each aspect of their lives before doing assessment tests. This information coupled with testing and career planning materials gave them an accurate idea of their future. Invariably, they told me that the clearest ideas about lifestyle and career plans came in the visualizations we did. This is because the unconscious mind knows you the best and will tell the truth. This doesn't mean you'll always like what you hear. Oftentimes, participants would visualize themselves as forest rangers and marine biologists, or even loggers and commercial fishermen. They would say, "But I'm supposed to be a doctor, a lawyer, or a corporate executive." As an adult, you may still have some of these tapes playing in your head. My advice: erase them, or better yet, shred and throw them away. The only thing stopping you is your own fear. Throw that away, too.

EMOTIONS DURING PRACTICAL PLANNING

No matter how busy you are planning your separation or divorce, feelings will still come up. Even if you don't particularly want to have emotions surface, they will. It's actually healthier to give yourself the time and space to have these feelings. If you do everything to avoid the fear and anger, then you're only postponing their eruption. You have the potential for an even bigger catharsis, explosion, or depressive episode. The other thing that may happen, and did happen to me, is that feelings such as excitement and relief may come up, especially if you're the one leaving. But then weeks or months later, the fear, anger, and especially the sadness can hit unannounced. This can be quite challenging. Why not notice and experience your feelings right now and deal with them, using the tools of turning inward, letting the feelings surface, writing in a journal, and reflecting on your responses. One workshop participant, Della, separated from her husband of twenty-seven years, says, "I have a vacation coming up. I haven't done any crying yet, but I'm planning to do it then." Of course, you can also talk with a therapist or friend to help you gain needed perspective.

Fear

Review the detailed section on fear in chapter 1. My guess is that you may be experiencing one of the types presented there. After the discussion of economics in this chapter, you may be feeling some "financial fears." This is only natural now that you are dealing with what it means to "divide" two people who are legally joined. It isn't just about the emotional separation, but the splitting of all mutual property as well. After reading the above section regarding joint-property assets and liabilities, what are your feelings? If you have some financial fears, list these in your journal, beginning with "I'm afraid that . . ." Now reread them, noticing which are realistic and founded in your experience. In other words, they either have been true in the past or you think they have a strong chance of coming about in the future. Star these fears. Next, write what you can do to help, change, or prevent the situation. An example comes from the story Jenna, married for thirteen years, told me. One of her greatest fears was losing their house, having to sell it and split the money in order to have the capital to buy other homes. This is exactly what did happen, but Jenna never used the money to buy a house; she needed it to get out of debt and pay for the day-to-day expenses. Looking back, she and her ex-husband, Marty, wish they had refinanced the house, allowing Jenna and the children to stay there. Marty had an excellent job. He could have rented for a while and then bought a new house. As it is, nine years later, Jenna is still in debt and does not own a home. So, if one of your fears is having to sell your home, get advice from a financial planner, have the house appraised, and proceed from there. Using the information provided in this chapter, take each realistic fear and create an action plan to address it. Rather than lying awake worrying, you can be sleeping soundly, knowing you are consciously addressing each potential problem and taking appropriate action.

How do you know if some of the fears you have listed are unrealistic? For instance, if you wrote in your journal, "I'm afraid I'll lose my house, my job, my car, my children, my sanity, and end up asking for spare change on the street," take this statement apart piece by piece and look at the reality of each loss: house, job, car, kids, sanity, and self-respect. From what you know right now from listing your assets as well as your expenses and debts, your potential income from the divorce, and any other factors, does this fear seem realistic? This technique to dispel fear involves taking the fear to the limit of absurdity. At this point, people can often laugh at their irrational beliefs. The concern about having less money as the result of a divorce, fed through a fearful mind, becomes losing everything and being homeless. You may be experiencing other fears, too, such as leaving your children, or facing the unknown. Retrace your steps back to the most reasonable, realistic fear, and ask yourself if you can live with it. Look at each irrational fear with this discerning eye, noting what may be logical fears and which are illogical ones.

Anger

As you plan to leave your relationship, you or your partner may be feeling and expressing anger. Another therapist recently told me that anger is the emotion she sees most when counseling couples who are divorcing. She believes that anger is essential for the distancing and separating process and important for a person's eventual healing. I agree. Review the methods for communicating anger in chapter 2, especially the part about fair fighting.

Also, it may be safer to be angry with a third party present, such as a mediator or therapist. At one point in the planning stages of my divorce, my husband became extremely angry at me. I was glad our mediator was there to diffuse a potentially ugly situation. At other times, my ex-husband probably didn't get angry enough, or at least express his angry feelings, which he had a right to do.

It is healthy to express this anger and hurt when it's happening, or at least as soon as you can for your own emotional well-being and for honesty in the relationship. Be sure, however, to use "I" messages as well as the other communication techniques suggested. If you're so enraged that you can't think clearly, it's best to take a time-out, leave the room or the house. Tell your spouse how long you will be gone and that you want to talk after you've calmed down.

If you or your partner do not choose to express your anger to each other, then do tell someone how you feel, or at least write these feelings in your journal. I spent many months writing daily in my journal, recording my anger, hurt, frustration, and sadness. By getting these feelings out of my body, I healed more quickly emotionally. Also, doing deep breathing helped, as did meditation and physical exercise. Do whatever would help you release pent-up emotions. If you haven't much time, dispel angry feelings by screaming while alone in your bedroom, in your car, or at a deserted location in nature. Also, I scream into my pillow and have been known to throw rocks and break bottles into a trash can. I used to hit a raquetball when at my most angry, but during my divorce, and even now, I go on long bike rides and ride hard and fast. I literally sweat the anger out of my pores. Many people I know are runners and find this exercise to be excellent for working out any issues, including anger. You return feeling unwound and a lot more clear-headed. If you need other suggestions of ways to release emotional tension, turn to chapter 7, Self-Care.

Some people tend to stuff their anger and don't say how they feel at the time. One woman, Miranda, married for eleven years, says of this, "While my ex-husband and I were preparing to separate, I never raised my voice. I never expressed my feelings at all. Looking back, I see how ridiculous this was. He was leaving me and our two young children for a woman he barely knew. And, yet, I smiled and wished him well. It has taken me sixteen years, many of them in therapy, to feel and express my anger, but still not to him." Elena, mentioned in chapter 1, is still married; she calls herself a "stuffer" and talks about anger in her marriage. "I had lots of anger for years. I couldn't really admit this even to myself and not to my husband. I stuffed it down deeply. I got this modeling from my parents, whom I never saw quarrel. This went on until four years ago when I just stopped pursuing my husband and realized I couldn't change him. I was so angry, that I refused to sleep together for quite a while. My anger has dissipated, as I have focused on my own life. Now, we're closer, but I have no idea if we'll still be together in five years when our kids are gone. I need to wait and see."

Chanté, separated for eight months, admits she became violent as a way to express her anger. Her husband, Ben, spent all their money on drugs and nearly lost their home. She says, "I didn't care that Ben was suicidal and very sick. At the time I left him, I was so angry he'd jeopardized everything we had for a stupid high. More than anything, I was angry at the lying. For two years we'd been going to therapy and supposedly improving, while the therapist and I never knew he was 'using' or emptying our accounts. I hit him in the face and scratched him pretty badly before walking out." Chanté has calmed down, but Ben, who has successfully completed rehab, won't talk with her.

It's very important to strike a balance between swallowing your anger and throwing it in your partner's face. First, acknowledge that you're angry, write about it, perhaps talk to a therapist about your feelings, study the communications skills in chapter 2, and if it is safe, tell your partner. The way you choose to release appropriate anger is up to you, but the process helps release tension in your body and in the relationship.

Excitement

Usually it's the person planning to leave who feels this emotion. This is because the process has gained momentum, action is being taken, and the end seems to be in sight. You are the one who has been dreaming and thinking about leaving for weeks, months, or years. Now it's finally here. Even the person who is staying in the home, who did not initiate the separation, may feel elated. Karl, who lived with Mary Claire for two years, threw a party the night she left, saying he'd never felt happier and more relieved. Rhonda, married for thirty years, now divorced, cheered when her husband left, and she found herself singing as she changed the sheets.

I clearly remember the weeks before I left my husband. I couldn't wait until the newspaper arrived to look at the want ads for housing. I drove around looking at places where I'd like to live. I hummed as I packed boxes, made cassette tapes, created a new address book, sorted clothes, and set aside furniture. Meanwhile, my husband watched me pack, and wandered around the house like a ghost. I didn't feel compassion for him. I didn't even try to hide my feelings or at least mute them a bit. I was not being conscious or centered in love. In my excitement, I was completely self-centered.

This reflection is, perhaps, overly critical. For twenty-five years I had been living a role. Like Sleeping Beauty, I'd been dazed, ensnared, if not by thorns, by societal convention and the duties of wife and mother. These bound me just as tightly, offering, in part, the security and protection I had craved as a twenty-two-year-old. Unfortunately, the safe castle walls became a prison, and years later when I felt more confident to venture into the world, I couldn't seem to move. It took numerous kisses to wake me, one from graduate school, one from a women's support group, one from the death of a parent, and many from loved ones. The spell was finally broken. After so long a sleep, I felt brand new, excited and eager to leave the fortress and begin a new life. I truly felt like someone who had just escaped death, who now fully valued life. I couldn't wait to leave. And I know this hurt my husband deeply. I've since made amends for my insensitivity, and have talked with him at length about why I had to leave. It's a relief to know he finally understands and forgives. As he said recently, "It's all in the past. I realize you needed to do what you needed to do."

Packing my car with everything important to me, I felt joyous, ecstatic. I was moving into a house of my own, alone for the very first time. I would be able to breathe. I did not mean to be cruel. It was just my honest expression. Often after years of stalemate, boredom, resignation, fighting, or whatever has been happening, it feels good to be changing this pattern and moving on. Change at this point is energizing. If you're the one who feels exhilarated, and your partner does not, just be aware of his or her feelings and be as sensitive as you can. Some would caution that this initial excitement phase is really a "pink cloud," and darker ones may be on the horizon. As will be seen in the next chapter, Separation, this is often true. The excitement waned for me, to be replaced by peace and, at times, terror. I knew, however, even during the anxious times, that I had made the right decision.

SUPPORT SYSTEMS AVAILABLE TO YOU

As you go through the stage of practical planning, many resources are available to you, most of which have been mentioned briefly. Here is a chance to see them together and know all the support you have. When appropriate, these will be listed in Resources, with addresses and phone numbers, or call 1-800 information or the general information number for local and national assistance.

National Organizations

American Association of Marriage and Family Therapy
American Bar Association
The Association for Conflict Resolution

Debtors Anonymous
Family Service America
Joint Custody Association
National Organization for Men
National Organization for Women
TRW Complimentary Report Request
United Fathers of America
Women Work: The National Network for Women's
Employment

Local Organizations to Call or Visit

The services and people I found useful in my divorce were a credit union, a therapist, a mediator, and a paralegal. By necessity, I had to call or visit the bank, gas and electric company, the phone company, post office, and an appraiser. You can split the cost of a house appraisal with your spouse. I worked on my own career and financial plan, found a place to live on my own, and asked friends to help me move. For further help, turn to Divorce Assistance in the yellow pages of your phone book. There you will find attorneys, paralegals, appraisers, tax accountants, bankruptcy experts, mediators, therapists, and others. The organizations below are listed by their California names. Other titles may be given them in your own county, state, or country.

AFDC (Welfare or financial support for low-income families) Laws have changed recently, but help still exists for mothers and children. More emphasis now on retraining women for jobs, including money for school and childcare.

Attorneys To represent you legally, especially if you need to go to court or your joint property is very complicated. Otherwise, I recommend a mediator.

Banks or Credit Unions To close or separate accounts, and open new accounts in your name.

Career Counselors To assist you in finding and pursuing a new career. Often on college campuses or run privately. Your county may have free services if you fall below a designated income level.

Financial Planners To help organize assets and expenses and create short- and long-term goals.

Gas and Electric Company To have utilities put in your name and turned on at the new home.

Marriage and Family Therapists Trained counselors for individual or couples' work.

Mediators Professionals specializing in the communication and negotiation process. They use counseling and conflict-resolution skills to help couples come to a joint-property settlement and a spousal and child support agreement.

Moving Companies To move your possessions.

Paralegals Trained to handle the paperwork of divorce and other legal matters. They will type and file your divorce papers inexpensively.

Telephone Company To remove your name from a previous account, and order a new line and number at the new address.

Post Office To request change of address forms; post-office box.

Real Estate Appraisers To assist in inspecting and estimating the market value of your home before selling it, or in order to determine its worth as part of the settlement.

Rental Agencies or "Finders' Organizations" To help locate housing.

The above companies and the people who work there are in business to be of service to you. Take ample advantage of their expertise and willingness to help you. In fact, this entire chapter has been written to help you plan your divorce, understand the financial ramifications, and take appropriate action. Divorcing can be so emotional that the financial details can seem overwhelming and confusing. I hope that this chapter has demystified the financial aspect and that you now have ways to process your feelings *and* think and act rationally. This balance of emotion and reason will serve you well as you create your conscious divorce.

OPTIONAL RITUALS
FOR PRACTICAL PLANNING

You may find some or all of the following rituals useful. Most of us need a great deal of support and stamina to leave a relationship. I hope you will be sensitive to your needs and nurture yourself.

1. *Listen to your body and its needs.* In addition to a good night's sleep, you can nap, meditate, or just close your eyes in a chair for a few minutes. Recently, I read that a twenty-minute nap each day will increase your life by ten years. Also, moderate exercise helps to release tension. This could be walking, dancing, swimming, skating, whatever is fun and gives you pleasure.

2. *Ask at least one person for support.* You are not alone. You have a wealth of resources to call upon. If you truly feel you have no one you can trust or ask for help, cultivate someone. Begin to talk with at least one person, even if you need to pay them in the case of a therapist or attorney. It doesn't matter. What does matter is your emotional well-being.

3. *Be good to yourself, preferably every day.* This might mean a hot bath, a stroll in a flower garden, a massage, a haircut, a new outfit, a rest on the chaise lounge, a soak in a hot tub, a vacation to a beautiful place—whatever feels like a treat.

4. *Begin letting go of the relationship and your old life through severance rituals.* These could be as simple as cleaning out drawers, cupboards, the garage, and storage rooms, getting rid of what no longer serves you. Give away as much as possible to others; this in turn creates a cycle of giving and receiving. Other rituals might involve burning photos, letters, and other memorabilia.

5. *Say or write prayers or affirmations to call in new energy for housing, a career, anything that you need.* You could say, "I can easily find a place to live that is perfect for me." In terms of career, you could say, "I am easily finding a fulfilling job."

6. *To create financial abundance, do one of the following, depending on what feels comfortable to you.* Experiment.

- Give money or time to a worthy cause or charity. This giving will rebalance your energy and the flow of money. Give willingly.
- Write down what your financial needs are in the form of positive affirmations. Then, read them each day. You could say, "I want great abundance that comes in safely and positively for all involved." Or, "Abundance comes to me effortlessly."

4

Separation

At the gate,
    I turn to
all I love:
    children,
apple trees,
    and cats,
to redwoods
caught by first light;

to you
my oldest friend.
All I Need

Separation is that moment of parting, of leaving or of being left, either as a pause on the way to reconciliation or as a stepping-stone to divorce. From interviews it's clear that this moment of separation remains with us forever; every detail, every nuance, imprints itself on the map of memory. I remember the date of my leaving: September 15, 1994, the day blue-skyed and warm, the air unmoving. I can still see my husband and children at the gate; even our dog and cat were there to say good-bye. At the time, we all thought it was a temporary separation; I would find what I needed, or "come to my senses," and be back home to make a soufflé or dust the oak table. Part of me agreed it was just a phase, a time to create the space to write and discover my identity outside the

ruts and roles. The other part of me, quieter and more myste-
rious, knew I would not be coming back. At the time, this
thought was too blasphemous, far too rebellious and terrifying, to bring to consciousness. And so, we smiled with
strained politeness, my family trying to be understanding but
looking puzzled and hurt. I loved them deeply, and I loved
myself enough to walk through that gate, get in the car, and
drive away.

At that moment, it all seemed like an incredible adventure.
For the first time in years, I felt alive. My own spirit lived
inside this body, not my parents' and husband's voices, or my
children's words. I felt stabs of guilt as I pulled out the drive, a
twist of nostalgia in my stomach as I looked back at my home
and loved ones. But, quite honestly, the greatest feeling was
unbridled joy that I could be at the center of my own life. This
may sound selfish to some, and it may have looked selfish to
those watching me leave. But I had rarely if ever been selfish in
my life. My greatest goal had been pleasing others, making
sure they were happy, even though I often ignored my needs.
These thoughts followed me as I turned onto the road.

Many of my clients and colleagues also recall this moment
of leaving and the feelings involved. Some were, like me,
walking away, and others were standing at the gate. Turner,
married seven years and recently divorced, remembers the
day he finally left. "I was sitting on the couch just kicking back,
on the same couch I'd been sleeping on for nearly two years,
thinking about the woman I truly loved. I didn't plan it; I had
no idea it would happen, but I got up, went into the bedroom,
and began packing a duffle bag. I didn't say a word, got into my
car, and drove away. I had nowhere to go, but I knew I had to
get out of there. I finally realized I couldn't stand living a lie
any longer, even if it meant leaving my two children temporarily while I set up my new life." It is often "a straw" that
pushes one person out the door, something small and simple

that is the catalyst. However, it is not a snap decision; the one leaving has been thinking about it for some time.

The person being left also remembers the time and place of the final parting with haunting accuracy. "We were having breakfast, toast and coffee, with our children before work and school. Suddenly, Jacob stood up, picked up his black briefcase, and said, 'I'm leaving.' I remember telling him to have a nice day and the kids kept eating Cheerios. But then he said, 'No, I'm really leaving. My clothes are packed and already in the car. I'm not coming back.' I could hear the hall clock ticking, the floor squeak as I shifted my weight. The children held spoons in midair." This remembrance comes from Ann, who has been happily remarried for many years. Yet, she still recalls the feelings of shock and emptiness on the day her former husband left.

A final story comes from Leslie, married for eighteen years, who recalls not only the final day with her ex-husband, but earlier moments as well. "One day I was looking for something in my husband's car and noticed the glove box was locked. Curious, I opened it and found a tube of Astroglide lubricant. We never used it, and so I confronted him in our room that night, asking him if he was having an affair. He said he was, and I told him I wanted him out of the house. But it was Christmas, and our youngest was only four. Somehow we made it through the holidays, but on Christmas Day he quickly opened presents and went over to his girlfriend's house. That day I cried for hours in the closet so the kids wouldn't hear me. At one point, I heard a loud crash and came out to see a ceramic wall hanging in a million pieces. It had a verse on it about love and relationships. I knew it was a sign I had to let go, that it was over. On January fourth we told the children, and Craig drove away."

At times, separation is used by one partner as a "wake-up call" to the other spouse, a way to say, "This isn't working, and we need to make some important changes." A relative in my family left her marriage three times, more as a way to get her husband to stop his abuse and neglect. It worked each time, but only for a few months. Then she would leave again. The final time came after he threw her into a glass door. She never went back, and divorce followed that separation. Like my relative, many partners leave in order to make a point, and some choose to reconcile after negotiating and making promises.

The leader of a marriage enhancement workshop, sponsored by a Christian church, told me that a large percentage of those couples who attend are separated and even legally divorced. At least half of these participants reconcile or are remarried after the workshop. And so, the term "trial separation" means just that. Individuals live apart in order to defuse the situation, gain some perspective, and see if they can reconcile or not. Our separation began in this way. We continued to see our therapist for several months, and we talked about whether or not to get back together. One month after I left, my husband took me to a wedding and said he sensed I had made up my mind. Actually, I didn't want to return, but I wasn't ready to discuss divorce. Our separation began in September, we filed for divorce in June, nine months later, and the divorce was final the next December. The process of our separation and divorce took fifteen months.

Professionals say the time period varies. Legally, a divorce can become final in several months, but in reality, the process rarely is completed in such a short time. In some cases, it takes several years to negotiate such issues as division of property, child custody, support, and visitation. As advised in the previous chapter, an attorney should be contacted before the actual separation. A lawyer may suggest that you seek a "decree of legal separation." You remain legally married while living apart, but all the issues that are involved in the divorce decree, such as joint property, child custody, support, and visitation, become clearly outlined in a legal document. We separated before meeting with a mediator to work out spousal and child support, but my husband and I had a verbal agreement that he generously followed. If you can trust your partner and can communicate well, this sort of verbal agreement may be possible. Overall, though, I recommend drawing up a separation agreement before leaving the relationship.

KINDS OF LEAVINGS

Peaceful Partings

The examples of leave-taking given above are fairly mild. The separations were understandably emotional but were conducted peacefully. In most of the cases, the couples had been communicating for some time about the state of their marriage, and most had been to family therapists. This doesn't guarantee a calm departure, but it helps.

It is rare, however, that both spouses are at the same stage in the decision-making process. The initiator of the separation has had time to ponder whether or not to stay in the relationship; the other spouse often feels caught off guard. It then takes time for couples to regain equanimity, through discussion, counseling, and mediation. The period of separation can be strained and emotional, but neither spouse should be abusive.

Violent Leave-takings

If your wife or husband has a history of violence or is emotionally unpredictable, be careful. This moment of leaving needs to be planned. Some professionals recommend a public place such as a restaurant or a park so behavior can be regulated and the situation kept safe. In addition, morning has been found to be the best time to talk about separating, and to actually leave. People in general are calmer and more rested in the early part of the day and less apt to become violent or reactionary. Some believe the worst time and place to talk about leaving or to actually leave is at night from your bedroom.

Evening is a time when most people are tired and compromised emotionally, and the bedroom brings up too many memories and feelings of intimacy. It is also, according to police statistics, the site of the most domestic violence. So be cautious. As recommended earlier, leave immediately if you suspect your spouse could become violent. Some of those interviewed told their partner on the phone or in a letter.

If you need to stay somewhere temporarily, or go to a shelter, make arrangements and move out of the house when your partner is gone. Many attorneys and mediators are specialists in helping clients leave marriages safely, even if it means getting a restraining order or legally removing the other spouse from the house. Such a specialist, Laika Grant Mann, comments, "I've been doing quite a few more restraining orders and kick-out orders (where my client has been trying to get the other spouse out of the house for weeks or months and feels that he or she needs the court's help). Mostly we try to fix the emergency problems and get things calmed down. If you've had someone abusing you for years and years, and they're abusive in the separation, there's a lot of anger."

If you sense that your partner could become violent, verbally or physically, contact an attorney or mediator to discuss your options. Call a crisis hotline for immediate help. Look in the yellow pages under Crisis Intervention. Saving or improving your life is the highest priority. It's about loving yourself enough to take action.

EMOTIONS DURING YOUR SEPARATION

If, after the initial leave-taking, you make a decision not to reconcile, each person begins the process of unraveling the relationship. The period immediately following separation is most characterized by discomfort. Suddenly, after being a unified couple, a person is separate, single, and with this comes anxiety, as if a part of you has been lost. The degree of distress may be greater, in part, for those who are most attached to their spouse, but nearly everyone experiences some turmoil, even if the relationship was difficult.

It is true that many individuals experience separation anxiety, but eventually there are positive elements of the separation, such as the emergence of a new identity. Two years after his divorce, Conrad remarks, "I thought my life was over when Bette left, that it would never be the same again. Now I realize it all happened to wake me up, to make me take a good look at myself. I know what's really important in my life, and I'm not wasting any time." Conrad is recovering from his separation and divorce. For most people, recovery takes between one and three years, but the length of time also depends on the individual.

Many helping professionals cite five stages that people experience while dying, stages that can also be seen in a separation and divorce. This is because separation is a kind of death—in this case, the loss of one's husband or wife. Briefly, these stages are denial, anger, bargaining, depression, and acceptance. A powerful emotion weaves in and out of the stages: grieving, the deep sadness for all that has been lost. Grieving will be discussed in chapter 6, Loved Ones. In my case, and in the lives of those interviewed, these stages do not always come in this order. At times during my separation, I felt angry, and a moment later I would be crying hysterically or praying for it all to change, and then I would feel enraged, and, a while later, numb. As human beings, we are unpredictable, our emotions ebbing and flowing in what seems to be a random manner.

If we look closely enough, however, most of us can see a pattern in ourselves. For instance, if something is difficult for me to accept, I often ignore the feelings about it or distract myself with cleaning or yard work, food or films. At this point, I'm in denial. Then, suddenly, usually at night, while trying to sleep, the feeling hits me. I either cry into my pillow or feel agitated and must get up and write. For me, anger is often the first level of emotion, masking the deeper sadness. I stomp around banging things and may shout a bit, but then the tears fill my throat and I begin to cry. Acceptance comes when I've emptied the anger and sadness and realized the truth. It might be similar for some of you. In any case, looking at the stages of loss should help prepare you for the possible emotions during your separation.

Denial

Denial is a normal and necessary reaction to a situation that feels overwhelming. Denial allows us to escape from reality long enough to heal emotionally. After you or your partner has left, you may be in denial for a while. I recall keeping very busy moving out of my house and into a new home; in fact, I kept myself compulsively busy arranging and rearranging furniture and doing yard work. This was my form of denial, of keeping the feelings from surfacing, at least until I sat down to rest or tried to sleep. Night was the worst time because my imagination ran wild; fantasies about what my husband was doing filled my thoughts. Was he alone? Was he thinking about me? What would it be like if we reconciled? I missed my home and fantasized about lying under the apple tree or cooking in my kitchen. In fact, my denial led me to my old home to cook for my husband and son one night a week. I even house-sat when my "ex" went to visit his new woman-friend in another state. I slept in my old bed with my cat and cried. For some reason, I thought I could go home again even for a weekend. I looked forward to the feelings of familiarity, to the joy of being truly home, but reality struck. I didn't live there anymore, and I wasn't ever coming back. My denial or fantasy shattered.

My symptoms of denial were several: fantasizing about my ex-mate and former life; living anonymously and in hiding, not telling people I had left, because I couldn't face their judgment;

being ambivalent about whether to go back or not, stalling because the weight of my decision was so enormous. I was terrified to say, "I want a divorce. I'm not coming back," and so I just said I needed more time. In some ways I wanted to live separately from my husband, and yet not divorce. I feared my decision to leave could forever jeopardize our friendship. During the separation, we celebrated birthdays together as a family and tried to have one last Christmas, but it was very difficult. Neither of us wanted to believe the marriage was over, and so we came together for special events as if nothing had happened.

My former husband experienced his own denial, living alone in the house we had shared for twenty years. He seemed to be in a daze, and moving in slow motion. Also, he believed I would be coming home soon. He called me almost daily, invited me to parties and to the movies. In general, my male clients seem to experience greater emotional distress during a separation and divorce, perhaps because some are more isolated socially. I found this to be true two decades ago when two colleagues split up. I found myself talking with each of them separately. Tanya, although feeling sad and angry, was sharing her feelings with many people, and she was able to function in her daily life because of this support and connection. She now says of her ex-husband, "Roger felt envious of my many friends and all the love I received. He said I was lucky to have people to stay with and talk to. He felt like he had no one, and he described himself as a ghost drifting from room to room in our house."

Men and women may escape into denial by working more or even drinking to excess, whatever it takes to forget. If you or your partner has an addiction or a potential addiction, this is an important time to be wary. Malena, divorced after fourteen years of marriage, worked at least twelve hours a day after her husband left. She buried herself in books, reports, papers to write and to review. She even ate at her desk and showered at work. She couldn't face going home to an empty house and found her work safer than people. A friend, who works as a waiter to pay for graduate school, tells me stories of the customers who, when going through a separation or divorce, almost live at the bar, drinking all afternoon and into the evening. He says, "It's sad they're here drinking themselves into oblivion. I talk to them about what's going on, but it isn't enough. Can life be so bad that you stay drunk for the rest of your life?" I know that I stopped eating during my separation. This was my way of dealing with the loss. My husband worked more than ever, and my teenage son was rarely home. He buried himself in school and sports, dealing with the family crisis by following our modeling, keeping compulsively busy.

Ask yourself if you are escaping reality by abusing any substances, overworking, watching TV all day, "surfing the net," or finding other distractions. This might be a good time to open your journal and answer the questions: "How am I in denial?" "Do I have any addictions or ways to escape that could become problematic during my separation?" Then write whatever comes up for you about your denial. Be honest. Read back what you've written, and see if there's anything else you want to add. Finally, write some solutions, what you could do in place of your addictions or escapes. For instance, if you put "overworking," perhaps you could call a friend, go for a walk, talk with your therapist, and so on. Or, better yet, you could sit still and let the feelings come up. You might cry or feel angry, then write in your journal, call a friend, or whatever intuitively you need. Write realistic alternatives, ones that you would really do. Being honest about your denial now will help you become aware of any potential problems later.

Even if, at first, you feel excitement or relief after the separation, you may also be in denial about your deeper feelings. For nearly everyone, this initial exhilaration is temporary. This was true for me. I blissfully decorated my new cottage, rode my bike, and went to work feeling happy and free. A month or so later, however, I realized the enormity of what I'd done. Fortunately, enough time had passed that I could better handle these realities. Most of us need the cushion of denial at first in order to survive the impact of separation. Those interviewed report some specific examples of denial: not being able to drive by their old home; getting sick and taking leaves from their job; not being able to sleep in their marriage bed; keeping mementos like photographs and their mate's clothing; keeping the house just the way their spouse liked it; waiting for the phone to ring, or wanting to call their partner each day; sleeping with an article of the spouse's clothing or a romantic keepsake; and the list goes on. These are ways of dealing with intense grief, of making things seem less frightening, less permanent. With each passing day, week, and month, it becomes easier to face the truth. We open the shades, pull back the curtains, and see that the sun still shines, the grass still grows.

Anger

How do you know if you're angry during your separation? Some clients report a feeling of tightness in their chest or stomach. Others say they move more quickly, even slamming things into place; speech can quicken and be sharp and terse. Still others become quiet and withdrawn. They may be swallowing their anger and exhibiting the signs of depression. Depression, as will be seen shortly, is anger turned inward. During a separation it's common and normal to feel irritated, and not only the person being left feels this way. The spouse leaving may feel intense anger that things became so intolerable that he or she had to leave.

Reread chapter 2 on communicating angry feelings, if this is a skill you need. At this point, you may decide to release your anger, in a journal, to your therapist, alone in nature, or at home. If you wish, open your journal when you're feeling angry and write: "I'm angry/furious/upset/pissed that . . . ," and continue to record your feelings. Write everything you're angry about even if it seems irrational or in the distant past. Just write it all, and in doing so, you get the tension out of your body. If you don't release the anger somehow, it can manifest in illness, in everything from stomach pain to headaches and, some say, to more serious ailments. Author Louise Hay speaks of a time when her shoulder actually burned with pain. She realized this burning was about anger. She sat down and thought about it, and finally beat a few pillows until she realized what she was angry about. Her shoulder pain soon disappeared. Don't forget that the word *disease* divided into syllables is *dis-ease,* meaning, "deprived of comfort and care." Care about your physical and mental health by learning how to release your anger. The connection between emotions and bodily ills will be presented in more detail in chapter 7.

When you deny or "swallow" your anger, it keeps you from feeling at peace with yourself and others. During your separation, you might find yourself snapping at your children or others. Your anger is leaking out and splattering innocent bystanders. When you notice yourself becoming enraged by something trivial (you spilled your coffee, forgot to pick up the dry cleaning, broke a nail), it's usually a sign you're angry at something deeper that you're not acknowledging. Just be aware of your words and actions. Apologize to the innocents, and take some quiet time to discover and unleash your distress. A divorced mother says, "I found myself yelling at the kids all morning for every little thing. As I got ready for a birthday party later, I realized that my 'ex' would be there with his new fiancée, and I was nervous to go." The greatest gift to yourself and to the people in your life is to realize you're angry, and take action to release it appropriately.

It is therapeutic to tell your ex-mate how you feel, but I recommend doing this with a third party present. I can recall several therapy sessions, during my separation, at which we both felt safer to express our anger. My husband needed to tell me he'd been mad at me for several years and now felt betrayed and abandoned. He repeated the phrase: "I can't believe you left us. How could you?" I had trouble expressing anger as well. During my marriage, I literally gritted my teeth and smiled no matter how angry or sad I really felt. I didn't think I had a right to be angry. In the same therapy sessions, I said how angry I'd been for years. My former husband never believed I could be so angry and hurt that I would leave. He had never taken me seriously before. It's unfortunate that it sometimes takes an event as drastic as a separation for spouses to truly listen.

Bargaining

Bargaining, the third aspect of the process of loss, occurs with frequency during a separation and divorce. When my mother died, I remember praying for her return, promising to be more attentive, spend more quality time with her, move her into my home—"anything, God, just send my mother back." These pleas are unrealistic, perhaps, but when grieving for a loved one, you try anything. The same thing is true of separated spouses; in fact, it seems more plausible because your beloved is alive. I've seen bargaining work with individuals who truly want to change and make their marriage succeed. In most cases, it takes time to make actual changes and to build trust again. For instance, if one partner drinks heavily and promises to quit, the other spouse may have heard this thousands of times. It takes courage to give it one more try, and the alcoholic must be willing to admit his or her problem and get help. For my client, Lisa, married "twenty-plus" years, it was too late. She had already heard all the promises that her husband would quit drinking, and she had given him all the chances she could. Now they are divorced, he is getting help, and they are good friends, better friends now than during the marriage.

Sometimes it is too late for couples; one spouse is now willing to spend more time with the other, is willing to work less or to take a romantic vacation, but it's "too little, too late" for the other partner. In the case of Charlene and Alan, however, bargaining has worked; Charlene moved back home, and Alan has kept his promise to travel less. He took a decrease in salary in order to be at home more and be able to spend quality time with his children. So far, after six months, things look good. The spouse doing the most bargaining, promising the impossible dream, is usually sincere, but he or she may be desperate and unable to fulfill all these promises.

There is no magical formula to apply to these situations, to tell you when to agree to the bargaining and when to refuse to negotiate. My recommendation is to follow your intuition. If you are contemplating a separation or are currently separated, ask yourself the simple question, "Do I want to reconcile or not?" The answer may not seem simple, but I believe it can be if you close your eyes, turn inward in silence, and wait for an answer to come. Usually it will be "yes" or "no," but sometimes it will be "maybe." Open your journal and write about your answers. It helps to put down the reasons you do or do not believe in the bargains being offered or to elaborate on the "maybe" answer. Why do you wish to reconcile, and why do you not want to try again? Overall, what is your gut telling you to do? Do you have any fears about this choice? Write about them. Are there solutions for your fears? For example, if you wrote that you don't want to return to the marriage, but you're afraid you can't make it emotionally or financially, then list specifically what your worries are. Also, return to previous chapters for concrete ideas to help with your feelings and issues.

Depression

Feelings of depression are common during a separation. We may feel powerless, as if we have no choices left; we may feel incredibly sad or unable to express our pent-up anger. When my husband and I separated in September, I felt exuberant and positive about my decision. By November, as this newness wore off, the initial feelings of freedom and strength were replaced by panic. What had I done? As Thanksgiving approached, I began doubting myself completely. I missed my home and family. The cute cottage I had rented became a lonely, silent box. I missed the noise and confusion of our children and pets, the familiarity of everything I loved. Suddenly, I found myself depressed. As the weather turned gray and the ocean stormy, I cried myself to sleep. I couldn't eat and began to lose more weight. Dark circles lined my eyes. What had I been thinking? November began at least six to nine months of depression.

I didn't take Prozac, but at times I wished I had. I did see a therapist regularly, went to personal growth retreats, and spent a great deal of time talking to friends and walking by the ocean. Nature and meditation became my Prozac, but if you're depressed and it's not improving, talk with your doctor or therapist about medication. I developed a sleep disorder, too, and did briefly take a prescription to help me sleep.

Depression for me has always been tied to feeling power-less, unable to control my life, as if I have no options or ways to change things. Symptoms of depression vary, but for those interviewed, depression means feeling fatigued, listless, blah, without emotion, sluggish, and heavy. These can result from stuffing down anger and other feelings. The key to lifting depression, then, is to release the suppressed emotions by writing in a journal, by talking to someone, and by physically moving your body. Sonia, separated from her partner of six years, says of her depression, "The simple act of walking to the kitchen exhausts me; all I want to do is crawl in bed and pull the covers over my head. But if I go outside, especially away from the city to a beautiful place, I feel somehow more cheer-ful." The walking, running, or other exercise you can do outdoors also activates your endorphins and can make you feel energized. For many of my clients, recovering from depression is tied to moving their bodies and mouths in about equal parts, exercising muscles and releasing pent-up thoughts and feelings.

Overall, taking action, no matter how little, helps lift depression. Often, making a list of what must be done, then checking or crossing off each item can make us feel empowered. Even making that phone call we've been avoiding can make us feel relieved and more confident. Experts suggest that we follow a familiar schedule during a separation in order to lend stability to our lives. There's been enough disruption, especially if you've moved. Try to keep your life as simple as possible and keep the routines you are used to. Just waking at the same time, having a cup of tea, or reading the paper can be comforting. This is true unless the routine used to involve your partner. Then, it might feel better to establish your own rituals. Joanna, divorced in midlife, always fixed breakfast for herself and her husband. After the separation, she found she needed to get out of the house in the morning, take a walk, and have coffee and a muffin at a local café.

In addition, consciously changing our thoughts can lift a depression. A friend often reminds me that attitude is everything, and that at times I need an attitude adjustment. It's true that we can consciously change negative thoughts to positive ones, and immediately feel more energized and optimistic. We can use our thoughts to heal ourselves emotionally and physically. Specifically, we can say and write affirmations to change pessimistic thoughts to affirming ones. First, it's important to clean the slate of negative or self-limiting beliefs. Open your journal and write, "I am depressed because . . ." or "Right now, I feel. . . ." Write quickly, in a stream of consciousness style, everything that comes to mind. Repeat the opening phrase whenever you feel stuck. When you are finished, when no more thoughts, beliefs, or feelings are coming up, stop and reread your list. Other emotions may have surfaced besides depression, feelings like anger, sadness, and guilt.

Many therapists see guilt as the root of our pain, for guilt seeks punishment and receives it in our self-hatred and physical symptoms. For those of you who have left your spouse, or who feel responsible for the separation, guilt may be the emotion that is causing your depression. As soon as the guilty feelings are released from your mind and body, the heaviness and inaction lift, and you feel better. In other words, first discover the reasons you feel guilty, then write or talk about these feelings and use affirmations to forgive yourself.

On a clean page of your journal, write affirmations that will help dispel the depression and negativity and create positive energy instead. Remember to write affirmations using "I" and your name in the present tense, as if the statement is already occurring. You are, indeed, making it "firm" within you by asserting this belief over and over. I suggest writing each statement, or one of your own, until it sounds believable. Some positive affirmations to lift depression during your separation might be:

1. I, _____, care about myself.
2. I, _____, am taking action to improve my life.
3. I, _____, deserve to have the life I desire.
4. Each time I take action, I, _____, feel empowered and positive.
5. It is safe for me, _____, to feel my feelings and then release them.
6. I, _____, let go of the past and live in the present moment.
7. I, _____, forgive myself. I know I'm doing the best I can.
8. I, _____, accept and love myself exactly as I am.

Of course, for severe depression, you'll need additional help. If you feel incapable of following any of these suggestions and are feeling self-destructive, see your doctor or therapist immediately. Some self-destructive behaviors may be: under- or overeating; not being able to sleep or sleeping excessively; drinking more alcohol, smoking more, taking drugs, or indulging in other addictive behaviors; having recurring suicidal thoughts; or engaging in self-mutilation or any other punishing behavior. A doctor may prescribe medication and other interventions to help you through this crisis.

Excessive isolation during a depression is not healthy. Perhaps ask your therapist about local grief and loss support groups. If you're not ready to join a group, at least call a grief counselor or a therapist and talk to him or her individually. As a suicide prevention speaker recently said to me, "Suicide is a permanent solution to a temporary problem."

The emotion of grieving, as part of the process of loss, will be addressed later, in chapter 6, as will the fifth stage, acceptance, in chapter 8.

HOLIDAYS, ANNIVERSARIES, RESTAURANTS, AND KNICKKNACKS

You're doing fine. It's been several months since you separated from your partner, and you're finally feeling normal, more relaxed, and happier. Then, it's Thanksgiving, Christmas, each of your birthdays, your anniversary, the kids' birthdays, your parents' birthdays, Valentine's Day, Easter, Mother's Day, Father's Day, and the Fourth of July. You get the picture. I wasn't prepared for the hundreds of special days to survive during and after my separation and divorce. I didn't even realize I would need survival skills. And because I didn't have these skills, I want to give them to you. Not that these holidays won't test your new reserve. They will. But my hope is that you'll at least be ready. Holidays and anniversaries hold so much emotional energy that they seem to trigger feelings long after a breakup.

Marilyn, who's been divorced for fifteen years, says, "I remember those first holidays when I went to my ex-husband's house and his wife was doing what I used to do, especially the nurturing. I felt like I was looking through a peephole at the scene and feeling so displaced, so replaced." Even now, Marilyn says she feels pangs of sadness during the holidays, but luckily she's not "divorced" from her children or her in-laws, whom she loves deeply; they see each other regularly and spend one day of the important holidays together.

Of all the holidays, Christmas and Hanukkah seem to be the hardest for those interviewed, followed by the wedding anniversary and birthdays. Especially if you have been married longer than two years and have cemented your relationship around traditional events, these special days bring up so many memories and nostalgia. If I begin thinking about "how things were," I cry. What I've realized is that I miss things and people that are no longer present. I miss the ideal of the way things were, or how I perceive them in my mind, which is no longer realistic. At times I palpably long for the days when my children were little and believed in Santa. I spent hours sewing outfits and bedding for Cabbage-Patch dolls, and I watched with delight as the children found their presents from "Santa." What I miss cannot be recaptured. My children are grown and leading their own lives. I miss what no longer exists. When I can realize this in time, I save myself a downward spiral on holidays. Of course, I still cry a little, but it's not about wanting to return to my husband or to the marriage.

Now we have Christmas at two houses, and the same traditions that we all remember are still in place. As a blended family (new husband, children, grandchildren, and stepchildren), the seven of us go up the hill to a Christmas tree farm, cut down trees, and spend the day decorating the house and making cookies. My children choose to spend Christmas Eve with their father, then spend the night at our house and are here for Christmas morning. As adults, they still wake early to find their stockings hung on the stairs, only now they drink coffee instead of cocoa. The love doesn't change; it continues no matter where you are.

In dealing with places and objects, you have many choices. Jeff, divorced for one year, says he packed up all the pictures of his ex-wife, including ones in his wallet. He went through the house and took down all knickknacks that reminded him of her and gave them away. He hasn't been able to throw away the pictures, but they're in the garage. Arden, who is separated and awaiting her divorce decree, says she's finally got all her things out of their house except the pictures. They still have to divide those. She adds, "Sometimes I just feel so sad about everything; it just comes on so suddenly." Arden does not want to return to her ex-partner, but she occasionally feels the nostalgia for the past. Ross, married briefly to a woman much younger, and now divorced for five months, is repainting his entire house a bright white and has bought a new bed. He says of this, "Doesn't it look great? I want to be here more now that the place is spruced up. It's brighter." Of those interviewed who stayed in their house, all have done some remodeling. My ex-husband has added bay windows and painted and redecorated. This, in part, is to exorcise the ghost of the spouse who has left. Patrick has a different feeling about objects from the relationship. "My partner and I bought many works of art that are still in my house. I look at them fondly with positive memories. The other day I showed someone a picture album filled with photos of my 'ex' and me together, and I was fine."

Places can also evoke memories. For those who leave, it might be difficult to pass the house they lived in together. At first, it hurt every time I drove by our old home. Then I would avert my eyes, and now on most days, I don't even look; but there are times when I feel the lump and prickle in my throat. Some people can't go to the same hotel or restaurant, or to a park, theater, furniture store, or other place that reminds them of their ex-partner. Others make it part of the closure ritual to return, feel the feelings, and then keep returning until it feels normal to be there. Only you know what would work for you. Use your intuition and then follow it.

This rational thinking does not discount your sadness, especially in the first two years following a separation and divorce. You will be affected by holidays and anniversaries, some people more than others, depending on the depth of connection to spouse, family, and tradition. If you're currently in a separation and dealing with holidays and anniversaries, or will be soon, here are some ideas from those interviewed to help you:

1. Face the feelings head on. Go ahead and cry. Remember the special day with fondness and grieve the loss of this time. Set aside a private place and enough time to fully release your feelings. Write in your journal or talk to someone afterward if you wish. You will feel better.

2. Ritualize the day somehow. One woman created a memorial on her property, and on every anniversary she places flowers there to honor the years together.

3. Create new traditions for your life now. Begin to celebrate in a whole new way. If you always cooked on Thanksgiving and would like a break, go on a family picnic and have everyone bring something; go out of town, or have the holiday at someone else's house or at a restaurant. Those who have done this report feeling a fresh and uplifting mood. My former husband, his wife, and his stepdaughter have Thanksgiving at our house one year, and we go to their house the next. Our grown children love this time when we're all together enjoying the day.

4. Buy something for your home that you've always wanted but your spouse disliked, or get something just to please yourself. For instance, Marsha always wanted a dog but her husband never wanted animals, and so, she got a dog. Plant the garden you've always wanted; build that workshop; put candles in your bedroom and flowers on the table—whatever you'd enjoy.

5. If appropriate, acknowledge your ex-spouse on his or her birthday or even your anniversary by sending a card and even a small gift. My "ex" and I do this for Mother's Day and Father's Day as well. It's a way to say, "I value you as a parent"; or "I value the marriage we had"; or "I'm glad you were born." Be sure of your motives. If you want something, such as more money or to get back together, and you know your "ex" wouldn't want this, don't give a card or gift. Your motives should be pure and love-centered, not ego-centered. Your former partner will sense the difference anyway.

CLOSURE AND RITUALS

Although I encourage clients to use closure ceremonies as they separate, I only know one couple, Turner and his wife, who used rituals at each stage of their divorce. They reminisced about their life together, visiting favorite haunts, looking at photo albums, and playing nostalgic music. They openly cried together, acknowledged one another, and asked for forgiveness. Why is this so rare? For one thing, partners are often hurt and angry, and at different stages in the separating process. One spouse may feel resolved enough to want a rite of passage, but the other person is not ready. Separation is often so emotionally charged that couples do not feel healed enough to ritualize the experience. I wanted to create a ritual with my husband, and I wrote a poem about burying our rings beneath redwoods we planted on an anniversary. He wasn't ready for this sort of closure, and so I performed ceremonies on my own.

Emotional healing sometimes occurs spontaneously, and other times is orchestrated. One man reports crying with his mate months after separating. "It wasn't planned. It just happened, and it cleansed us both. I didn't realize that the divorce was as hard on my partner." Turner and his wife revisited places they loved while married. They cried on beaches and at cherished bed and breakfasts, returned to mountain cabins and quaint towns. There, they strolled, talked of their years together, and held each other at the day's end. Now, they have a friendship and are raising two children with mutual love and respect. This is the ideal, to be able to honor the marriage and the other person, even as we let go.

Ritualizing our closure can take other forms as well. We can send a letter to make amends, or call to say thanks for the good years, mail a birthday card, or call to say "thank you" for sending the mail. Especially if you have children, but even if you don't, it's important to keep working on your relationship. This sentiment is echoed by attorney Robert Frandeen, who says that a relationship is never really over. "It comes back to working on the relationship they are trying to get away from. Their best friend in this whole process is time. Time will actually heal more things than I ever will and twelve attorneys staying up all night for you. I mean a metaphysical or spiritual sense that time is not passive, that we are really in the hands of something bigger, and issues do get resolved in the passage of time."

If you want to, and your spouse is willing, it can be healing to say a prayer together, asking for a blessing for one another. Also, you might write your own separation vows if you wish. If words are not your medium, then you could throw flowers into the sea or into a canyon; pass on pictures to children, other family, and friends; or light two separate candles representing the beginning of two lives, as you may have burned one at your wedding. You can create the ritual that is best for you whether or not your partner participates. Just intuitively choose what would best reflect your marriage and separation. For instance, if you surfed together or walked on the beach, perhaps take a lei of flowers into the ocean and let it float away. If you loved going to the symphony, perhaps go one last time, or play a tape of your favorite pieces in the background while saying a few words to each other. I do suggest doing something meaningful to mark this moment, to acknowledge your years together in this time of separation. Any gesture, however simple, illustrates your desire to create a conscious, love-centered separation.

5

The Divorcing Process

A gulf is widening,
a chasm deep within
sharp rock,
sides slippery with
oozing moss.

Across the empty space
in ice blue rain
our eyes meet
and say,
"I wish there were
a bridge."

Impasse

I usually arrived early for our mediation appointment, parked the car in the shade, and tried to relax. I'd watch my husband arrive and go into the building. Then, I'd take a deep breath and try to compose myself as I walked into the attorney's office. During each session, despite my guilt and my husband's anger, our mediator helped us communicate clearly and negotiate honorably. In a sense, our attorney helped us build a bridge from a long-term marriage to a separation and divorce, a bridge we learned to cross side by side.

The original title of this chapter was Learning the Law. However, after talking with mediators, attorneys, and those divorcing, I realized that terms like "law," "legal system," and "litigation" emphasize conflict rather than cooperation. In a recent newspaper ad, an attorney offered potential clients a "traditional adversarial approach," presenting divorce to the public as antagonistic and conflictual. Marriage is a legal system, but, perhaps more importantly, marriage is a complex familial connection that must be unwound with care. Thus, the title "The Divorcing Process" offers you a positive sense of neutrality and normality. As couples, many of you want to bridge the gap; you want a better way to handle your divorce, a way that is less stressful and more unifying, but the legal system doesn't always offer a collaborative approach.

Attorneys interviewed believe that most of our systems in this country, including the legal one, have capitalism at their base, which is individualistic and competitive. There is an emphasis on right and wrong, a plaintiff and a defendant, and eventually a verdict declaring innocence or guilt. The premise in the world of law is that a power struggle is at the root of relationships. The legal profession assumes that conflict exists, and the attorney's job is to prevail in the conflict. Such a competitive approach often leads to further antagonism and increased stress for couples and families.

The Civil Code encourages this adversarial approach and was used by attorneys in divorce proceedings until recently, when family law codes were established. But attorneys are still rated by how powerful and successful they are, by how often they can win against another attorney, establish their client as the victor, and make a fortune. The two-attorney system encourages competition and power struggle, which do not belong in family disputes. This system ignores your ability to collaborate with one another in your own family system.

I believe that, except in cases of violence, addiction, or insanity, when it's impossible to communicate and negotiate, you can use trained paralegals and mediators to handle your divorce, not separate attorneys. Statistics show that the majority of citizens agree. At this time, thirty-nine states require mediation, and more than half of the states have a court-sponsored mediation program. In 1997, approximately 300,000 family-law actions were filed in California, and in the past several years, approximately sixty percent of all family-law filings in any given year were by parties representing themselves. Couples are taking the power out of the equation—using collaboration rather than competition, mediation rather than litigation, to negotiate a settlement advantageous to both parties.

In doing so, you can avoid impasse by walking across the bridge and meeting one another halfway. This choice supports the premise in Ashley's Hierarchy of Love, that you can follow inner wisdom to meet your needs while being supportive of partners and children. You can communicate and create an equitable and peaceful settlement, a divorce of highest consciousness, with love and integrity at its heart.

LEGAL DOCUMENT ASSISTANTS OR PARALEGALS

In every state, Legal Document Assistants (LDA's) can fill out and file your legal paperwork with the court system. In my case, I avoided the expense of an attorney, and the effort of trying to do the paperwork myself, by having an LDA do it for me. Basically, paralegals fill out and file papers for legal separation, divorce, child support and custody, restraining orders, annulment, guardianship, paternity, adoption, and other categories. Shop carefully for an LDA. Ask your friends for names or call a mediator or attorney for suggestions. The most qualified LDA's have university degrees and certification, as well as years of experience working with the court system, attorneys, and clients.

LDA's must now register with their county clerk and post a $25,000 bond, which entitles them to give you written information approved by an attorney. Choose an LDA you can talk to and who can provide you with self-help publications, which should answer most of your questions. One LDA says that women are often afraid they can't take care of themselves financially, and it's important to find someone who will really listen and help alleviate any fears. If you don't have a recommendation from someone you know, look for the heading "Paralegal" or "Legal Document Assistant" in your local phone book. Interview each one on the phone until you find the person with the qualifications, experience, and personality you desire. Remember to follow your intuition, too.

Usually Legal Document Assistants fill out and file the initial petition for dissolution of marriage based on information you give them. At the time of publication, the cost to prepare this document is approximately $300 to $400. When papers are initially filed with the court, a filing fee is paid to the court, not to the paralegal. Be sure to ask how much each filing fee will be. Then, if it is a simple marriage settlement agreement, involving a house and simple assets, a paralegal can file this paperwork for approximately $200. A child custody agreement will cost about $100 to type and file. These are just the charges paid to the paralegal. Most LDA's will have a pamphlet or handout with a list of services and costs. Go over all of this before deciding to use their services.

One type of divorce, the summary divorce, is less expensive (about $200), is only three pages long, and has specific criteria. You must be married less than five years from the filing date; you must have no real property and no children by that marriage; and you must have no assets greater than $25,000 and no debts greater than $10,000. This does not include your car. Not every state has summary divorce. Research the requirements by calling or E-mailing your state bar association. Numbers and addresses appear in Resources.

If you are unable to afford a paralegal, mediator, or attorney, check with your state bar association to see if you have a family law facilitator in your county. Anyone, whether able to afford representation or not, can be seen by a family law facilitator. If you are on public assistance or meet low-income guidelines, you can have your filing fees waived.

One woman, Rachel, a teacher divorced after ten years of marriage, did most of the divorce herself and used a paralegal to do the final typing and filing. Her divorce in 1996 cost $500. She comments, "I went to a bookstore and bought one of those do-it-yourself divorce books, read it, filled out the practice forms, asked questions of my cousin who is a lawyer, and didn't use a paralegal until filing the marriage settlement agreement. If I can do it, anyone can."

MEDIATION

A mediator is usually an attorney or mental health worker who is trained as a neutral facilitator to help marital partners negotiate and reach an agreement. The difference between mediators and regular attorneys is that mediators have you and your spouse in the same room and help you share information, communicate, and negotiate a mutually agreeable settlement. Mediators can help you stop blaming one another and, instead, accept reality and strive to achieve the best outcome. In contrast, a traditional attorney would represent you, and a second lawyer would represent your partner. Attorney Robert Frandeen explains what brings clients to his door. "Once love falls apart, it's amazing. Voids get filled mostly with fears and doubts, and suddenly you're imagining the person you loved is doing the worst thing possible. Fear drives a tremendous part of the animosity." What happens to "light the powder keg" could be canceling a spouse's credit card, or taking the money out of a joint bank account; this may be done as a fearful, defensive maneuver, but is perceived by the other partner as aggressive. What is missing here is ongoing communication. If you are in this stage of increasing tension, see a counselor, use the communication skills in chapter 2, and talk to one another. By the time one partner makes a threatening unilateral decision, trust is lost, and it's very difficult to regain.

At this point, spouses usually take action to protect their rights and dispel the rising fear. After paying separate attorneys thousands of dollars in retainer fees, individuals, in fact, often feel more anxious. At this point, lawyers are separately gathering data for each spouse, called discovery, which increases the suspicion and mistrust; couples stop communicating altogether and only do so through their attorneys. Is there a way to avoid such a situation? If partners see one mediator together instead of hiring two separate attorneys, this could prevent the paranoia and divisiveness. In fact, as soon as you call a mediator to set up an appointment to share mutual information, especially about financial issues, the fear will begin to dissipate. Mediation offers you the option of communicating and negotiating, of retaining mutual respect for the marriage and for one another. This is the basis of a conscious divorce.

And, so, what is the mediation process? First, you talk with the mediator on the phone, and he or she answers questions about mediation and sets up the number of sessions you want. Most mediators recommend a fact-finding or informational session with both of you present. If your partner refuses to attend, the mediator will usually give him or her a tape about mediation to listen to in order to understand the process. Mediators stress that the informational session is collaborative, not competitive or strategic. This is the only way you can maximize your benefits, by seeing your spouse not as an enemy but as a partner. It is in your interest that your spouse have all the information.

Mediators such as attorney Chip Rose often use four stages with couples in an average of six to ten sessions over six to twelve months.

1. Data gathering and communication
2. Option development
3. Modeling a settlement
4. Negotiating a successful outcome

During the ninety-minute sessions, mediators will teach you how to use "I" messages to express your feelings and needs and model how to listen to one another. If one of you says something that causes the other partner to become defensive, the mediator helps the speaker rephrase the sentence so the listener not only hears it, but responds with the same respectful attitude. The result is that you learn to communicate about difficult issues in a safe, neutral environment that supports inclusive decision making. My former husband and I took just three sessions to resolve our issues of joint property, spousal support, child custody, and support of our one minor child. Clearly, mediation was the bridge we needed.

Most mediators charge on a sliding scale and bill on an hourly basis, approximately $100 to $350 an hour. They don't usually require retainers. A divorce using mediation costs approximately $1,500 to $5,000, with another $1,000 or so to draft the agreement. Mediators rarely charge more than $10,000 for their complete services. Currently, no uniform licensing requirements exist for mediators. In other words, anyone can say he or she is a mediator and begin a practice. When interviewing potential mediators, be sure to ask about their credentials and experience. Call the organizations listed in the Resources dealing with mediation and conciliation, or contact the state or national bar association for a referral.

The only criticism I have of mediation is more about my own attitude. I wanted to rush through the process in order to avoid my feelings and move on. This is a common mistake shared with those interviewed. One person, usually out of guilt and pain, gives up something in order to speed up the process, and later regrets this. Turner signed over investments to his wife in order to "get her out" of his life. Now, three years later, he is sorry. Carol, married nineteen years, rushed the process and asked for minimum financial support for herself and three minor children; when her ex-husband failed to give her any money, she never complained or reported him. Since then, sometimes working three jobs, she is upset about her decision. Similarly, because of the length of my marriage, I was entitled to thirteen years of spousal support. I took one year. Also, I agreed that my husband should keep a portion of assets accrued during our marriage and not split them with me. I did this so he wouldn't be upset. My advice is to be cautious and take all the time you need to come to an agreement. You have your entire life to reflect on these decisions. Make them good ones.

THE LEGAL SYSTEM AND TRADITIONAL ATTORNEYS

How do you feel about the legal system? About attorneys? Many people express fear and dislike of the law and lawyers, even when they have never been involved in the legal system prior to their separation and divorce. This is partly because of the stereotypes concerning the judicial system, and also because of real stories about the financial expense and emotional havoc. As one man states, "Attorneys are the folks people love to hate . . . until they need one." Even though my preference is to use paralegals and mediators for most divorces, the family law attorneys I interviewed seemed genuinely concerned about their clients.

Robert Frandeen, who has practiced law for over twenty-five years, has been divorced for ten years and is coparenting four children. He says, "It wasn't easy at first. I can definitely empathize with my clients—the craziness you go through, the fear you go through. My ex-wife and I see each other often and talk several times a day. She is an incredible woman. Our children flow easily back and forth." Most attorneys feel that they are, in a sense, a last resort, especially around the issue of child custody. One lawyer said that often his clients have tried counseling and mediation, and now are hoping he can help them solve their custody disputes. Lawyers, in a sense, can be used for the most difficult cases, after other avenues have been tried.

The average cost of seeing an attorney is $200 to $500 an hour, and the fees will only go up. In addition to hourly rates, attorneys require a retainer of approximately $5,000. This means if each of you hires a lawyer, you are spending a minimum of $10,000 at the beginning of your divorce, money that could be divided in your settlement. Initially, if you feel the need to see an attorney, make sure you're organized. When making an appointment, ask what the attorney charges an hour. Ask whether or not he or she is trained in mediation. Find out what to bring to the first meeting and, in general, what you can do on your own to expedite matters. Write your questions ahead of time, have all the necessary paperwork ready that the attorney has told you to bring, and let him or her know how much you are willing to spend on fees. These strategies will not only save you money, but will empower you as well.

DO YOU NEED AN ATTORNEY?

If your situation is straightforward—if, for example, you have no children, have minimal property and assets to split, and are communicating fairly well—you probably don't need an attorney. Seeing a paralegal or mediator will be all the help you need, or you might use an attorney for part of your divorce. It depends on each unique situation. Some experts advise hiring an attorney while you are married, before you physically separate, to draw up an agreement of legal separation, noting such important things as division of property, child custody, and support payments so these issues are honored. Then, when you divorce, this legal document can be used as a basis to draft the final divorce settlement agreement.

Mental health mediators should be used when the issue is child custody. This is because custody arrangements often evolve as children grow older and their needs change, or one parent disagrees with the other's new request. Ross has been divorced for six years and has been the custodial parent of his daughter since she was one. He is back in court facing his ex-wife, who now wants full custody. For him, it is a nightmare, and he cries openly when he says, "I have taken care of her since she was a baby, and I had to plead with my 'ex' to come and see her. I have always had custody. My ex-wife is from a wealthy family and they have hired a powerful attorney. What am I going to do?" In the past, what helped this couple, according to Ross, was psychotherapy, and he hopes the court orders it this time. Meanwhile, he neglects his work and is an emotional wreck. He is hoping that his years of love and support of his daughter will count in court. At this point, in his deteriorating relationship with his ex-spouse, he feels he has no choice but to hire an attorney.

After hiring a paralegal, a mediator, an attorney, or a combination, it's time to negotiate the key issues, which are joint property, spousal support, child custody, visitation, and child support.

NEGOTIATION OF PROPERTY

Joint property is also called marital or community property and represents all the holdings accrued together during the marriage. In most cases this includes money the two of you earned while married and anything either of you bought during that period. Some mediators and attorneys first divide the separate property into "piles" that represent items that are individually owned by each spouse. Separate property is what you owned individually before you married, or anything you acquired after your separation or from an inheritance or gift. Lists are made of all the mutually owned possessions and their value, and then these assets are divided. Finally, each couple must share the cost of debts, termed community obligations, accrued while married. Rachel made a list of what she considered to be their separate and joint property, as well as their debts, and then presented this list in a letter to her husband. The letter is included at the end of this chapter. She did not touch his hobbies or investments, even though, under the laws in California, she was entitled to half of all joint property or community property. It was more important to her that they have an amicable and expedient divorce.

Most experts advise that you put everything in writing, not count on verbal agreements such as, "Of course, honey, you can have the silver coffee urn we got as a wedding present." Be conservative and safe, and create a legal document to ensure the agreement will be binding. It is also advisable to have help in separating assets; it is a rare couple who can do this by themselves at the kitchen table. It might be less stressful to engage a paralegal or mediator. As our mediator said during divorce negotiations, "When we finish dividing the joint property, it is important that each of you come as close as possible to the standard of living you enjoyed during the marriage. Equity is what is important here." The items of property to be negotiated include:

1. *Income* earned by either of you during the marriage. This refers to money received from a career while married. If you have what is called passive income, which is current income from property owned before the marriage, it is usually seen as separate or individually owned and not divided in the divorce. You will need the most recent tax return to show your yearly income, and pay statements from work to illustrate the latest figures.

2. *The home (and contents)* you have shared. In most states, couples are allowed to establish their own agreement about how the worth of the home is divided fairly. In some states, however, another piece of property or assets of equal value must be traded for the house, or the partner leaving must receive half the worth of the home. This is often difficult financially and many couples end up selling their home and then splitting the profit.

This is what happened with Connie and Larry, who could not afford to keep the family home, but they came up with a way to give their four children stability for a year after they separated. Each of them found a small place to live and traded off staying in the family house with the children. This way the kids never had to go back and forth between them in the early stages of the divorce; they could feel secure in the home where they grew up. Eventually, the house was sold, but by then the children had grown used to the idea of their parents being with them separately and the transition was not as difficult.

If you need to sell your home or take out a second mortgage to pay your spouse half the market value, you will need to get the house appraised. First, a real estate agent can give you an estimate of the fair market value of your home. If you're going to refinance or sell, however, you will need a certified appraiser. This can cost hundreds of dollars, so shop around for someone reasonable and qualified. It helps to get a recommendation from friends, mediators, or financial planners. Be sure to get advice from legal or financial experts before deciding to sell your home. There are substantial tax penalties and real estate costs to consider, and most couples should not make this decision alone.

3. *Other possessions* will need to be divided, including the cars, boats, planes, hobby equipment, and other items shared during the marriage. This can be very emotional, and sadly, the marriage seems to be reduced to a blender and CD collection. Of course, these possessions are not just objects; each holds emotion and memory. The hardest for most people are the presents from birthdays, Christmases, and anniversaries, as well as the photos and paintings of family. It may seem challenging to be open and generous, because it feels as if so much has already been lost. Suddenly, a vase that once held a dozen red roses on Valentine's Day seems to be the most important object in the world. I have seen siblings fighting over their deceased mother's glass collection, and it is more about keeping a part of her and feeling some power in a powerless situation. Divorce creates similar feelings in people. If you find yourself in an emotional struggle with your spouse about an object, take time to think about the hidden meaning, and do some writing in your journal. Allow yourself to experience the deeper feelings behind the desire for a chair or breadbox.

If your spouse is sensitive enough to be approached about it, tell him or her why you really want the object. I wanted a trunk that had come from my husband's family but always held my sewing. Tied to this wooden chest were memories of all the Halloween costumes and prom dresses I had made, and images of the room where I sat creating. I told my husband, "I'll never live in this house again, but I'd like to keep the trunk." Be as kind to yourself and to your partner as you can be.

4. *A jointly owned business* that was bought and established during the marriage must be split equally. If, however, one spouse owned the business before marriage, or spent more time working there after the marriage, he or she will feel entitled to a greater share of the worth. This is debatable, the situation quite complicated and volatile, and it should be handled by a mediator or attorney. Also, the tax laws related to family-owned businesses are quite complex and could present problems for the average person. Get legal assistance. In one case, in which a couple owned a sporting goods store, it was decided that Alan keep and run the store because it had been his before the marriage and he loved being there. His wife, Mary, was content to receive generous spousal support, which came from the success of the shop. This is the ideal outcome when negotiating a settlement: individual satisfaction and mutual harmony.

5. *Retirement benefits.* If you or your spouse have retirement plans tied to your place of employment, then these are part of the community property and will be negotiated during the divorce. Some spouses think this is highly unfair, as Marcus, married for twenty-two years, describes. "I work hard. I have always worked hard, and now I'm supposed to just give my money to her. Who says?" Marcus has strong feelings that are understandable, and yet, the law in many states supports the splitting of all property, especially in long-term marriages of over twenty years, when one spouse, usually the woman, has stayed home as a homemaker and mother.

Dividing pensions or retirement benefits can be a complicated and lengthy process. The partner who earned the benefits can agree to give the other spouse a lump sum for half the worth or defer this until retirement. Younger individuals usually prefer the "buyout" method and those older spouses, the second alternative. Of course, the pension plan can just be a piece to negotiate on the Monopoly board. Its worth can be traded for something equally valuable. Again, equity and standard of living should be the guiding principles. A mediator or attorney can help you put all the "trading cards" on the table and they can be swapped depending on value and desire. Each marriage and each settlement is different. If you decide to divide the retirement benefits, a word of caution. It is an exceedingly complex and frustrating process, at least it was for me and for many of those with whom I spoke. Ask your mediator or attorney to explain the concept of a QDRO (pronounced "quadro"), which means a "qualified domestic relations order." This legal order tells the administrator of the retirement plan that a portion must be paid to the ex-spouse. The administrator can take up to eighteen months to approve this; in my case, it took nearly three years to receive the money in my account. You need legal assistance to handle the division of a pension plan and to complete a QDRO. Be persistent if this is something you feel you deserve.

6. *Social Security benefits.* In a phone interview with a customer service representative at Social Security, I found that if you have been married at least ten years at the time of your divorce, you are eligible for half your spouse's Social Security benefit when you reach retirement age of sixty-two to sixty-six years old. The representative also said that if your ex-spouse dies and you have not remarried, you can receive 100 percent of the benefit. A pamphlet entitled "What Every Woman Should Know," recommended for women, can be picked up at your local Social Security office. You can contact the Social Security Administration at their toll-free number: 1-800-772-1213.

7. *Investments.* All the investments the two of you have made during the marriage are joint or community property. Be sure to have lists of these investments as part of the negotiating process, not just their current value but their projected future worth. If you are the partner who has not handled the stocks, bonds, IRA's, mutual funds, annuities, or other investments, make an appointment with a professional trained in financial planning. There is a lot to learn about the tax consequences and the difference between investments. Do whatever is necessary to take care of your financial future.

8. *Spousal support.* This issue has been discussed in chapter 3, but it is included here as part of the negotiation package. The attorneys interviewed stress that the spouse who has been the homemaker, or the partner making less money, is entitled to support. In general, spousal support depends upon the number of years of marriage, the ability to pay, the need of the requesting spouse, and the overall health, age, and standard of living of both partners.

Attorneys emphasize that those receiving support must show need for the assistance, for instance, money to pay for school tuition or retraining in a new career. In other words, most attorneys currently favor temporary support, rather than permanent assistance, to help the spouse become self-sufficient. The stereotype that women want to bleed men of all their money and be supported to eat bonbons and watch TV still lingers. Films such as *Divorce American Style* make fun of these stereotypes but instill them as well. In the movie, the men drive beat-up Volkswagens and wear clothes with patches and holes, while ex-wives live in posh homes and wear flowing silk. Leading male characters advise other men to beware of wives who want to destroy their finances and their manhood.

It's important to dispel such stereotypes, and also to let fairness be the guide in awarding spousal support. When one partner makes three times what the other does, as in the case of Raymond and Patrice, the mediator helped Raymond realize he needed to give financial assistance to his wife, especially while she completed nursing school. So far, he has given her spousal support for tuition and living expenses, including travel, for the past three years. Their agreement stipulates that the support will continue until Patrice has a full-time job, not to exceed ten years, but they have verbally agreed that when she is self-supporting, the payments will cease. Financial support may be a difficult issue if resentment still exists between you. Try to remember the ways each of you has contributed to your marriage and family, listen to your mediator's recommendations, and recognize this service generously.

CHECKLIST AND ADDITIONAL LEGAL TERMS

1. First, decide whether or not you will use a *paralegal, a mediator, an attorney,* or a combination. To save time and money, write down questions before you go, and take all necessary documents with you. As mentioned previously, you will need income tax records, retirement benefits information, bank statements, and records of all other assets, including recent appraisals of your home. The paralegal, mediator, or attorney will tell you all this.

2. Next, you must file a *petition for dissolution of marriage*— or it might be called a *complaint for divorce or legal separation.* This document contains basic information about you and your partner and asks if you have any children, what your assets are, and whether you are filing for a divorce or a legal separation. This is the paperwork that Rachel did herself, but a competent paralegal can do it for you. Do-it-yourself divorce books complete with the appropriate forms are listed in the bibliography. The petition then needs to be filed with the court, and again, a

paralegal can do the filing. With the advent of no-fault divorce, it's not necessary for you to prove "fault" or find grounds for the divorce in order to file this petition. Some states still have fault-based grounds for divorce in addition to no-fault divorce. Be sure to call your state bar association to clarify the current laws in your area.

3. The *court clerk* files the petition and the summons at the same time. In the past, the summons had to be served by a marshal, but now the spouse who did not file can pick up the summons at the attorney's office, or it can be served by someone over the age of eighteen or by a process server. In this document is notification that you have filed for divorce and the time given your spouse to respond, usually between ten and thirty days. If your spouse files and you receive this summons, it says you are being sued. Don't panic. This is the language of the codes. My ex-husband filed, and I received the summons, so I remember the impact and the feeling of "Oh, my God, this is it." If you are the one receiving the summons, you might need to talk to someone about your feelings, or at least write them in your journal.

4. The *respondent* or person receiving the summons used to file an answer or response within thirty days, or the time period given. However, most uncontested divorces today are by *default* and a response is never filed. This saves approximately $200 in court filing fees and decreases the amount of paperwork and waiting time involved. The state where children reside has jurisdiction over them; this means that in a custody situation, the court will favor leaving children where they are, in the same state, city, and even in the same home, in order to give them the most stability. If your spouse cannot be found at the time the summons is being delivered, you can still be granted a divorce, again by default. Child support payments cannot be collected from him or her, but by reporting

the situation to the district attorney, you can be assured that the DA's office will be recording the amount owed and trying to collect what is due when your spouse is found. New state and federal laws allow agencies to use the Department of Motor Vehicles, Social Security, and other means to track down a spouse who is not paying support. Again, call your state bar association or the State Office of Child Support for specific help.

5. The *discovery process* is the information gathering or fact finding that occurs between the issuing of the summons and the final settlement. Mediators call this an informational session with both persons present. All the financial issues will be discussed, such as community property and all joint and separate assets. It is vital to bring accurate records to determine what property was accrued in the marriage, and what each of you owns individually. It is less expensive and more efficient to have the financial documents literally on the table between you. Otherwise, you will have attorneys gathering data, called *discovery,* and it will be very expensive. Attorney Robert Frandeen explains that the old concept of discovery was part of the Civil Codes, but now family law is based on *disclosure.* He cites several cases in which discovery is being used by attorneys in order to collect high fees. If you engage separate attorneys, be careful that they do only the research necessary. Have your attorney document the hours and fees, and ask to see this record weekly. It is preferable to mediate rather than to litigate, choosing the process of disclosure rather than discovery. Then, you will feel more in control of your divorcing process.

6. *Temporary or interim orders:* While a divorce decree is pending, it is vital to make sure that temporary agreements are negotiated, legally written, and filed to cover such important issues as child custody and visitation, child and spousal support, payment of debts, and access to house and property.

Although it's often tempting to make verbal agreements with your spouse, it is not advised. Especially if you have children, it's wise to have an agreement written up by a paralegal, mediator, or attorney. Paralegals indicate that such agreements are looked upon favorably by the courts because they show that parents are cooperating. Informal agreements can easily be written up by your legal representative, signed, and filed with the court. As in the case of a legal separation, interim or temporary orders can be used as a model for the final divorce agreement.

7. *Restraining orders:* The summons contains language describing a restraining order that applies to both parties in a divorce. What this means is, neither of you can move away or take and spend the joint assets, such as the money in bank accounts, in life insurance policies, and in real estate. At times, in an atmosphere of fear and mistrust, one partner may be tempted to take the money and run. A high school student and client, Andrew, discusses his mother's illegal actions: "She left once when I was ten and then came back two years ago, but she still hadn't settled down. They were separated but not divorced yet. My dad was a sucker for her promises. One day while he was at work, she emptied their bank account, every cent he had, took the stereo and some paintings, and split. I hope she never comes back."

The second kind of restraining order will protect one spouse from the other, at least on paper. It will prevent a partner from contacting the spouse at home or at work, and prevent harassment in any form. If the partner was aggressive or violent in the marriage, he or she could be even more so in the divorce. Several authors of divorce books describe the "craziness" that people feel and express during a divorce, and sometimes they can go berserk. If you sense your spouse could become violent, stay at a shelter or safe place where you cannot be found. Also, do not meet with your partner except in the presence of a mediator or attorney. One young woman, Marissa, knowing the history of her partner's alcoholism and his potential for outbursts, got a restraining order and full custody of their daughter. She made sure she was never alone, staying with different friends and family, until the situation deescalated. She wisely took care of herself and her child. Unfortunately, in a recent murder case in California, a husband killed his wife, who had just announced she was leaving. Friends were shocked because the woman always described her husband and their marriage as ideal. Then one day, with the children in the house, he stabbed her to death. Be aware that divorce can cause people to respond to stress and fear by acting in ways that are uncharacteristic. For your own safety, note any signs of escalating tension, aggression, or violence, and get a restraining order.

8. *Kick-out orders:* Many women and some men have problems getting their partners to leave the house at the start of divorce proceedings. If the party served with *Kick-out orders* does not obey them, in most states, the person can be arrested and told to either stay away from the spouse, or go to jail. If you have a recalcitrant spouse, you have the right to have your attorney draw up a legal document to evict him or her from the house. If you are afraid of reprisals, then move to a safe house or shelter until things become calmer.

9. *Child custody:* This is a term that many family law attorneys feel is outmoded and divisive. They prefer the word *parenting,* which has a cooperative, child-centered focus. This positive philosophy is echoed by Donald Saposnek and Chip Rose in their chapter "The Psychology of Divorce" in the book *Handbook of Financial Planning for Divorce and Separation,* edited by D. L. Crumbley and N. G. Apostolou. "Indeed, the family going through divorce does not break up, but rather is

restructured and reorganized." In the same chapter, the authors present custody data, stating that approximately sixty percent of divorcing couples have minor children and of these, about eighty-five to ninety percent successfully work out a custody agreement. Only ten to fifteen percent of these couples cannot agree.

In 1981, California began to mandate mediation for child custody, and other states have followed suit. This means that every couple with minor children must meet with a court-ordered mediator to discuss their custody and visitation arrangement. The attorneys interviewed stress that the focus, from the perspective of attorney, mediator, psychotherapist, and judge, should be the children. The more centered on the children's best interests everyone is, the more successful the mediation and custody agreement. Child custody should be gender-neutral, recognizing what is best for the child rather than for the mother, as has been the focus in the past. Legally, fathers have the same rights as mothers, but the attorneys I've interviewed agree that judges often favor mothers in child custody cases. In fact, nationally, physical custody is still granted to mothers in ninety percent of cases. Because of this, many father-advocacy groups have sprung up around the country to help fathers in their fight to have at least equal time seeing and raising their children. More will be said about this in chapter 5, and lists of fathers' rights groups appear in Resources.

The major types of custody are *physical custody* and *legal custody*. Physical custody means where the child lives at any given time. Legal custody means the right and responsibility to make major decisions about the child's health, education, and general welfare. These may be further characterized as:

Sole Physical Custody or Sole Legal Custody
Joint Physical or Joint Legal Custody
Split Custody

Sole custody, when the child lives with one parent who is responsible for raising him or her, is very rare and accounts for only 10 percent of cases. Sole physical custody means the child will live with and under the supervision of one parent, subject to the court's order of visitation for the other parent. *Sole legal custody* means one parent has the right and responsibility to make decisions about the child's health, education, and general welfare. Sole custody does not mean that one parent should be prohibited from seeing his or her child, unless the child's safety and welfare are at stake. In one case, Jessica, never married to her child's father, received sole physical and legal custody because her partner was a violent alcoholic. Visitation with the father had to be supervised and was limited to once a month. This mother wishes she had more financial support but says that her daughter's welfare is the most important factor.

Joint custody accounts for about 90 percent of cases, and means that both parents share legal rights and responsibilities. *Joint physical custody* means that each parent has significant amounts of time with the child, not necessarily split equally. *Joint legal custody* means both parents share the right and responsibility to make major decisions about the child's health, education, and general welfare. It is the opinion of many researchers and of those interviewed that joint legal custody is best for children. Parents, in this case, share major legal and vitally important decisions regarding their children, but not always joint physical custody. Clinicians disagree about whether or not children should be "shared" physically between two homes. A marriage and family therapist colleague says whether or not joint physical custody works depends on the family and the personalities of the children. She recommends that parents who want to share significant amounts of time with their children do so for a minimum of one week in each home. Otherwise, it is too disruptive for children.

Joint physical custody takes work and cooperation for parents to create a schedule, and they will see each other more frequently, but children can benefit. This form of custody means that children see both parents regularly, bond with them more deeply, and miss them less. Also, parents must work on improving their relationship when they see each other more often; this means less conflict between them, and less stress for families.

Some children and adolescents like joint custody less than their parents do, according to those interviewed. One boy, Terry, who is twelve, says, "I don't mind it in the summer. But during school it can get weird. I forget my homework at Mom's or Dad's and always leave my jacket or shoes or something. When I was smaller I got pretty confused and couldn't always keep straight where I was going. I guess it's okay. I want to see both my parents, but mainly they want to see me." One teenager, Rose, a former client, decided to live with her father full-time even though her parents have joint custody. "It was just too crazy," she says, "going back and forth, and I chose the house closest to school. I do miss my mom, but we have dinner once a week." Of course, the degree of conflict between ex-spouses has a great deal to do with whether or not joint custody is successful. Seeing one another weekly can at times be problematic, but if parents can continue to work on their relationship and parenting skills, with children as their focus, joint custody can be very supportive for kids.

Split custody is probably the most controversial of custody models, and perhaps the hardest on siblings. In this case, one parent takes one child or more, and the other parent, the rest of the children. Therapists interviewed advise avoiding this kind of custody if possible because of the feelings of loss children experience. Joanna, a former client, now an adolescent, who was separated from her twin brother at the age of ten, still wakes up in the night missing him. He lives with their father in another state and they visit each other once a year. According to Joanna, this has been the greatest loss of her life.

10. *Child support:* Refer to the discussion in chapter 3.

11. *Ex parte motion* is very common in family law. It is the legal request for emergency help from the court, usually due to financial crisis or fear of physical harm. Temporary orders will be issued by the court to make sure you receive support payments or to protect you from injury.

12. A *hearing* must be held in court before a judge in order to approve documents of your divorce, but you need not be present. This is not a trial, but a formal meeting with attorneys and the judge. During pretrial hearings, some judges will request the attorneys meet in his or her chambers to push for pretrial settlement. These judges want to avoid a trial and work to get attorneys to reach an agreement. Sometimes a family law attorney specializing in mediation will be called in to help resolve any conflict and speed up the settlement process.

13. *The trial* in a divorce case usually does not involve a jury. As a rule, by the time a divorce case goes to trial, the child custody issues are already settled. Such a trial, held in front of a judge with attorneys and clients present, is about property, income, and spousal support, and the more wealth the parties have, the more heated the argument. If this is the only way for one spouse to obtain a fair settlement, then a trial is necessary. However, the price is high, not just the increase in trial-based attorney fees, but the emotional havoc of facing one another in court in such a tense environment. In a conscious divorce, you can reach an agreement with a mediator, so the settlement is achieved more amicably and without a trial. It takes two conscious people to do this. If your spouse is unwilling to negotiate, then you have no choice but to engage a skilled attorney and proceed from there.

14. *The judgment* is the final ruling in a divorce, and it usually

comes in the form of the *marriage settlement agreement.* You cannot assume you are divorced until you receive a file stamped "Judgment" from the court, indicating the date your divorce judgment was entered. You and/or your spouse must have submitted the necessary paperwork to the court before a final judgment can be made. The earliest date a divorce can be final varies from state to state; the average is six months and one day after the date the respondent was served with the petition, and you cannot remarry until you receive this final judgment telling you you're divorced.

EMOTIONS DURING THE DIVORCING PROCESS

Relief

Some people feel relieved to have the legal process finally under way. This stage is filled with action: appointments, paperwork, phone calls, thinking, and more action. For those of you who have been waiting some time for this and just "want the whole thing to be done with," the stage of filing, negotiating, and settling with your spouse feels good. Be aware that one moment you may feel relief, and the next, sadness or fear, anger or remorse. There is no formula, no pattern except your own. Go with the flow. Don't get mad at yourself if you feel moody or "all over the map," as one young woman, divorced after eighteen months of marriage, expressed. If it is relief that you feel, then just breathe more deeply, relax those shoulders, and enjoy the moment.

Fear

You might wish to review the categories of fears in chapter 1, because these may surface during your preparation for divorce. With the stark reality of this action-oriented phase can come apprehension. You might wake up and say to yourself, "This isn't what I want!" as I did on several occasions. My fear prompted me to attempt a reconciliation with my spouse, even though I knew it wasn't the right choice. Actually filing for divorce made me feel irrational, crying hysterically one moment and hiding in bed the next. In other words, I felt terrified by what I had initiated. These fearful emotions are normal, whether you are leaving or being left; they are about being vulnerable and alone, being unsure of yourself at times and having to go on anyway into the unknown. Authors Donald Saposnek and Chip Rose, in "The Psychology of Divorce," comment that those divorcing feel unusual pressure, insecurity, and panic, arising because they are no longer part of a stable couple and family.

These feelings will shift and change as the divorce becomes finalized and things begin to settle into a new routine. At times, because you're human, you may feel fear and panic, but these moments will become fewer as you move into a post-divorce stage that promises more optimistic feelings. If you have anxiety, let yourself feel these emotions, realizing that it's healthy to get these feelings out of your body. Then, use the journaling techniques described in earlier chapters. Write down what you're afraid of, and what action you can take to dispel these fears. Also, it would help to talk with a therapist. Sometimes, just voicing our concerns, bringing them into the light, is enough to make us feel better. As you meet with your attorney or mediator and with your spouse, remember that your fear may not be based in reality; it is a response from the ego that makes you want to fight or flee, even when the threat is nonexistent.

You may find a deeper reason for your terror than is first apparent. If, for instance, you're afraid of being alone, it may stem from an earlier experience in your life. This is the case with my client Justine, married for thirty-eight years and now contemplating a divorce. "All I've ever wanted is to be loved, but it hasn't happened. I guess I got used to being neglected by my father, and then by my husband. Even though I'm ignored, it's what I'm used to, and it seems better than being totally alone." Your fear can actually be a catalyst for transformation. Justine's friends have noticed that she is taking action, which has lessened her fear. They tell her they love her new hairstyle and encourage her to attend singles dances. Although she feels it's happening slowly, Justine sees her progress, too. "I like that I'm getting back into sculpture and feel creative for the first time in years. I've even sold a few pieces." You may wish to use the rituals at the end of each chapter to help you feel more peaceful during stressful times.

Confusion

Even with an excellent mediator to help, I often felt confused by the legal terminology. If you feel confused during the divorcing process, you may still be in shock. Divorce is a tremendous change, and for most of us, it is a great loss. At times, you may feel dazed or scattered and not as focused as usual. Be sure to ask for clarification from the person assisting you. Ask as many questions as you want. You are the client. Don't be intimidated by the language or the demeanor of attorneys. Use your journal to sort out the confusion by writing down questions to ask your mediator or attorney. Perhaps begin with, "What am I confused about?" Then let the words pour out. The process of writing can often help you end the confusion by concretely seeing what the real and specific questions are.

Powerlessness

More than one attorney mentioned this emotion when talking about separation and divorce. Clients often express feeling "out of control," "powerless," or "victimized." Powerlessness is one thing that drives people to hire attorneys, and as mentioned earlier, this protection is a myth. An attorney cannot actually protect you from the feelings that will ensue. What can help you feel more powerful is the owning of your part in the situation. Rather than continuing to believe your spouse is a monster and you are an angel, see that each of you is partly responsible for the dissolution of your marriage. No one is bad or good, completely right or wrong. You each did the best you could, based on the modeling in your own family and on your own emotional health and readiness for marriage. Giving up the role of victim will give you the energy to move through your divorce with honesty and into your future with confidence. Taking action is what truly dissolves powerlessness. The two of you can meet with your mediator and share information that will dispel fear and increase feelings of control.

Powerlessness can feel like depression, the realization that there is nothing you can do to change what is happening. It is true that you cannot control what your spouse is doing, saying, or feeling about you. What you can control are your own thoughts, words, and actions. You can think that what is happening is the worst thing in the world, or you can reframe it as an opportunity for great transformation. This change of perspective takes time to develop as part of the healing process, as a former colleague, Jerome, divorced after nine years of marriage, expresses: "Recovering from a divorce has its own internal clock; each person begins to feel better at different times and in different ways. It's been nearly three years, and I feel happier than ever and really excited about my life."

If you are feeling powerless and out of control, then perhaps say the Serenity Prayer mentioned in chapter 1. You could also write down what you cannot change and what you can, making a list for each category. You may want to write the things you are powerless over on pieces of paper and put them in your let-go box, as described in chapter 1. Then, those things out of your control can be continually "turned over" to Highest Consciousness, or perhaps to the universe itself. There is nothing you can do about them. Lying awake dwelling on your spouse's words or actions, or imagining what he or she is doing right now, can literally drive you crazy. Instead, picture the words and scenes disappearing in wisps of smoke or put the images in a balloon and let it float away. Practice letting go of each disturbing word and image as it appears in your mind. Replace them with phrases of your own, such as, "Go to peace," "Let go," "I accept my life as it is," "I turn over my fear; fill me with love and serenity." Ultimately, letting go of what you cannot change and taking action in the ways you can will help you feel less anxious, more energized, and more accepting of what is happening.

Anger

According to Saposnek and Rose in "The Psychology of Divorce," anger is what is called a secondary emotion, the surface expression of other feelings beneath. Often, anger masks the feelings of fear and hurt. It also can be used as a protective device or a defense mechanism to keep other feelings from surfacing. Anger puts distance between spouses, and the person who is upset may feel safer or less vulnerable when angry. Hannah, divorced for seven years, left her husband because his anger could erupt any time no matter what she did. He was this way in the marriage and in the divorce as well. She tearfully recalls a time when she tried to connect with him. Her touch made him explode in rage, "What do you want, bitch? You're just like my mother!" Hannah says of Randall, "He was a classic abuser and I was the classic victim; I left because he couldn't stop hating me." During divorce negotiations, Randall would alternately scream and cry, enraged one moment and despondent the next. Finally, while awaiting the divorce decree, Hannah took care of herself by allowing no contact with Randall.

Feeling angry during a divorce is understandable; everything in your life is changing, often without your permission. The feeling of powerlessness can often cause anger to erupt, especially in the person being left. Some of the best therapists to see for anger work, in my opinion, are "process therapists." They have clients act out their feelings in various ways, but the action and movement seem to help release the emotions from the body. Sometimes pillows are used for the client to pummel with fists. At other times an "empty chair" is employed; the client imagines a person in the chair, and then talks aloud to him or her. This is a way to release the words and the underlying feelings.

Remember, you're free to scream in your car, pound the pillows on your bed, or take up a sport or hobby that is active or competitive. You might wish to turn to chapter 2 and follow the suggestions for releasing anger through writing in your journal. Just begin with the phrase, "I'm angry that . . ." Write until nothing else surfaces, and you feel complete. Do whatever is necessary to release the rage before talking with your spouse. You may need a counselor to be present while you express angry feelings to your partner. It might feel safer this way, and could give you the courage to express yourself.

Sadness

With the taking of legal action can come the reality that the marriage is truly over, and with this awareness comes deeper sadness. Sometimes after a session with your mediator or attorney, you may feel especially sad. For me this was triggered by driving there in separate cars, hardly talking outside, trying to discuss finances when I still felt raw emotionally, forcing myself to be strong and not cry. Then after my husband drove off, I would sit in my car and cry before I could leave. It felt so sad to be talking about our house and children, a life together, now being reduced to numbers on paper. Surviving a divorce isn't easy and it isn't instant, and the sadness can come in waves, completely unexpected.

Cynthia, divorced for two years, remembers that during their divorce she would wake up from a dream with tears on her face and reach for her mate, but no one was there. Jan, divorced for seven years, says he still gets postcards from his "ex" every few weeks, sweet and sad vignettes about their life together. His ex-spouse has never really let go, even though she is remarried. Andrea says her ex-husband put letters under her pillow while they were divorcing, sad notes, love notes, and angry ones, and she hasn't been able to throw them away. She will take the bundle out, read the letters, and cry. This is after being divorced for eighteen years and remarried for fourteen of those years.

If you are feeling sad during the divorcing process, be sure to give yourself total permission to have your feelings and the time to do so. Cry, talk to friends and professionals, and write in your journal. I filled several notebooks during my divorce. This process, in part, kept me sane. Begin with the phrase, "I'm sad about . . ." and let yourself go. Cry and write and write and cry. Do this until all the feelings have been expressed.

OPTIONAL RITUALS FOR
THE DIVORCING PROCESS

1. A day before meeting with your legal counsel, spend time alone getting centered. Close your eyes and imagine a circle of light surrounding you in a bubble of protection. To save time,

you could sit in your car for a few minutes before the next session, take a deep breath, relax, and surround yourself with soothing light.

2. If you're a person who has found prayer comforting, pray before each session, using whatever words come to you. This may help you feel more peaceful and accepting.

3. Between sessions, say and write affirmations to "make firm" a positive attitude to carry into each meeting. You could use these or phrases of your own: "I am strong and able to handle all that happens"; "I am clear about what I must do"; "Truth and integrity are my guides"; "I trust the process and my own intuition"; "I am helping to create the best outcome."

4. Write your feelings in your journal before and after sessions with your spouse. In this way, you will empty yourself on paper, and feel lighter.

5. After each legal session, schedule time alone to unwind and process your feelings. Be careful while driving. You may be more preoccupied than you realize.

6. Schedule therapy to help you deal with what is happening during the divorcing process. Don't wait until you're in crisis to ask for help.

7. Listen to your intuition and tune in to your physical self. Are you hungry? Tired? In need of exercise, a massage, fresh air, a change of scene? Do whatever will be therapeutic mentally and physically to help you stay healthy during your divorce. Refer to chapter 7, Self-Care, for further suggestions.

RACHEL'S LETTER TO HER HUSBAND WITH A MARRIAGE SETTLEMENT PROPOSAL

Dear Bill,

It is clear to me that our marriage has no possibility of change, and that our priorities and life goals are too different. Our needs will be better met living apart. Therefore, I have filed the appropriate legal papers in court for an uncontested divorce. It is my desire to achieve this amicably, with no ill will whatsoever.

Here is my suggested marriage settlement proposal:

Legally, we are each entitled to half of all that is considered joint or community property, which is defined as, "Anything earned or acquired by either spouse during the marriage that is not separate property. Community property belongs to both spouses equally no matter who earned it." In our case, this would be our home, bank accounts, automobiles, home furnishings, computer equipment, musical instruments, etc. However, contingent upon a mutual agreement not to retain lawyers (avoiding potentially astronomical costs), I have another proposal for your serious consideration.

We need to figure out the details of car insurance, new bank accounts for house payments, changing utility bills to your name, changing health insurance, taxes, and setting a timeline for removal of my personal property, as well as the division of community property. Essentially, I am proposing that we split the market value of the house, minus what is owed, and divide the furnishings, and I will leave the rest alone. Let me know if you accept this offer.

In friendship,
Rachel

6

Loved Ones

I no longer live in the house
down the road
where my children
were born,
but memories linger
of
tea parties
and picnics in pastures,
wishing on birthday candles
and first stars;
ripe blackberries in June
and apples in September,
toothless Christmas smiles
and cocoa
left on the mantle for Santa.
Nostalgia

Divorce deeply affects the people and things we love, including children, of course, but also other family, friends, pets, home, and our dream of marriage. At the time my husband and I separated, I naively thought he was all I left. At least in that moment of driving away, I didn't understand the full impact of my actions. In reality, I said good-bye to my partner, our daughter and son, family pets, the apple trees and stream, my country home, and the image of growing old by the wood stove. It took two months for the grief to set in, and seven years later, I still have moments of deep mourning.

Now, I see human relationships as huge, intricate webs. Every breath of wind, every spider's step affects each strand. This spiderweb is like a family system; the behavior of each member affects everyone else and influences the stability of the group. And so, my leaving affected an entire system of loved ones. This is not to say I would or could do anything differently. But the leaving of a marriage has a profound effect on everyone and everything in the "web."

CHILDREN AND DIVORCE: AN OVERVIEW

Children are the innocents in the divorcing process, and much of the literature on divorce is devoted to their response and well-being. During my research for this book, the topic of children evoked the most diverse feelings. Most clinicians believe that divorce has a profound effect on children. They concur that it doesn't have to ruin children's lives, but it has a far-reaching effect. My colleagues feel empathy for everyone in a divorce, especially the children in difficult custody battles. They further observe that society provides few meaningful guidelines or any preparation for marriage, parenting, or budgeting family finances. Change, according to these professionals, must occur in the entire society and would greatly benefit couples and children.

One attorney offers another perspective. He maintains that kids can suffer in a bad marriage, too. In the final analysis, he stresses that kids are resilient, are receptive to counseling, and do not have to suffer in a divorce.

In a conscious divorce, parents continue as coparents, keeping the welfare of their children at the forefront through cooperation and mutual respect. Partners may divorce, but they do not divorce their kids. They must learn new ways to relate to one another and to their children. There is no reason for outmoded and negative ideas of divorce to remain prevalent. It's time to replace terms such as "broken" or "split" family for terms such as "bi-nuclear" and "blended" family, showing that the unit is not lost but restructured, that the bonds of kinship continue long after a divorce. Especially with fifty-one percent of first marriages and sixty-five percent of second marriages ending in divorce, it's important to reframe our concepts of dissolution to fit the times. We need to normalize divorce and the family of divorce, using positive terminology and concepts that show continued health rather than demise.

TELLING YOUR CHILDREN

This positive focus does not discount the challenge of divorcing when you have children. Even though most of the adults interviewed whose parents divorced when they were children say they are happy with the decision now, they recall the moment of separation with poignancy. One young student in her twenties, Rory, whose mother and father are in successful second marriages, thought her world was ending when her father left. As my fifteen-year-old client, she had stormed into a session, yelling, "I'm never getting married or having children, *ever.*" After Rory calmed down, she told me her father had announced he was leaving that morning before school. She had idolized her dad, and in her grief, she made a decision not to speak to him again. This, in part, is due to the way in which he left, without talking to anyone in the family ahead of time, including his wife. Rory says of this, "It would have been hard to deal with any way he did it, but I think I could have forgiven him sooner if he had at least made an effort to explain."

Is there a preferable way to tell your children you are separating or divorcing? And, perhaps a more immediate question might be: Is there preparation to be done before talking with your children?

WHAT TO DO BEFOREHAND

Your attitude, conveyed through your manner, is actually more important than what you say. In other words, how you appear to your children individually and as a couple says a great deal to them. If you're angry and agitated, or in conflict with your partner, this isn't the best time to talk to your kids. In fact, you might need some quiet time alone first, calmly thinking about what to say. If you feel upset with your spouse, then write about it in your journal, or talk with a therapist or friend, before trying to meet with your partner and children. When you feel more at peace and ready to discuss what to say to the children, sit down with your husband or wife. Agree to agree, if for no other reason than for the welfare of your kids. Then decide on a good place and time to talk, the earlier in the day the better. Your children will be more rested in the morning, and they will have the entire day to reflect and talk with you again if necessary.

Prepare for the discussion with your children by trying to understand how they might be feeling. Let yourself feel this empathy and deep love for them. You may still be nervous to face them, afraid of disappointing them and being so human, but you're doing the best you can. Ellis says he still remembers the time before he told his children of the divorce. "Beforehand was horrible. It was the hardest time in the divorce for me because I kept imagining the worst situations: they would hate me or not want to ever see me again." Ellis adds that actually telling them was easy because "they were so wonderful." It may be tense at first, but over time your children will eventually appreciate your sensitivity and honesty, your focus on their needs, and, of course, your love for them.

THE IDEAL WAY TO TELL CHILDREN

Most books on divorce advise telling the children together as a couple. This is ideal, but not always feasible. Most of the parents interviewed talked with their children separately, some discussing what they would say ahead of time, and some spontaneously saying their own personal truth. From my own experience, I suggest that, if possible, you plan what you'll say, and tell your children together. This is what Ellis did with his wife, Maggie, now divorced for sixteen years. They met three times alone over tea at a local restaurant. During these meetings they talked about their marriage and then planned what they would say to the children. My son and daughter asked me why I was leaving, and I told them as much as I could at that time. My husband told them what he believed to be the reason, but his answer differed from mine. Then both children told me what their dad had said and wanted me to explain the discrepancy. This was quite confusing for them and upsetting for me. If we had discussed what to tell the children before meeting with them, it would have been better for all of us. In fact, it would have been best for us to have told them what was happening all along, at least in general terms.

Children know more about what's going on than we realize, and we should be as honest with them as possible. Frank, married for nine years and divorced for three, thought his children were too young to realize that he and his wife had not been intimate for two years and planned to separate, but his six-year-old daughter, Monica, said one day, "Daddy, why do you sleep in the back room? Don't you like Mommy?" If you're not getting along with your spouse prior to the separation, it would be good to tell a child this, and to do so based on his or her age and capacity to understand. Then it isn't such a surprise, as it was for Rory and for my children. They will be more prepared for what is to come because of your honest communication.

KEEP IT SIMPLE

When the two of you meet to discuss what you'll say, keep it simple and age-appropriate. It might be best to tell all the children together if they are close in age, for instance, all of grade school age. If you have one in elementary school and one in junior high or high school, it may be better to tell them separately; otherwise, what you say may be too basic for one or too complex for the other. Ellis sat down at the kitchen table with Maggie and their son and daughter, aged five and seven. Ellis told them, "Things are just not working out with Mommy and me. We're going to live separately, but neither of us is leaving you."

First, you might want to tell them how much you love them, that you had hoped the two of you could stay together and work things out but you haven't been able to. Then state the situation as honestly and simply as possible. For example, if this is a trial separation and you will be working on a reconciliation, you might say, "We've decided that we can't live together right now. We're going to live separately at least for a few months and then see if we can be together again. This doesn't mean either of us is separating from you. We love you and always will." If this is not a trial separation but the beginning of a divorce, be honest. There's nothing worse than giving kids false hope. If you are too optimistic, especially to spare their feelings, then it is much worse when they realize the truth. Be honest, not brutally so but direct and truthful. "As you know, we haven't been getting along very well for a while. It's reached the point that we've decided to separate and divorce. This has been a very difficult decision because we both love you so much, but we just can't live together anymore."

Crystal, divorced for eight years, still remembers what she and her ex-husband said to their children. "We had it planned. We said, 'We need to divorce; we don't know how to make each other happy, and we have too many problems we can't resolve. There is nothing you guys did that caused this. We love you so much. We just hope we can be friends after this and get along better if we're apart.' And then we all cried."

WHAT ELSE CAN YOU DO?

During the time you meet as a family, remember to listen to your children's questions and comments. If you need to review chapter 2 on communication skills, do so before you gather. Be as ready as you can be to verbalize your views using "I" statements and to practice compassionate listening. Your children may be sad and angry at this meeting; they may do everything from listening in silence and refusing to talk, to throwing a full-blown tantrum. Even if they say they hate you, begin yelling, or become hysterical, know that it is done out of deep pain and disappointment. Children hate change, especially radical change that so disrupts their lives. They crave consistency no matter how dysfunctional the family has become; it is all they know. So, as hard as it may be, try to remain calm, and don't become devastated by what your children do and say. They are working out their own feelings about the divorce, as you are, and it's a newer reality for them. Give them time to go through the stages of loss you've already been dealing with and will face in the months to come.

CHILDREN'S CONCERNS

Children tend to worry about many issues during a divorce. As parents it's important to take their fears and reactions seriously, listening openly and answering their questions as honestly as possible. Children worry about where they will be living and with whom, how often they will see you, and if all their siblings will be together. They may even worry about money, especially if they know or sense it has been an issue before. I overheard a friend's son say to her shortly after her divorce, "Mom, you can have the money in my piggybank and I could get a job; I know how to do lots of stuff." Her son is seven. He sensed her concern even though she tried to be upbeat and nonchalant.

Watch for your children's tendency to want to take care of you. Assure them you're doing fine. If you aren't doing well and find yourself confiding in your children, be careful with your boundaries. You should be seeing a therapist and unloading there, not with your children. Kids should not be expected to take care of us. Get help for yourself and allow your children to have a childhood.

Children, especially those in elementary school, have a deep fear of abandonment during a divorce. They may show this fear at bedtime, fearing the dark, a closed door, or a closet. Also, they may not want to stay with a babysitter or relative they once loved to visit. This is a normal reaction to the fear of losing you. Just be patient if they are more clingy than usual or fearful of small changes. This will pass as they become more secure in their new lifestyle and surroundings, especially if you are there at the center of their world.

Besides the fear of abandonment, children fear the unknown, just as their parents do. They want to know, as specifically as possible, what is going to happen next. Ellis says that his children were very confused and kept asking why Mommy and Daddy lived apart. Ellis and Maggie never fought, and treated each other with respect, so the children couldn't understand why they had separated. Ellis talks about his commitment to his kids: "It was clear that I wasn't leaving the kids. Once we separated, I put so much time into the kids. It was really important." Jackie, divorced after nine years of marriage, with two daughters, prepared a calendar with marks in one color for the days at Mom's and another color for the days at Dad's.

In general, children want to be told where they will be, when, and who is picking them up from school. They want clarity and order, to know their life has some sort of plan, and they need to be told about the plans in advance. This gives children security, and with security comes confidence, a belief they are valuable and important to you.

Children, especially adolescents, worry about what their friends, teachers, coaches, and any important person may think about the divorce. For years my children joked that they had a boring family, and they wished they could get double the presents like their friends with divorced parents. Then when we did divorce, they were embarrassed, even mortified, that we were separating after so many years. They told their friends it was just a time for me to be alone for a while, and I would be home in a week. Often, children have a hard time explaining to teachers and others that their parents now live apart. In fact, one divorced dad, Andrew, says, "It would really help if teachers didn't assume every kid has parents who are together when they hand out dittos and mailings that say, 'Dear Mom and Dad,' or 'Dear Parents.' This was sad for my daughter, Malika."

As parents, you can keep reassuring your children that you love them, that you will always be there to support them, and that no amount of change will alter this. If you feel you cannot deal with their concerns, or they shut you out, then make an appointment with a therapist who works with children. Ask friends or your own therapist, mediator, or attorney for a referral. It's better to get help for them now rather than wait until the problems escalate. One of my colleagues has reached the point where she won't see a family with an adolescent who has never had counseling during an earlier divorce. This is because by the time a child becomes a teenager, his or her issues are so problematic, and the damage so severe, that the case is just too stressful. She further believes that every couple with children should go to family therapy at the beginning of and during a divorce.

CHILDREN'S BEHAVIOR DURING DIVORCE

The earliest period, lasting about one year from the making of the decision, is difficult for many children. One reason is that it's challenging for parents to focus on their children when they are so intensely focused on themselves. During this stage, according to therapist Michelle Samis, children either withdraw so they don't add more stress to the family dynamic, or they are symptomatic to draw attention away from their parents. In other words, younger children may become quiet and withdrawn, tiptoeing around their parents, or they may begin acting out, having tantrums, crying, wetting the bed, expressing nonverbally and verbally their anger and sadness about their parents' separation.

Madeline's son, Jon, who was four at the time of their divorce and is now nineteen, just seemed to fade away as a preschooler whose father had left. He rarely talked and seemed almost autistic, preferring to sit alone in a corner staring into space. His parents saw it as shyness, as a manifestation of independence and individuality. Friends and babysitters, however, saw something amiss. Their childcare provider, looking back fifteen years, comments about Jon's initial behavior: "I worried about Jon's passivity then and told his parents that he seemed depressed or in a trance most of the time. He never had an opinion and let the other kids decide everything for him, including what to eat. Most of the time he sat by himself indoors. I always spent extra time with him, trying to get him to talk, but he usually just shrugged his shoulders or nodded yes or no."

Young children under twelve are egocentric, seeing themselves at the center of their world, often faulting themselves
when a parent leaves. They often blame themselves and become
hypersensitive to the potential of abandonment and rejection.
Turner, quoted earlier in the book, says his preschool child,
Brandon, asked him a question that nearly broke his heart:
"Dad, you aren't divorcing me are you?" In reply, Turner told
his son, "Of course I'm not divorcing you. I'll always be your dad
and I'll always love you." On a positive note, both of Turner's
sons, Brandon and Taylor, are doing extremely well a little
over a year after the divorce. Teachers, friends, and family all
say the boys are happy and well adjusted, mainly because
Turner and his ex-wife, Jill, get along well, talk nearly every
day, go to school functions at the same time, and plan to have
the holidays together in one home.

Many therapists, such as psychologist Donald Saposnek, see
the importance of focusing on very young children of divorce
and their needs. They want parents of infants to realize the
potential impact of a separation and divorce on them. Clinicians are specifically concerned about babies six to twelve
months of age who need to attach or bond with at least one
parent in order to develop normally. Saposnek tells the story
of a divorcing couple with a six-month-old baby. One parent
was moving to Hawaii and the other was staying on the main-
land, and they wanted to fly the baby back and forth every
month so they could have joint custody. They could only focus
on their own needs, ignoring the potential impact on their
child. Interrupting a child's development in this way and not
allowing for attachment can create sociopaths, who may later
act out their distress violently. If you're a parent, seriously
consider your effect on your kids. Preferably, see a child psychologist at least once during the divorce to set up a parenting
plan. This isn't a scare tactic, just a realistic prevention strategy.

This early stage can be problematic for young children unless parents are focused on their kids, and that means working on their own coparental relationship. Sometimes what parents need is someone to talk to, a therapist or other parents in a support group. As parents, it's important to get your own needs met, whether this is through expressing your feelings, getting occasional childcare, exercising, or whatever helps you cope best when you're interacting with your former spouse or your children.

During this initial period, adolescents are also at high risk. They are getting ready to leave home, yet they may feel as if they have no solid foundation. If parents can respond enough to notice that their kids are acting out, then the issues can be dealt with. High-risk behavior in teenagers can be increased drug and alcohol use, sexual acting out, truancy, and breaking the law. Adolescents often are angry when their parents separate, and they express their feelings by doing something to "punish" their parents or at least to say, "Hey, pay attention."

Candace has been divorced for six years, ever since her youngest son was three and her oldest was thirteen. She explains, "Travis has had the hardest time with the divorce from the very beginning. As a preschooler he didn't have the words to say how he was feeling. He just sat quietly watching TV or eating. But at night he would cry when I put him to bed and want to be held. He has a weight problem now, and I can trace it to the time of our separation. The oldest, Anthony, didn't want to come home. Luckily, he played sports and just kept busy all the time. Thank God he didn't get in trouble." Also, as parents we must pay attention to children's actions and to what they're *not* saying. Edward, divorced for thirteen years, regrets that he was so preoccupied with his new relationship and his own feelings, that both his children fell through the cracks. Damage can be averted if you are conscious of your adolescents' behavior, aware of their needs, and willing to spend quality time with them.

Adolescent females seem to express their sadness by crying and moping, while males tend to express their grief through anger. Often, boys have a harder time with divorce than girls, especially when their dads leave. It's important for fathers to realize the impact they have on their sons, and to be there when their children need them.

Researchers say that male adolescents suffer most when their mothers leave, and they take out their distress on their mothers, not their fathers. When I separated from my husband, my teenage son seemed fine, visiting me often and not really verbalizing his feelings much. Instead, he focused on school and sports, got a 3.5 grade-point average, and ignored his feelings. It was nearly a year later when his anger erupted, and he began verbalizing his frustration and hurt. Initially, I had talked with him about my reasons for leaving, but he kept expecting me to come home and never believed we would divorce. By the time he realized it was a permanent change, the anger surfaced. We worked through this rocky period with honest communication and weekly therapy.

During the first year, do your best to take care of your own needs and, at the same time, be there for your children. It can be quite a balancing act, but your effort to be present for your kids is essential for their recovery and well-being.

The next stage is a transitional period, which begins one year after the separation and continues for approximately two years. During this phase, response to the separation and divorce is not as extreme. Children have expressed much of their anger and sadness and realize that things are not changing back to the way they were. During this period, children are adjusting to the many changes, from moving between two homes, to changing friends and sometimes schools, to settling into a new pattern of living. Also, economics may shift during this stage, putting more strain on an already delicate transition. All these changes can affect children emotionally. One child I knew during his parents' divorce, Ben, only wet his bed at his dad's, and this continued for two years. His father had a series of girlfriends living there, which upset him, and for this reason, he felt more secure at his mother's house.

This phase is one of adjustment for everyone. I found a larger house so I could have my younger child with me. He loved it there and moved in full-time. I wish I could have lived there longer than six months, because he now says it felt like home, as if he were finally settled. When I moved again, he had to go back to living with his father, and he felt angry and displaced. Create as much stability as you can in the first three years, because children need routine; they need to know that something is stable and can be counted on. After all, their entire world feels upside down.

It's also hard on children at this time if parents get back together and then separate again, or engage in constant conflict. Ben's parents were divorced and yet saw each other often, even making love occasionally and conceiving Ben's sister, Sara. This closeness was very confusing for Ben, who says he just wanted his parents to do one thing and stick to it. Such ambivalence creates false hope for children and does not allow them to heal from the divorce. Also, parents who fight continually in front of their children, who criticize each other, or who try to enlist their children as allies or messengers are negligent as parents. The most heartbreaking story comes from six-year-old Lisa, who hides in the closet when her dad comes. "I just put my fingers in my ears and sing to myself. Sometimes when I can still hear the yelling, I wrap myself in my mom's coat."

From my perspective, the transitional stage is an easier one than the initial phase in terms of stress, but it still takes vigilance to make sure your children are doing well emotionally. Jeffery, divorced for three years after seven years of marriage, says, "Just ask them how they're doing. Sometimes they'll say, 'fine' when you can tell that something's wrong. Then I say, 'You can tell me anything; don't worry about it; just tell me the truth.' We've had some great talks, usually while on hikes."

Some of children's negative behavior may be linked to a divorce, but probably not all of it is related. Rather than focusing solely on the risk factors and the negative behavior in children, focus on what you *can* do to help your child. This means stopping what you're doing, spending quality time with each child, and having heart-to-heart talks in which you truly listen. It's not the divorce that is potentially devastating for kids, but how you deal with them and the other parent. In other words, the less conflict, the fewer problems in kids. One of my colleagues tells the story of a client who lived several states away and now wanted full custody of his toddler without thinking about what was best for her. At this point, my colleague felt like reading the Bible verse about the two mothers fighting over a child. The king said unless they decided soon he would cut the baby in two, and give each of them half. Finally, one mother said to give the child to the other woman. Of course, this was the real mother because she cared most about the welfare of her child. This is what my colleague wishes parents could understand.

In other words, as parents, you should resolve your differences and forgive one another, or at least put aside ill feelings, for your children's sake. If you can't do this, then act as if you can, and do it anyway. Your children's future success is at stake.

Finally, at the end of five years the family is a single-parent one or a blended family. At this point children have adjusted to most of the changes, including the economic and social ones already mentioned. Even after two or three years, children seem to have acclimated to the divorce, according to those interviewed. Their positive adjustment, of course, is tied to the lack of conflict between parents and to the degree of focus on the children's welfare. The more parents make it all seem normal, the better for the kids.

One aspect that has not been addressed is the involvement of parents with new partners and the effect of this situation on children. This discussion belongs in the final stage because most professionals advise waiting a few years before becoming involved with a new partner, especially if there are children. Laurie, who had a daughter at twenty-two and has chosen not to marry the father, has remained unmarried, saying that her focus on her child has always come first. This may be the extreme, erring on the side of caution, but those who begin relationships too soon after a separation, may adversely affect their children.

Ideally, you should not introduce a new partner to children for at least six months after separating. Children fear that the new partner will replace the divorced parent. The new person can just be a friend to the child for one to two years and not try to be a parent. It is best that the new partner not sleep at the house when your children are there. Otherwise, it tends to be confusing to younger children and sexually overstimulating for older children. It puts all children in painful loyalty conflicts. Overall, it's best if you do not remarry for at least a year and a half to two years after separating—the longer, the better.

One reason second marriages fail is that children unconsciously or consciously try to get rid of the new person by lying, playing tricks, and undermining the new partner in hopes that their mom and dad will get back together. This especially happens if the relationship has materialized too quickly. If you are involved with a new partner, make sure you talk to your children about their feelings and introduce this new person gradually. In my current marriage, we have four children and two grandchildren between us. For at least a year I just met my husband's children casually at parks and at the beach, and we were able to build a friendship. We married two years after these initial meetings, and now I have a loving and trusting relationship with each child. They call me their second mom and MaSue, names I cherish.

TYPES OF DIVORCED PARENTS

What sort of divorced parent will you be? My colleagues and I use the research of Constance Ahrons, which categorizes divorcing parents into five groups. Fifty percent of divorces come from the first two groups, perfect pals and cooperative colleagues. Nearly fifty percent of parents are either angry associates or fiery foes, and less than one percent are dissolved duos.

1. *Perfect pals:* These folks were usually good friends in the marriage and would have been better as friends than mates. These parents celebrate together, go out together, and even bring their new partners along. Children often appreciate this feeling of extended family and cooperation. The only problem is that kids don't understand why their parents divorced, and they may ask this from time to time.

2. *Cooperative colleagues:* These parents relate in a business-like manner with one another. They may not like each other, but they respect one another as parents. They may go to school events at the same time but not together. They maintain better boundaries than do perfect pals.

In my divorce, we began as perfect pals mostly for our children's sakes, but also because we were still disengaging as a couple. After twenty-six years together, it seemed easy to share Thanksgiving as an extended family, to give one another gifts, and to attend family events at the same time. In the past two years, however, we have become cooperative colleagues, declining invitations to holiday events and weaning ourselves from so much contact. Now, both children have left home, and it seems more comfortable to have less contact. This is also out of respect for new partners and events with them and their families.

3. *Angry associates:* These divorced parents fight one another, call each other names, and bad-mouth each other both alone and in front of their children. Every attorney interviewed deplores this sort of behavior and its effect on children.

4. *Fiery foes:* These are similar to the category above, only the intensity of their behavior has escalated. It is not uncommon for these parents to return to court anywhere from several to twenty-five times in a single year. These parents fight constantly, and often the police are involved. The ones who suffer most are the innocent children who must witness and be in the middle of this conflict.

5. *Dissolved duos:* These parents involve at least one who has moved away, especially dads who have left, relocated, and even remarried with a new family. They may not even tell their new spouse of their first family or be in contact with their ex-spouse and children.

As coparents, the two of you can consciously decide to work together harmoniously. You can choose how much to interact by trusting your comfort levels and boundaries until the parental relationship feels just right for everyone.

THE SINGLE-PARENT FAMILY
AND WHAT TO EXPECT

Every family is unique, but the single-parent family does have different characteristics from a dual-parent one, and different needs. First of all, one parent suddenly does everything alone that used to be shared. This can be quite demanding and stressful, as well as liberating. Some single parents try to keep everything exactly as it was in the two-parent household. This means doing the job of both parents at once. Not only is this impossible, unless you clone yourself, but it's exhausting. Instead of having one centered, happy parent, your children would have a burned-out, resentful one. So, do what you can, realistically, to be the best parent you can be, but also take care of your own needs. On a positive note, now you can make decisions that you feel are best for your children, in the context of your home and way of life there. When large decisions develop, it is best to discuss these with your ex-partner. The everyday ones, though, such as the schedule of meals, bedtime, and leisure-time activities, can be easier to decide as one parent.

In your new home, try to keep things as normal as possible, especially during the first few months to a year. The worst things for children at this time are inconsistency, broken promises, and too much change at once. Of course, some changes can't be helped, especially if you must move and your children need to change schools. If possible, stay in the same house where the children have grown up, in order to give them added stability. But if you have to leave, try to be accepting of this change, and don't feel guilty and upset with yourself. You're doing the very best you can. Tell your kids that you know it's hard, but you're doing everything you can to create a loving home for them. They'll know this from your words and actions. My son and daughter were very sad that I moved out, because they felt I had created the nurturing feelings in our home. Now, however, they feel this love and comfort in my new home and realize that their dad is happy in the old house. Children need to feel that at least some things have remained the same; some things can be counted on, especially the constancy of your love.

At times, especially if you have more than one child, you can feel stretched pretty thin, with everyone wanting a piece of you at once. Be sure to ask for help from family and friends now that you're divorced. Grandparents, if close by, often enjoy being asked to help. Join a carpool, enlist babysitters from among young adults in the neighborhood, or do trades with other parents to create some free time for yourself. This networking, bonding, and joining of friends into a new family system is a positive result of divorce. Lynda, who is single, has joined other mothers and families for several years to help her with her parenting and provide a larger, joyful extended family for her daughter.

Also, you can let your children help you according to their capacity. Many professionals support the theory that we should allow children to do for themselves whatever they are able to do. Don't baby your children, even though you may be tempted to do this during and after your divorce. The divorced parents interviewed say they have a tendency to buy too much for their children and give more time and energy to their kids than before. Turner speaks for these parents: "We love our kids so much, and we still feel bad for disrupting their lives. We want to show them how much we care, and let them know we're sorry." Give your children love and nurturing, but don't cater to them out of guilt or pity. Let them pitch in and help the family, and feel important and needed in the process.

I have seen many divorced parents spoil their children to make up for the pain they have just experienced. Remember, you are the parent, and your children count on you to be consistent and set limits. Many stories exist about Saturday and Disneyland dads. Of course, both mothers and fathers may be tempted to give children special treats, trips, gifts, whatever says to the kids, "I love you most," or "I want you to love me (or love me best)." The danger is in the negative competition between parents using materialistic bribes, which make children feel more powerful, yet even more insecure. Even though it can feel threatening to let your children go on a trip with your exspouse, don't be tempted to compete, especially with money.

Just be yourself. Give love and your time, set limits, and, above all, check in with your intuition to see if what you're doing for your children feels right. If it doesn't, then change your behavior. While raising my children, I often did more for them than I wanted, in order to "earn" their love. At times, I sensed I was going against my inner judgment, but I ignored my intuition. Since the divorce, I've become more secure, giving when it feels right and being able to set my boundaries and say "no." Both my children say they respect me more now, and our love for one another is honest and strong.

A FINAL WORD ABOUT CHILDREN

If you have children, then you have probably worried at some point about the effect of your divorce on their lives. Divorce clearly has an effect on children as well as adults; it is second only to a death in terms of a life-changing event. Your children, who are imaginative, sensitive beings, go through the same mourning process that you do, without the ability to make sense of it all. What they need are parents who can listen to their fears and concerns, who can answer their questions and reassure them. The way children react and adjust has a great deal to do with their own resiliency, and this differs from child to child, even those raised in the same family. Ellis comments that each of his children responded differently to the divorce, based, he feels, on the difference in their personalities. His son, who was the youngest, is very mellow and flows with life, and he seemed able to handle everything with ease. His daughter, who was two years older, felt a lot of anger and rejection, but with communication with her dad and a helpful therapist, she is doing fabulously.

In summary, what do the parents interviewed recommend to help your children through and beyond the divorce?

1. Give your children affection and reassurance. Show them and tell them you love them.
2. Tell them the general truth, in language they'll understand.
3. Keep your promises. If you can't do it, say so right away.
4. Each week, spend quality time alone with each child.
5. Let children help to make decisions that affect them, and let them help in other ways, too. This will make them feel good about themselves.
6. Be patient with the healing process your children are going through. Their process, and the time it takes, is their own.
7. Be available to answer your child's questions about the divorce and related issues. Be willing to set aside enough time for this.
8. Take time for fun. Lighten up, and spend a day together doing what you love. If you have rarely done this, now is the perfect time.
9. Take care of yourself by scheduling a day off alone or with friends in order to recharge your batteries. You will be a better parent when you get home.
10. Be assured that through all the stages, things will continue to improve. Even if your children don't say it now, they will eventually appreciate all you've done.

FAMILY AND FRIENDS

Children are not the only ones affected. Other family members and close friends are also shaken and shifted by a divorce. People in general tend to want to create order out of chaos, to see things more clearly or logically in terms of black and white, right and wrong, good and bad. This is often done in order to alleviate fears about change that feel threatening. Many people still married who see family and friends divorcing fear this could happen to them. They try to figure out what happened in a logical way in order to keep the issue in perspective, so they can eventually say, "I see why they divorced, but it won't happen to us." Also, they may align with the person to whom they feel the most loyalty, or if this loyalty has been equal prior to the divorce, it shifts with the "rightness" of one spouse's claim. From my observations, family and friends side with the one they perceive to be the victim or the one most innocent or "wronged" by their partner.

I've been guilty of this tendency to polarize, to judge and to take sides. When one of my best friends divorced, I blamed her husband, who was also my good friend. I "hated" his new wife for years, because by trying to make sense of what happened, I completely blamed her as the "homewrecker" or "the other woman." Years later, my good friend has realized her part in the ending of her marriage but says she got lots of attention and love from playing the victim. Now, she no longer needs to be in that role and can realistically see what she did to cause problems in her marriage. While going through my own divorce, I made amends to the woman I had so unfairly judged, explaining to her how I had responded out of fear and a lack of understanding.

After a divorce, people tend to line up next to one partner. Family, especially, will remain loyal to their relative, and sometimes shun the ex-son- or daughter-in-law. In the case of Abby, separated for one year after twenty-eight years of marriage, her in-laws are definitely ex-laws. She is separated from their son, Russell, and has filed for divorce. Abby once had a very close relationship with both of Russell's parents and his siblings, but now they won't answer her letters or phone calls. "It is," she says, "as if I am dead." Part of the problem, Abby adds, is that she is in love with another man, and they have moved in together. Her ex-in-laws, according to Russell, see her as an adulterous woman who betrayed the family, and they want no contact with her. Russell told them much of the gossip that fueled their feelings, and, according to Abby, he seemed to enjoy hurting her with the "excommunication." When this happens, it is especially hard on the children, and grandparents may later regret severing connections with their own grandchildren. Again, if adults can put their egos aside, everyone can benefit from this multigenerational exchange.

In other cases, there isn't so much animosity, but a gradual and more subtle letting go of the relationship. Turner still maintains a cordial relationship with his ex-in-laws, writing to them and sending gifts. They are not as close as before, but "the ice is thawing, and by the next time they visit this area, I think we'll be able to go out together." Unfortunately, one of Turner's siblings has "sided" with his ex-wife and has barely spoken to him in years. This is a case of one spouse playing the victim and being perceived by family and friends as the wronged one, even though no one outside the family knows what really happened in the marriage. Turner tends to be philosophical. "You find out in a crisis who your true friends and family members are. They know who you are inside and don't abandon you. Maybe the others weren't really friends at all."

Crystal wrote to her in-laws for many years, but recently the relationship has been strained because of money issues. Her ex-husband, their son, borrowed money while they were married and never paid it back to his parents, and now they are holding Crystal partly responsible for the debt. Her children had maintained their connection to these grandparents, but this crisis threatens to sever the ties for good.

In one large family of seven grown children, three of the siblings are divorced and the ex-spouses maintain a close relationship with the ex-in-laws. These parents have successfully separated themselves from their children's issues and can maintain a blameless and open relationship with all their daughters-and sons-in-law. This is a perfect example of keeping love and forgiveness at the center of our hearts, rather than blame, which is fueled by ego and fear. Rachel wrote a letter to all the family members on both sides, telling them about the divorce and her wishes. Writing a letter is a good idea, and Rachel's sample is included at the end of this chapter.

Jessica is just as close to her ex-husband's parents as when they were married, except that they don't see each other as often. When they do, it is a warm and loving reunion. His parents have even told her that they love her as much as their son, and consider her their real daughter. When I divorced, my mother still saw my ex-husband once a week, and they continued to have a friendship until her death. He came to her funeral and seemed to truly mourn her loss as his "other mother." I feel lucky to be close to my new mother-in-law, who somehow balances a warm relationship with me and a continued respectful friendship with her ex-daughter-in-law. She does this mainly for her grandchildren, who benefit from all the good will among us. In fact, it's often the children who help heal any rift in the family during a divorce. They so much want everyone to get along and be happy, that for their sakes, we can put aside our pride and hurt feelings, our petty beliefs, and be at least polite to one another.

If you've been ostracized by family members, don't lose hope that they can eventually see in you all the good qualities they once saw. These attributes are still present. It's just a judgmental perception that keeps others from still loving you; it's their inability to forgive that blocks this love, and this inability causes pain and sorrow. They may blame you for their pain, but truly, it is their hoarded love, and lack of forgiveness, that hurts their hearts.

MORE ABOUT FRIENDSHIPS

In terms of friendships changing during and after a divorce, expect that some people will remain your friends and some will not. From my perspective, this has to do with the depth and strength of the bond before the divorce, and to which spouse the friend is closest. I was in my forties when I divorced; by then I had outgrown the friends who did not truly care about me. At the time of my separation, I had a core of friends who loved me unconditionally. They supported me night and day, and I am deeply grateful for their love and loyalty. The only friends I "lost" were really acquaintances who were wives of my ex-husband's colleagues. Sometimes, I wonder how they are and miss the social interaction with them, but none of them was truly my close friend.

Only one person, my ex-husband's best friend, was also my friend. I didn't call him because I thought he had chosen sides and wouldn't want me to contact him. Finally, after nearly four years, I called him. To my surprise, he sounded genuinely happy to hear from me and said he had no ill feelings or judgment whatsoever. Our imagination can work overtime, and we erroneously think that someone dislikes us. Our fear keeps us from reconnecting with those we love and miss.

It may seem that those who leave a relationship are often judged more than those who are left, or perhaps they worry more about being judged. In speaking with "leavers," some say they are abandoned by friends because they left their spouses. Lars, who initiated a divorce from his wife, Estelle, after fourteen years of marriage, says, "No one really shunned me after the separation, even though we had the same circle of friends; but I felt a coolness that wasn't there before, which I guess was judgment for what I did. It lasted for a year or two, until they saw that Estelle and I were still friends and our children were fine. I know my second wife felt some of this coolness and thought some people blamed her, but she's a strong person with her own friends and didn't let it bother her."

Patrick, divorced after seven years of marriage, feels judged by old friends for being the one to initiate a separation. He says, "They only heard my wife's side of the story, because they'd call there and she'd tell them her feelings, even things that were untrue, just to get their sympathy. It's taken me a year to regain two of these friendships, but another two are dead; they wouldn't return my calls or cards and refused to see me. That hurt. But I've got enough old friends and new ones who are here for me." Jocelyn, who's been married three times, says her first two marriages were very amicable during each divorce, probably because there were children involved with the first and a good friendship in the second. These two ex-husbands still call her and send letters, and they have a deep bond that has never been severed. She is friends with their current partners, and the three ex-mates have maintained mutual friendships that span thirty years.

The secret to these unbroken connections, according to Jocelyn, is, "a love and respect for one another, for each person's spirit, that remains constant and lovable no matter how long it's been or how far away we are." She believes in the premise of this book, that marital bonds are never completely severed, especially if you have children. Exterior lives may change, but the essence of the relationship, the love you gave and the love you received, still exists.

If you have friends who seem to have rejected you during your divorce, give them time. If you have contacted your friends and they still want no connection, you have to let go, at least for now. Nothing you can do outwardly will change them. You can, however, ask the universe or Highest Consciousness for a change of heart, or just send your friends love and light, asking for their highest good and happiness. When you pass their houses, think of them, or if you see them, send love from your heart to theirs and wish them well. I do this every time I pass my former husband's house, mentally surrounding the home and people with light, sending them good wishes. This is different from my prior behavior, passing the house and feeling sad and angry, and projecting these feelings. When I did this, I closed my heart, and I felt the sadness and pain inside. Now, I no longer want to do this. You can't change your friends, but you can change yourself, keeping your heart open and continuing to love no matter what.

PETS

Kali, recently separated from her partner of thirteen years, misses raising goats, dogs, cats, and other pets together. She says her grief is as much for her animals as for the relationship. "Much of the positive memory is of a time together in the country living simply with our animals. When I left a few months ago, I took both dogs and left the cats. Since we don't have children, this felt like dividing up our kids, and I cried many nights for the loss of our family. The dogs have been grieving, too. I've been taking them everywhere with me and they have to sit in the car, but they just don't want to be left." And so, for many of us with animals, separation and divorce is also about leaving them or dividing them up. Most people try to do what is best for their pets. Some animals, such as cats, usually don't like to move; it means coming to a new territory and competing with animals already there. Also, the safety of the new location has to be taken into account.

In my case, I left a cat and dog. The dog really was my son's and was staying there with him, but the cat belonged to all of us. I wept when I left her and thought seriously about taking her with me, but I lived in a tiny house in a neighborhood full of cats; she could stay in the country where she had lived since kittenhood. Sadly, she was killed a month later. For at least a year, I felt guilty for leaving and not taking her with me. Noel, divorced for one year, knew he had to take his dog Drake with him. Not only was Drake his dog before the marriage, but Drake hardly left his side, riding with him in his truck and sleeping next to his bed. Leaving Drake would be "like leaving my kids, if I had any." If you have children who are leaving with you, think about taking the pets they are used to; otherwise, they'll miss them terribly. Pets can tell when we're feeling sad, and they try to help with wet noses and kisses.

Finally, after four years, I have two dogs and a cat, and my life seems normal again, the house messy, but cozy. The grief, though, can be deep when you leave your animals, or your spouse takes them. This is one of the effects of divorce, but when the time feels right, you can find another pet to love. Kali now has a kitten and four hens, in addition to her two dogs, and is looking for a country cottage for her "family."

HOMES AND LAND

Most books on dissolution focus on the relationships with children, family, and friends that are affected by a divorce. From my own experience, however, the loss of one's home, land, and animals can be almost as difficult. For the person leaving, especially, or for those who must sell their homes, the situation can be heart-wrenching. It was for me. I've never cared much for houses; my love has always been for the land itself, in this case, three acres with redwoods and a stream, old fruit trees, and sloping meadows. After living there for twenty years, I knew every rock and blade of grass, had worn paths to the stream and stained many shirts with wild blackberries. Since childhood, nature has been my refuge, even my church, and this land had special spiritual significance for me. And so, I've mourned nearly as much for the space I left, for it wasn't just space, but a temple where I worshipped. The house was also important, not for its antiques or polished wood floors, but because my daughter played with pots and pans in the kitchen; my son was born in an old four-poster bed, and outside his window, a lilac bush blooms over his buried placenta. It isn't just a house, but a holder of memories.

I've talked with many others who've left their homes or have sold them. One man, Joseph, married for twenty-seven years, says he put his soul into his ranch, planting every tree and building all the fences and barns with his children at his side. His wife, with a more powerful attorney, has kept the house, one he says she never really cared for, but she lives there now and Joseph has bought a condo. He says he hopes to be able to buy some land and build again in a few years. In the meantime, however, he feels bitter and heartbroken.

With the cost of housing soaring, divorcing couples are frequently forced to sell their homes and split the money. Colin, married to Kim for four years and divorced for eleven, has just sold their home and has given her half the money. Instead of selling immediately, he was able to give her spousal support and let the value of the house increase. Emotionally, it was the best decision, too, as Colin couldn't handle the disruption during the divorce. Ginny, whose husband moved out of state, leaving her with their heavily mortgaged house and three small children, had to sell the house by herself, give away their pets, and move into a tiny apartment, all while finishing her education and trying to work. This experience, as she explains, nearly killed her. If you need to sell your home, let yourself grieve. Know that the grief lessens but might come in waves for a few years, triggered by seeing the house, looking at old pictures, or hearing about it from someone.

I've done some things to ease the grieving process, such as visit the house less. This was difficult when my son lived there, but now he's moved to another city. However, my daughter lived on the property for four years, and I saw her often. On most days it didn't bother me to go there, but at times, I'd start to cry the second I pulled into the driveway. We solved the problem by meeting at restaurants in town. It's been a slow process of mourning and letting go. Two years ago at Thanksgiving, my former husband invited me to dinner. Initially, I accepted, but I felt so upset and nervous for days beforehand that finally I realized I couldn't go. To be served turkey on "my" china at the dining table where I had sat for so many years was too highly charged. It didn't seem to matter that I'm the one who left of my own free will. The grief was still as great. Finally, I felt healed enough by Thanksgiving last year to accept my ex-husband's invitation. I thoroughly enjoyed being there with our children and new mates.

Admittedly, it has helped to buy my own home in the mountains, to plant fruit trees and hear the rush of a stream from every window. I've also realized that my longing for the past is not a desire to return to my ex-husband, or even to that house, but to be able to recapture the moments when my children were little, our pets were alive, and we all loved each other under one roof. The nostalgia is for something that no longer exists.

For those of you still living in the house you shared with your spouse, it also can be tricky. Most of those interviewed say it helps to make changes, even completely remodeling the house as economics permit. One client, Millie, divorced after eight years of marriage, has lived alone in the original house for the past fifteen years. Her children are grown, and she's never remarried. Now her son lives in a granny unit, and she'll wait two more years until he finishes college to sell the house. She says, "The house is too big and has too many memories. Look how tall the kids' trees are! We planted them when they were little and now they're touching the phone lines. It'll be hard to sell, but I really want a quaint little cottage with a garden and less upkeep. I know the kids will have a fit, but I need to do it."

Sometimes it isn't healthy to stay in a house you've shared with an ex-mate. This is the case of Veronica, married for nineteen years, who became a recluse when her husband left, hiding inside the large country home and often refusing to leave for days. On the day her ex-husband remarried, she became hysterical, and her daughter stayed with her for fear she would harm herself. Just recently, after being divorced for over twenty years, she sold the house, and she is doing much better. If you are currently living in the house as a single person, or will be doing so, how does this prospect make you feel? Eventually make a decision based on these feelings. But give yourself time. The first few months can seem difficult wherever you are. As time passes, you'll feel better emotionally, and you may be able to stay in your home with some renovation. Just do whatever supports you.

THE DREAM OF MARRIAGE AND FAMILY

You may still have your children, other family, and friends in your life, and you may still live in the family home with your pets, but you probably have lost the dream of what you thought marriage would bring. It's this image, this vision, the ideal of what you hoped you would have, that is gone. In a sense, this is what we mourn after a divorce—the dream of what our wedding promised. For most individuals, a wedding symbolizes joy and faith that this union will last forever, that we're not alone in the universe but supported and nurtured by our mate. Finally, we can relax, let down our guard, and be loved unconditionally by another human being. Perhaps it is this faith that feels so betrayed when we divorce. The one person in the universe you know the best leaves you, or you leave the person you've vowed to cherish no matter what. For those of us who take our wedding vows seriously, separation and divorce shake us to the core. "But," you say, "it's not supposed to be this way. All the books I've read and movies I've watched, the songs I've heard, all say that love lasts forever."

And the love does last forever, but not the way we imagine. We have cords that join us to our former mates, cords of commitment, of love, and connection that can last forever, especially if we share children. This connection does not end. It just doesn't look the way we thought it would. Many of the people interviewed truly thought they would grow old with one another, sit in rocking chairs on the porch, and wait for the grandkids to call. I know I did. A few months before I left, my husband and I talked about being old friends and grandparents, getting ready for thirty more years together. That we would be separating in less than a year never occurred to either of us. Divorce was not a part of the dream we carried.

Perhaps the expectation is too great, this dream that our culture feeds us from childhood. Perhaps it is too much to expect that one person can fulfill all our hopes, that two people can keep changing and still want to be together. Many experts on relationships do believe that couples can maintain a long-term marriage, that this commitment can be nurtured and preserved. With all the books and therapists, church workshops, and professional seminars on marriage, we should be learning more about relationships, and I hope we are. Divorce means the end of a dream, heralding the beginning of a new vision, perhaps, but still the end of something we've loved, and this hurts.

THE EMOTION OF GRIEF

The major feeling that accompanies the loss of loved ones, after many of the initial emotions have been felt, is grief. It's when we "say good-bye to children, apple trees, and cats," to all that has been familiar, that we truly begin to mourn what we've lost. Recently, while interviewing a therapist on the phone, she began to cry while remembering what she had said to her children before her separation. This happened nearly nine years ago, and yet the grief bubbled to the surface. "I didn't expect to cry like this. But I just feel so sad. You'd think after all this time I'd be over it." Even though she left the marriage as I did, the grief can still feel overwhelming. This is because the choices we make can change our lives forever. Things will never be the same, and we probably can't go back. Of course, this is true of the past in general, and most of us have mourned for our childhoods, or an old friendship that is lost, for a part of our lives that can never be recaptured. The good news is that grief and mourning come just before final acceptance. If you can cry, or in other ways deeply feel your loss, then you can eventually accept what has happened. You can heal and move on.

During this period of mourning, give yourself complete permission to feel whatever you're feeling. Going through the pain actually heals the pain of losing a loved one. Fully allowing yourself to grieve, which means feeling "bad," may seem foreign to some of you. This is because we live in a culture that does everything to suggest we escape physical or emotional pain. Many of us also want instant recovery with our microwave popcorn. Recovering from a divorce is actually more like a progressive dinner, in which you travel to different homes for each course. It takes time, patience, and a willingness to travel into new terrain. The rewards—a seven-course dinner, or a healed heart—are worth it. Many therapists advise that the only way out is through, and this phrase fits the grieving process perfectly. You may want to avoid it, postpone it, or deny it, but the only way to truly feel better is to go ahead and grieve.

This doesn't mean you have to do it alone, nor do you need to sink into a deep depression that is dangerous before asking for help. On the contrary, this is the perfect time to write in your journal, talk to supportive friends, and see a therapist. It might be helpful for you to open your journal right now and write about your grief, beginning with the phrase, "I am grieving for . . ." or "I am mourning . . ." or "I miss . . ." or "I remember . . ." This last one is very effective and can elicit buried memories and sadness. Then write whatever comes, stopping to cry when you feel like it. This can be incredibly therapeutic. You'll feel lighter and calmer after writing and releasing your emotions.

Also, schedule time to grieve, literally setting aside time to mourn. One friend, who feels the tears stuck in her throat but cannot cry, is going to rent the saddest movie she has ever seen and sit and watch it alone with a box of Kleenex. She wisely knows she must cry in order to breathe easily again, to feel clear and calm. Then she plans to write in her journal all the feelings and thoughts that surface. She knows that at any time she can pick up the phone and call me or another friend, but for now, she wants to do it alone. And this won't be the last time. Grief seems to be like an onion; you peel one layer, and then another one appears, and another. One client who dislikes onions calls it a rose that keeps unfolding, petal by petal. I've noticed in this process, though, that it gets easier to do. At least I understand what is happening, and it isn't as frightening as it was in the beginning. Now a small voice says, "You'll feel better if you just go ahead and cry."

If you don't grieve now, you will eventually. Until then it can seep out in sarcasm and anger, or you may feel sad when something unrelated to the divorce occurs. Evan, divorced for five years, lives alone and rarely leaves his house except to go to work. He drinks heavily and tends to have several beers alone after work, then go to sleep and start it all over again. He's still in love with his ex-wife, and even though she is in another relationship, Evan fantasizes about being with Joanna.

After the deaths of his parents recently, he has begun to cry and mourn the end of his marriage. It took the loss of his parents to help him grieve the earlier "death." His depression is lifting now and he's becoming more social, all because he finally let himself cry and acknowledge his deep sadness for his wife and their marriage.

Cooper has been divorced for three years and still hasn't grieved. Instead he works nonstop and has already remarried. His friend Mark says of this, "It's obvious he doesn't want to deal with the fact that Shari left him. He felt terrible for about a month and decided that was enough. He's always at work or away on business. Maybe he thinks he can escape his feelings several thousand miles away."

The next chapter is about self-care, ways to take care of yourself while going through a separation and divorce. To say it will pass is the truth, but it seems a shallow and disrespectful comment at this time. I encourage you to experience it all, as difficult as this is, because then you can truly begin life anew. As a mentor of mine told me, "To heal from the pain, you must first experience it, walk through it, like fire."

OPTIONAL RITUALS FOR LOVED ONES

1. Before telling your children of the divorce, write in your journal, listing any feelings and thoughts, so your mind is clear and you are as calm as possible. Then, write down what to say to your children.

2. Review chapter 2, Clear Communication, in order to be the very best speaker and listener you can be when talking with children, other family, and friends.

3. During the meeting with your children, keep breathing deeply, allowing yourself to feel your feelings, and encouraging the children to feel their emotions, too. Silently ask for

help when you need it, then pause and begin again. You're not alone.

4. Give yourself a break after the meeting, if you need some time alone to rest and regain your "center."

5. Write a letter to your family or friends about the divorce. You can look at Rachel's letter, included at the end of this chapter.

6. Set aside time to grieve for the loss of your marriage, for your dreams of married life, for your home, and for your family and friends.

7. If you're leaving your home, take cuttings from the plants you love most, or take rocks or other parts of the land that you want to have with you. When I left, I took wild violets and replanted them here at my new home. They are flourishing.

8. If you're staying in the house, after your spouse moves out, do a cleansing of the space. Open all the windows and doors and air it out. You can wash windows, change the shades and drapes, and, when you can, change the furnishings to bring in your taste and energy. If nothing else, put some flowers in the rooms.

9. Each night before you go to bed, either think, say aloud, or write a list of all you have to be grateful for. When we take the time to feel grateful for what we do have, we don't think so much about what we don't have. Gratitude brings in more joy, abundance, and the positive energy to take action.

RACHEL'S LETTER TO MEMBERS
OF HER FAMILY

Dear Family Members,

I would like to tell you that Bill and I have recently separated. As you know, raising a family has been a lifelong goal for me; Bill knew this when we married, but since then he has rejected the idea of having children, ultimately rejecting me. A successful marriage requires that both partners take each other seriously, and ours has not been such a marriage. Bill's unwillingness to confront this, and other serious issues (with or without professional help), has virtually eliminated any possibility of reconciliation.

Our separation is amicable, and we know that we can count on your love and support as we each begin anew. We know also that you will understand our wishes not to discuss this, in any more detail, as no one stands to benefit.

As always,
Rachel

7

Self-Care

This morning
lupin flowers
inside me;
redwoods fill my core.
I begin to heal,
to be home
inside my skin.

Body Love

Six years ago, while giving a final exam in a writing course, I suddenly felt nauseated, dizzy, and disoriented. Unable to continue, I found someone to take my class and went home. I did not return to work for eight months. The stress of my divorce had finally caught up with me; the sleepless nights, the inability to eat consistently, and my worry and fear all contributed to adrenal exhaustion. I had literally burned myself out. Being ill for nearly a year gave me time to think about my life and the importance of good health. Writing this chapter on self-care is my way of saying, "Please pay attention to your physical and emotional needs during your divorce. Choose to be well."

For a moment, remember Ashley's Hierarchy of Love from the introduction. Envision yourself just below the Creator, or Highest Consciousness, endowed with a complex physical body and the gifts of intellect and spiritual awareness. These gifts should not be taken lightly, but should be used to help you fulfill your greatest potential. To do so, you must balance your love for yourself with your love of others; you must focus on your own wellness in order to function fully and be of service to those around you.

Unfortunately, the emotional upheaval of a divorce may cause you to forget to care for yourself and, instead, to neglect your own basic needs. Divorce can put tremendous stress on your physical and emotional health, stress that can be alleviated by refocusing on your own well-being. This chapter will present the specific symptoms of stress and help you become more relaxed physically and mentally, so that you can stay that way long after your divorce decree is final.

We know from current research that approximately fifty to eighty percent of diseases are the result of stress or psychosomatic causes. Chronic illnesses such as cancer, tuberculosis, congestive heart failure, rheumatoid arthritis, leukemia, and diabetes, among others, are seen more often in those experiencing some form of stress. The autoimmune diseases are potentially related to stress when the immune system is overactivated. Lupus is a good example of this, and possibly multiple sclerosis, cancer, heart disease, colitis, hypertension, and migraines. Stress, then, can be the catalyst for life-threatening illness, but it can be managed and prevented.

Before further examining the stress of divorce and positive ways to cope, let's evaluate your current health. How are you feeling physically and mentally? Open your journal and answer the following questions about your level of stress, or answer them here in the book. All you need to do is follow your intuition as you have in other chapters. Answer quickly whatever comes to you first, putting a check beneath "yes" or "no." Your initial thought will be the right answer.

STRESS AND PHYSICAL WELL-BEING

	Yes	*No*
1. I wake up feeling tired no matter how long I've slept.		
2. My body aches when I get out of bed.		
3. My shoulders and neck feel tight.		
4. I have frequent headaches.		
5. I have heartburn or acid indigestion.		
6. My eyes look and feel tired.		
7. I don't have much energy during the day.		
8. I am nervous, fidgety, and restless.		
9. I don't feel like eating.		
10. I'm eating more than I need.		
11. My back hurts.		
12. I'm accident prone and keep hurting myself.		
13. I'm drinking alcohol or taking drugs in order to cope.		
14. At night I can't sleep.		
15. I want to sleep all the time.		

STRESS AND MENTAL WELL-BEING

	Yes	*No*
1. When I awake, my mind feels fuzzy or unclear.		
2. I forget people's names and lose things.		
3. I am crying more than usual.		
4. Lately, my moods change rapidly.		
5. Often, I worry or feel anxious.		
6. I have trouble concentrating on a task.		

STRESS AND MENTAL WELL-BEING

	Yes	*No*
7. It seems like I imagine the worst.		
8. I feel apathetic; I just don't care.		
9. I am often pessimistic or cynical.		
10. I have outbursts of anger.		
11. Life seems overwhelming and unmanageable.		
12. I have racing thoughts or voices in my head.		
13. It is difficult to make a decision.		
14. At night, my thoughts keep me awake.		
15. I don't care if I live.		

After checking either "yes" or "no" for each question, add up the number of "yes" responses and put the total at the bottom. Notice if the answers reflect the degree of stress in your life or are caused by something else. If, for instance, your shoulders are tight because you just started lifting weights at the gym, or you don't pay attention and you've always forgotten people's names, then don't count those in your stress total. If you have 0 to 3 "yes" answers, then you are experiencing little to no stress in your life right now. All you need to do is adjust your life to change the stressor. For example, if you are staying up too late, or watching horror movies before bed, you might feel tired or nervous in the morning. Just notice what you're doing on a daily basis that may be causing you to feel tired or scattered or whatever you marked. Your score, however, is nothing to stress about! In fact, you're handling your divorce extremely well.

If you checked 4 to 8 "yesses," this indicates a moderate level of stress impacting the quality of your life. Last, those of you who checked "yes" 9 to 15 times are experiencing a high level of stress and your physical and mental health may be compromised. After noting your score, please open your journal and answer this question, writing as much as you wish in reaction: "What does my stress total tell me about my physical and mental health during my divorce?" It's helpful to refer to specific questions in order to fully understand your needs. If, for instance, you checked "yes" for number one in both categories, then this says something about your sleep problems, which could be affecting everything else. Write in your journal until it feels complete. Later, you'll write about how to alleviate these symptoms and feel better.

This chapter is mainly for those of you who have moderate to severe stress and want to learn how to feel more relaxed physically and mentally. Of course, even minor stress is disturbing, and its elimination is a benefit to everyone. In addition to reading this chapter, please make an appointment with your physician and therapist if you scored moderate to high on this test. It should be of concern to you if you cannot function on a daily basis, are too tired or too anxious to enjoy your life and your loved ones. If you marked number fifteen "yes," then you may be in danger of harming yourself. Please take action by seeing a professional and discussing your feelings and symptoms. This is how to prevent symptoms from becoming chronic diseases. It is also how to love yourself.

Perhaps the best time to take stock of yourself is when you are emotionally "all in pieces." This means you are hurting and, thus, vulnerable and less stubborn, even willing to make some changes in yourself and your life. Once, several years ago, when my marriage and family were in crisis, I lay on a massage table and said to the practitioner, "My heart feels like it's breaking." She said, "No, it's breaking *open*." These words have come to me many times since then. Deep pain allows us to open in ways we never have before. At first, we may be willing to try anything just so the pain will go away, but as we heal, we can see the benefits of such change, and even admit that it feels good. My own therapist has spoken to me about the value of "falling apart." This may sound puzzling, perhaps, but what she means is, once we let go, give up, get down on our knees, positive changes can occur. As my sponsor in a Twelve-Step program said to me when I humbly asked for help, "Now you're teachable. Let's get to work."

During the upheaval of divorce, you are infinitely teachable. You can learn ways to alleviate your stress, to relax and take care of yourself physically and mentally; you can feel a sense of well-being and renewed energy. The good news is you have the remarkable capacity to heal yourself. Your body mirrors your inner thoughts and beliefs, which during a divorce can be depressive or negative ones. With new thoughts, affirmations, and actions, you can heal your body and mind at the same time. As you divorce and begin to move on, you have the capacity to understand the past, live fully in the present, and plan for the future. You can completely recover from a divorce, and transform your life.

SYMPTOMS OF STRESS DURING DIVORCE

Some of us may walk around, even go to sleep, while deeply stressed. Our necks and shoulders feel tight, heads and stomachs hurt, and we even grind our teeth at night. Part of this issue is cultural; as Americans, we work too hard and don't take enough time to relax. After living in New Zealand and the United Kingdom, where people seem less nervous to me, I've decided that stress is especially endemic to the United States. Everything here seems accelerated, from freeways to fast-food restaurants. We have E-mail and fax systems and the fastest computers. Even though technology is supposed to make our lives easier, at times it just allows us to work harder, until we arrive home after dark, exhausted, fall into bed, and do it all again the next day.

Depending on our professions, we may experience daily stress and never take the time to recuperate. Stress in itself isn't the killer; it's how we respond to it and how we manage it. In this context, what are the symptoms of stress in those divorcing, and how can this tension be relieved when it's partly a cultural factor?

First, manifestations of stress will differ from person to person. Some of you feel your stress exhibited in bodily symptoms, such as muscle tension, headaches, stomachaches, nausea, more frequent flus and colds, exhaustion even after a full night's sleep, too much or too little sleep, overeating or undereating, heart palpitations, chest pains, dizziness, and other physical symptoms. These conditions should not be ignored, especially if they're constant or recurring. You also may feel stressed mentally; a lack of concentration, short-term memory loss, racing thoughts, constant worrying, and a tendency to procrastinate are some examples. Of course, these physical and mental manifestations often work together, one feeding the other. For instance, during her divorce after eighteen years of marriage, Jan couldn't sleep at night because of the constant thoughts and images in her mind. Already a very thin woman, she couldn't eat, lost weight, and needed to be hospitalized for dehydration and weakness. Phillip, divorced after three years of marriage, found that during the first few weeks he felt like a zombie, moving around in slow motion. He couldn't remember if he ate or not and found himself distracted at work, unable to remember what he was doing and even how to do it. Finally, he took a week off and went camping, saying, "I needed to get out of my apartment and away from her presence everywhere. Being outdoors helped me get back in my body. Just sleeping on the earth and walking around seemed to ground me. I could finally sleep, and felt like I could focus."

This would be a good time to take out your journal and write down any symptoms of stress you notice, and whether they are physical, mental, or both. Then reread what you've written. Below this list, write what has worked in the past to alleviate stress. Whether you realize it or not, you are one of your greatest resources. You already know what has worked for you and what could work again to reduce the stress in your life. However, some of these "unstressors" may actually be addictions or coping mechanisms that have detrimental effects.

ADDICTIVE BEHAVIOR

Ellis, divorced for sixteen years, describes what he did to avoid his feelings and to keep the stress under control. He exercised daily, sometimes running and swimming several miles in one day and then drinking beer until he passed out on the couch after dinner. Now Ellis realizes he overdid it, but at the time, he felt so overwhelmed by guilt that he over-exercised and drank to escape. The stress of a divorce often causes people to use their drug of choice more frequently, in order to "numb out." Even if you haven't had a drink or used drugs in years, the upheaval of divorce can cause you to begin again. It's important to recognize the warning signs and call a friend or a Twelve-Step sponsor, and get to a meeting. If you have a therapist, make a phone call and an appointment.

You may not be tempted to drink or use illegal drugs to ease your stress, but might be comfortable taking prescription medication. Doctors often prescribe antidepressants to people going through a divorce. A prescription may be necessary for the short term, but be careful of becoming dependent on drugs. They are legal, yet highly addictive, and have side-effects that can alter your behavior in unhealthy ways. Talk to your doctor or therapist about natural alternatives to antidepressants.

During a divorce, those who have a history of food abuse, such as compulsive overeaters, anorexics, or bulimics, may stop eating entirely or overeat in order to cope. Many of those interviewed say that at first they felt too upset to eat. Later in the divorcing process, compulsive overeaters tend to overeat or binge to "stuff down feelings." For those of you who are food addicts, stress reactivates compulsive eating; you may reach for junk food, like sugar, which just makes you more nervous, jolting the body into a false high and then draining its energy. At the first signs of food abuse, see a therapist and ask about support groups.

Addictive behavior will not help the situation or you; all it does is mask what is happening for a while, and then as it wears off, the feelings come back, usually stronger. Instead of using a substance outside yourself, use your mind and body to help alleviate your discomfort, and feel healthier in the process.

HEALTHY WAYS TO ALLEVIATE STRESS DURING A DIVORCE

The following techniques can help in any stressful situation, whenever you feel tense, nervous, and in need of relief. You can use your own list of tension reducers from the journal exercise, or choose some of the ideas below. Create whatever formula will help you manage your stress and feel more relaxed physically and mentally.

The Magic Potion Exercise

Imagine that you have a crystal bottle in front of you and an infinite variety of life choices, attitudes, and activities to add to make the perfect formula for optimum health. What would the ingredients be? Close your eyes and think back to a time in your life when you felt and looked fantastic, when you were at your strongest physically and emotionally. When was this? Do you remember the year or your age? Where do you see yourself? What are you doing in the scene? Are you alone or with other people? What do you look like? Try to remember what you felt like. What words come to mind to describe your appearance and feelings? Why do you think you were so healthy then and felt so good about yourself? If you can't visualize this time and place, then recall or look at a photograph that shows you in your healthiest light. Take out your journal and answer the above questions. Finally, what were you *doing* to be so healthy?

I knew which pictures to pull out of the drawer, how long ago it was, and where they were taken. I looked and felt so energetic, my face radiant, my body muscular and strong from cycling. What I did to look and feel so healthy had many components. For one thing, I exercised regularly, at least four times a week, cycling, walking, and doing aerobics. Also, I lived alone and ate simply and sensibly, mostly vegetables, rice, some fish, and some bread. In one picture I'm standing with a good friend just before leaving on a trip to the California desert. I look excited and full of expectation, youthful and glowing. I had just begun to publish my poetry, and the writing was going fabulously. I was meditating daily, studying earth-based religions, and joining other women in a support group each week. I felt ecstatic, hardly able to sleep for all my joy and energy. My therapist even told me I was having a "spiritual awakening."

After writing down your own observations from memory or photos, reread what you wrote. What of the things you listed could be a part of your life now, or perhaps is currently in your life? I would like to cycle more than I do now. I know I feel better when I eat less, and when I wait until I'm hungry to eat. I need more time in nature, more time praying and meditating, and connecting with other women. If I wrote my daily formula for a magic health potion, based on past success and current lifestyle, it would look like this:

Prayer and Meditation + Quality Time with Loved Ones + Time in Nature + Relaxation + Writing + Exercise + Nutritious Foods = A Healthy Self

What would be your formula? Write it now in your journal, noticing that it is unique and may not resemble mine at all. That's because it's what works best for you. You may need to do the following exercise before a formula comes to you. Then write it down.

If you couldn't remember a time when you were optimally healthy, or find a picture, then you can envision yourself physically and emotionally at your ideal. Just close your eyes, and let yourself relax. See yourself as you would like to be, physically and mentally. Where are you? What are you doing? Are you alone or with others? See yourself doing something you enjoy, really experiencing this fully. Feel the sense of happiness and well-being. Also, notice the positive, joyful thoughts you're having, some of them about you and your life, because it is just what you want. Notice overall what it is you're doing in this ideal life that supports you so much: the physical, emotional, and perhaps spiritual components. When the visualization feels complete (you have seen and experienced all there is), open your eyes, pick up your journal, and write down what you "saw." Then write the formula that would create optimum health for you.

Next, we'll look at the specifics of stress reduction and good health, based on my experience and the advice of others. From this, you can choose to keep what you have done before, what you now see as your ideal, and/or the ways to feel good that follow. Remember, choose what you'll enjoy and what will really work for you in your lifestyle.

WAYS TO FEEL GOOD PHYSICALLY DURING A DIVORCE

The following ideas will help you feel more relaxed and healthier, too. For them to work, you have to work them, and this means having enough esteem or self-love to say "I deserve to feel better. I deserve to exercise, rest, eat well, set aside time to be social or alone, to meditate, be in nature, or wherever I wish." The key to feeling better is deciding that you are a priority; you are number one on your list of people to help and to love.

Take Your Body Out to Play

As John Steinbeck says in his last book, *America and Americans,* we are a people of extremes, who work to excess and then play with as much ferocity. We are full of energy in this young nation, energy that we don't always know how to use or contain. Exercise to many Americans means beating the body into shape. It's as if we fear that if we relax for one moment, we will age, become fat, and our chance to be loved will vanish. As Americans, we need a new approach to exercise, in order to enjoy moving our bodies rather than punishing them. What if, instead of viewing exercise as a fight with our flesh, we saw it as fun, as taking our bodies out to play. I experienced this concept in Judy Wardell-Halliday's workshop, called Thin Within. Judy encouraged us to find something physical that we enjoyed. We began to look forward to getting up in the morning and walking, cycling, going to a dance class, jumping rope, or whatever "tickled our fancy." The object, then, is not to believe we're fat and whipping our bodies into submission, but that we're lovable and deserving of a healthy body, mind, and spirit. What a concept.

For some of us, childhood was the last time we moved our bodies for fun. We can remember playing tag, dodgeball, kickball, softball, running races, and climbing a lot of trees. Most of the time, exercise was pure play. What immediately comes to mind that you've enjoyed? Have you done this recently? Open your journal and list some options for exercise, things that seem fun to you and match your fitness level. With desire and effort, you can usually work up to the skill level needed for each sport. You can narrow the field by seeing which ones fit your lifestyle and location and can be done fairly easily and with a minimum of expense. Of course, before you begin exercising, check with your doctor if you haven't exercised for a while, or if you have a health condition that needs monitoring. Then, when you have the go-ahead from your physician, start having fun.

While exercising, the brain releases endorphins, the "feel-good" substance, that can give you an enhanced sense of well-being. This contributes to your positive attitude and makes your head feel clearer and your mind sharper, especially if you are deeply breathing fresh air or combining breathing exercises in your regimen. Yoga, if it appeals to you, is an excellent way to stretch, tone, breathe, and relax, benefiting the body and mind all at once. Overall, moving your body can change your mental state from a negative to a positive one. Part of this is because you're taking action, and this raises your self-esteem.

No matter what physical condition you're in during your divorce, with help from your doctor, a physical trainer, or other professionals, you can find a way to move your body and lift your spirits. If you already know what you love to do and are healthy enough to do it, then start today to reduce your stress, and have a good time in the process.

Rest and Nourish Yourself

I remember at the beginning of my divorce staying in bed more, where it felt safe, cozy, and womb-like. This is normal, and if you feel like sleeping, then your body may need this replenishing. Balance physical activity with naps and a good night's sleep. If you are suffering from insomnia, you have several choices. Doctors and therapists recommend everything from warm baths, warm milk, and herbal teas to minerals such as calcium and magnesium, relaxation tapes, daily physical exercise, and getting up in the night, instead of fighting the insomnia.

To help you sleep, many herbalists and acupuncturists recommend drinking chamomile, valerian root, passion flower, wood betony, or Saint John's wort tea a half hour before bed. Physical exercise will help you sleep better if it's done at least three or four hours before bedtime. Otherwise, it could be too stimulating. You should also go to bed before ten, and make sure your room is a place of rest and not piled with work, or filled with other distractions. I sleep better when I take a hot shower or bath before bed, take calcium and magnesium, and drink tea made by mixing herbs, skullcap, and Saint John's wort. Of course, check with your primary health-care professional for advice before beginning a new regimen.

For those of you who are sleeping too much, fresh air and exercise could boost your energy level. If you feel unusually tired, please see your doctor for a complete checkup. Be aware that some of your need for rest could be a desire to escape your situation, one more coping mechanism like work and food. Crawling into bed is less harmful than drugs and alcohol, but any escape done to excess can interfere with your life. If you find yourself wanting to sleep all the time, it can also be a sign of depression and should be reported to your doctor or therapist. On the other hand, listen to your body very carefully at this time. If it's tired, rest it; if it's hungry, feed it; if it needs to exercise, move it; if it wants nurturing, support it. Your body needs your tenderness and patience.

It's best to eat moderately during stress, not tax your body with too much food and drink. The lighter you feel physically, the better you can cope emotionally. Avoid foods that over-stimulate the nervous system, such as caffeine in coffee, colas, and chocolate; and avoid decongestants and illegal drugs such as cocaine and amphetamines, which make the nervous system and body feel more hyperactive. Also to avoid are sugar, pro-cessed foods made with unbleached flour, and all fried foods such as chips and other snacks, which make the body work harder to process them. In general, balance your protein intake with complex carbohydrates, vegetables, and fruits, listening to your body to determine what it needs.

Many health-care professionals recommend a mostly vege-tarian diet, because it is really a lower stress diet, with mostly grains, vegetables, some fruit, soy protein, and fish occasionally. Many nutritionists and health-oriented authors recommend the taking of herbs, vitamins, and minerals to supplement your food intake, especially when you are experiencing increased stress. They suggest taking a good multivitamin and mineral supplement that is rich in the B vitamins and the antioxidants. Also, I recommend drinking a smoothie every day with fruit juice, nutritional yeast, flaxseed oil, and bee pollen. Nutri-tional yeast is at the top of my list, high in vitamin B, protein, and chromium. Personally, I have lessened my level of stress by taking vitamins and minerals, such as calcium, magnesium and zinc, a multiple vitamin, and extra B, C, and E. Again, check with your doctor before beginning any new health plan.

The taking of supplements is a controversial topic at this time in America. Some doctors say taking vitamins and miner-als is dangerous; others say they don't help at all and are a waste of money; and still others see the benefits in some vita-mins and minerals. My primary-care physician recently recommended that I take vitamin E for three months. Herbs such as Saint John's wort are being mass-produced by several companies because of the reported success in treating depression. Many local therapists and doctors are recommending this herb but say it takes a month to begin to work. If you are run down, or in other ways not at your best in terms of energy and attitude, then perhaps see a nutritionist, an herbalist, or an acupuncturist in addition to your regular physician. Gather their opinions about diet and supplements, and ask your own body what it needs; your intuition can be trusted to give you the best advice.

During the stress of a divorce, it's more difficult to listen to our bodies because of all the distractions. If, however, you can sit down quietly for a minute or two, close your eyes, and focus on your body, especially the stomach region, you can tell if you're hungry, thirsty, or nutritionally deficient. If your stomach feels empty and you're hungry, you'll know specifically what you want to eat and can prepare it lovingly and enjoy it thoroughly. What a gift to nurture yourself, to say "I deserve this time and my body deserves nourishment so it can remain healthy." You will find that with practice, you'll be able to tell if you're hungry, and then give your body exactly what it wants. If you realize you're not hungry, then wait a while. Your body will send you signals from the abdomen when it's truly hungry, and you will know exactly what you want to eat. This is how to eat consciously, and is another way to listen lovingly to your inner needs.

Perhaps you aren't hungry for food, but for other kinds of nurturing. You might need a hug, or to talk to someone about your feelings. You might need to lie down and rest. Rather than eating to satisfy an emotional longing, you can figure out what it is you truly want.

Decide Whether or Not to Be Sexual

During and after your divorce, you may or may not be feeling sexual, and unless you are already in another relationship, you may not be sexually active during this time. Some people choose to remain celibate during and after their divorce. Carla, divorced after eight years of marriage, has not been sexual for the past two years. As she explains, "The last thing I need is a man in my life right now. Things are complicated enough trying to raise two kids under five, and go to work, without another child to raise." Carla is in counseling to deal with her anger toward men, stemming from child sexual abuse and her husband's recent desertion. Until she's clear about some of these issues, she doesn't want a relationship, adding that any man she meets would just feel the brunt of her anger. Katie was married for ten years, and now has been divorced for seven. During this time, she has not been involved with any- one. She says she's needed all her energy to raise her youngest child, who was only six months old when she divorced. It's taken her five years just to be able to talk calmly to her ex- husband and to overcome a severe depression.

Gerry, divorced for six months, says he doesn't feel sexual for the first time in his life. "I meet women all the time, and I'm just not attracted." He isn't worried, and thinks his drive will return when he's ready. It's normal for some people to feel less sexual after a separation and divorce as part of the detachment from the relationship; it's a form of shutting down that may occur emotionally and physically. Also, if your previous relationship ended unpleasantly, you might feel repulsed by the thought of sex. It could take you time to exor- cise the negativity surrounding sexuality, realizing it was one experience with one partner and not the whole of who you are as a sexual being.

Choose Sensuality

Some people feel sensual during their separation and divorce, and find alternative ways to express this feeling. One thing I did was dance: at home, in aerobics class, and at the local pub on Friday nights. I danced to the point of exhaustion, but I didn't feel depleted. Instead, I felt exhilarated and energized afterward. Besides dancing, you can dress in clothing that feels and looks sensual; you can go swimming naked by the full moon, or walk barefoot on newly cut grass. The world offers an infinite number of pleasures besides lovemaking. If you're feeling sensual but don't want to be sexual right now, then ask yourself what would feel good to you. If you miss being touched, then you could get a weekly massage, or sit in a Jacuzzi and feel the bubbles pop against your skin.

Unspoiled nature seems to work the most magic, if you can find a spot that calls to you. Even if you live in a city, you can walk in a park or along the street at twilight, watching the sun fade and the lights come on. Some of us need to be near water—the ocean, a river, or a stream. Just hearing the rhythm of waves or a trickle over round rocks seems to lull and satisfy. It helps if you go alone and find a place to sit where you can absorb the natural sounds and feel nature's rhythms. If you wish, take your journal and write from your senses, what you see, hear, and feel.

This is another way to express your sensuality: writing your most intimate thoughts. You could buy a beautiful journal or decorate one to reflect your taste, using a pen in a seductive or exotic color. Then write away! If you aren't a writer, try listening to music that speaks to you on many levels. Music can elevate your mood, be soothing or exciting, make you smile or cry.

All these suggestions are about giving yourself sensual pleasure that will help you feel good. You can pamper yourself daily, or perhaps on weekends by waking early and walking outside, or sleeping late under down comforters; giving yourself a delicious breakfast; being spontaneous and letting the day unfold, doing whatever is most luxurious to you; ending with a warm bath by candlelight or a massage and soak in a Jacuzzi. If, for whatever reason, none of this seems possible to you, then think again. You may need to wait until the kids are in bed to have that bath, or trade with a friend to get childcare in order to go out, but please do something just for you, preferably every day. You're not just a spouse, a parent, a worker, and friend, but an incredible, sensual being of flesh and spirit who deserves the very best.

Become Sexual Again

If what you want is more overt sexual experience, you also have choices. Personally, I don't recommend going on a binge of one-night stands, not only because of AIDS and other sexually transmitted diseases, but because it may be another addiction and not good for your self-esteem. When I met Theresa, a colleague in the seventies, she was married to a coach and had one child. When they separated, she was devastated and began going to parties and bars. She slept with the first man she met, who turned out to be a nice person. He told her to get some help, stop drinking, and take some time before being with anyone again. Luckily, she took his advice, quit the bar scene, and went to therapy. Melissa is a regular every Friday night at a local bar. She's separated from her husband, but they're still living in the same house and raising three kids. To escape her reality, she begins drinking at 5:00 P.M. and meets men until the band stops playing. Melissa thinks she wants to find a man to take her away from her life, but the more she drinks and escapes with strangers, the more confused she becomes. She tells me, "I can't stand what's happening, and I just want to block it out for a while." Sadly, Melissa is addicted to alcohol and casual sex as a way to cope with her reality, and every Saturday, she feels worse. The last time I saw her she looked terrible, perhaps hitting bottom, and she says she wants help. I hope so.

Perhaps you met someone before your divorce, during either the marriage or the separation, and you have a sexual relationship with him or her. This happens frequently for many reasons—love, attraction, loneliness, fear, and everything in between. This new partner could have been the catalyst to get you out of the marriage, as was the case of Ellis, quoted earlier. His marriage had not been good for several years, even though he had two small children and was in couples' therapy. He met his lover, Maeve, on a business trip and carried on an affair with her for over a year before his wife became suspicious. Ellis says, "Looking back, I wish I could have done it differently, but I couldn't or didn't. Maeve and I were both in bad marriages and gravitated toward one another. Our affair meant the dissolving of two marriages and two families, but we wanted to be happy, too. We've been married now for eight years and it definitely was the right choice."

Natalie, married for eleven years, also met someone else in order to leave her marriage, but she has not ended up with that person. She had a brief, very sexual affair with him, but it only lasted a few months. She is now divorced from her husband and living with someone else. Natalie comments, "I needed something my husband couldn't give me, some excitement and romance. My marriage was boring, and I had been unhappy for a couple years before meeting Mark. The sex was fantastic and really showed me that my husband and I shouldn't be together." Perhaps some of you have found a new partner whom you love passionately, like Arden, quoted in chapter 3. She left a long-term marriage, has filed for divorce, and, at fifty years old, is now living with Martin, her love. What Arden wanted was sexual and spiritual passion, which she feels she has found in her union with Martin.

You may not have had a new partner in the marriage or during your separation, but would like one now. If you have children, keep in mind the suggested timeline of six months to a year before becoming involved with someone new. This is for your children's welfare but also for your own. Ultimately, in order to recover from a divorce and prepare emotionally for a new relationship, you need to figure out what went wrong, honestly see your part, and grieve your loss. This takes time, perspective, and maturity. If you want to avoid the mistakes of your first marriage, then take some time to get to know yourself and what you want and need in a relationship before actually starting a new one. This is the ideal.

Some of us, myself included, began relationships during our separations. What I had to do, however, was create a three-month no-contact period with my new partner while I sorted out who I was and regained my sanity. Before making this decision, I had no time to grieve for my first marriage or to understand my part in causing the separation, since I was already preoccupied with a new person. I advise taking as much time alone as possible for self-reflection, therapy, and healing. You have the rest of your life to begin another relationship. Let it be one begun by two whole, healed people. Of course, some of you have begun sexual relationships during or immediately after your separation or divorce, and things are going fine. Just make sure that you process your feelings together or with a therapist in order to clear the slate of your first marriage. Second marriages, remember, have a high rate of failure, often because at least one spouse has not gotten over or grieved for the first partner or marriage. Just be conscious of the long-range effects of your choices.

Pleasure Yourself

Another choice exists other than those above, a way to be sexual, and yet not involved too soon in a new relationship. This is the technique of self-pleasuring, or masturbation. This method is shrouded in controversy and myth, taboos and stereotypes, but for those of you who feel sexual but not ready for a partner, self-pleasure may be the answer. Several excellent books exist on this topic, my favorites being those by Lonnie Barbach. See the titles in the Bibliography at the back of this book. If you eventually want a satisfying sexual partnership, masturbation is a good beginning, because it allows each person to intimately discover what is pleasurable. Then this can be shown or communicated to one's partner.

WAYS TO FEEL GOOD MENTALLY DURING A DIVORCE

To alleviate mental stress, you can explore different ways of coping. It's essential to look at your environment to see what is upsetting you, from toxic world news to toxic friends. To feel less stressed, notice everything in your life that is not supporting you. Then, change this attitude or situation in order to create a more peaceful life.

Change Your Attitude

In therapy sessions, my clients learn how to "reframe" or change how they perceive something, usually from a limiting or negative perspective to something more expansive and positive. This reframing is actually a way to improve your mental health or sense of well-being. You can feel good just by thinking that you do. Begin in the present moment to change your negative thoughts, words, and actions to positive ones. It all begins in your mind. If, for instance, you wake up and say, "I don't want to get up; it's going to be a lousy day; nothing will go right; I hate my life," then guess what? You will unconsciously create all this misery for yourself just by taking action based on your thoughts. Sometimes we think our minds and thoughts control us, that we have no choice, but this is simply not true. Your mind is a computer and you are the programmer; you can change the program anytime you want, to one that will work the best for you.

This reprogramming of your computer-mind can work for any situation. If you feel judgmental toward people in your life, you can change your thoughts each time negative ones surface. One technique is to reshape the thought immediately from "I hate him/her," to "I release him/her to their highest good;" or "I let go of him/her." Another method of letting go of judgment is to mentally put people in a pink balloon or bubble of any size or shape, and then release them to their own destiny. This technique has helped me let go of my obsession with someone. If you have depressing thoughts about your current situation, your divorce, home, job, finances, or something else, you can use the same reframing method to change these negative thoughts to positive ones. For example, instead of saying to yourself, "I will never be loved again," "If I lose my house, I'll die," "I hate my job," or "Money always slips through my fingers," change the words to "I love and am lovable," "My needs are always provided," "I'm grateful for this job while my life's work unfolds," and "Money is energy, and I always have enough." Of course, change the wording to your own, making sure you say your name after the "I" and keeping it in the present tense, as if it's already happening. And it is.

Another aspect of attitude that may need changing has to do with letting go of your control. So much energy is wasted and so much stress is built up by dwelling on things you can do nothing about. This would be a good time to take out your journal and make a list of everything in your life you *can* control, that you can literally do something about. Then make a list of the things you *can't* control, that you are unable to change, fix, manipulate, or make the way you want them to be. You may notice that you can change things about yourself and your life situation, but it's not possible to change things about other people, such as their attitudes, their choices, and their lifestyle. If, for instance, you want to spend more time with your friends, this is somewhat in your control, as long as they have the time and want to spend it with you. All you can do is *say* what you want, and then it's up to them.

You can control what you think about and say to your ex-spouse, and whether you send him or her a birthday card. You can't, however, control what he thinks about you, or says to you, or whether he thanks you for the card. His or her thoughts, words, and actions are out of your control, even though you might obsess about how to change them to suit your needs. Put a mark by the things you want to control, or try to, but really can't. These are the ones that need to be released. As you read them over, you might feel emotional as you realize your powerlessness and need to let go, not only of the thoughts, but of the person. In chapter 1 I suggested making a "let-go box," and this would be a good time to use it. Write down on a slip of paper what it is you want to control, but now know you can't. Put the paper in the box as a symbol of turning it over to the universe or Highest Consciousness. Let it go and know that it will be taken care of, but not by you.

What you *can* do is take care of yourself and make changes within you. It may help you to say the Serenity Prayer, or any prayer of choice, and to turn to family, friends, and professionals for support. Stress is unavoidable, but you can learn to distinguish between the situations you can change and the ones you can't. Accepting what you can't control is a key to feeling less stress and more serenity.

Ask for What You Want, and Set Your Boundaries

Another way to reduce the stress in your life during a divorce is to know what you want, ask for it, and be prepared to stand your ground. Perhaps you have over-helpful siblings, parents, or friends who want to come over, fix your meals, and fix your life in the process. If this is too much for you, too invasive of your space, then thank them and tell them you don't need assistance right now, and when you do, you'll call them. If your ex-partner is calling or coming over and this isn't what you want, then you need to tell him or her you do not want contact, at least right now—or ever, if this is your feeling. When I remark how close Jade and her former husband are, she replies, "Yes, too close. I wish he'd get married again. I'm afraid he'll get sick and I'll have to take care of him for years." Yet Jade is reluctant to tell her ex-husband that she doesn't want him calling so much or dropping in unannounced.

In the case of an aggressive ex-spouse, who refuses to hear the word "no," an attorney will request a restraining order. You do have rights. You can decide exactly what it is you want and get it. Barb, who was married one year to Marvin, has finally told him to stop writing to her. She was deeply in love with him, and he betrayed her, and now she cannot reopen the wound each time she gets a letter. Just seeing his handwriting made her cry. For her own health and recovery, she is now refusing all his correspondence.

Carl had trouble asking for help from family and friends. He took care of his needs by joining a men's group, and it seemed easier to connect with strangers once a week. Now, three years after his divorce, he can talk about his feelings with two or three friends.

What is it you want? Open your journal and answer this question as quickly as possible, from your heart: "In what parts of my life do I need to take care of myself by setting boundaries and saying 'no'?" You might begin with the words "I need . . ." and when you are stuck, write "I need . . ." again. Then shift to "I don't need . . ." and see what surfaces. Write until nothing else comes up. Reread what you've written and decide when you will take action on each. It helps to put dates, the more specific the better. If, as an example, you don't want your ex-partner to drop by your house without calling, then set a time to say this. The sooner the better. Setting boundaries and becoming more assertive is a way to take care of yourself emotionally during your divorce, to let others know that your needs are important.

Create a Support Network

Many of us going through the stress of divorce, which seems like a death, have a tendency to isolate. Jerry has been separated for the past year and rarely leaves her house. She explains, "I just don't want to see anyone. I have to go to work, but when I get home I just stay here. I like it this way." Of course, some desire to be alone is perfectly normal. You have a lot to think about, and solitude is often the best backdrop. If, for several weeks, however, you find yourself in pajamas all day, with the drapes closed, watching TV, refusing to take calls or answer the door, then this is isolation, and it can be indicative of depression. If you want to feel better, you must reach out, return those calls, and ask for help and company.

I can remember not wanting to tell anyone we were divorcing. I avoided seeing old friends or calling them. But my closest friends were tenacious. If I didn't answer the phone, they came over, or saw me at work. They were worried, and they eventually made me see that their concern was deep love for me and my welfare. At first, begin slowly to socialize. Perhaps go out for lunch, for a walk, or to a movie. Those close to you will probably invite you over for dinner, and this might be a good first event. Overall, friends and family—people who love you unconditionally and support your choices—will be important to you during a divorce.

If friends or family are not supportive, and become negative and critical, avoid them. If they call and ask why you seem unavailable, tell the truth. Say, "I care about you, and at the same time, I really need people in my life right now who support me in a positive way. When you can do that, we'll be in contact."

In addition to people you know intimately, you can ask for support from professionals. At times this may be the best choice because you can feel free to "unload" on a therapist rather than burden a friend or family member. If you have a religious affiliation, make an appointment with your priest, minister, or rabbi. Part of their training is in pastoral counseling, and they usually have patient, sympathetic ears. Also, you can see your family doctor, if this is a person with whom you have a trusting relationship, and if he or she has time to listen. In order to function well on a daily basis, you may need to ask for help, at least for a while. This isn't a sign of weakness, but a sign of great personal strength and high esteem. Also, if you don't nurture and "fill" yourself, how can you give to others such as children, family, friends, and coworkers? It's really a very practical choice.

Meditate

More than twenty years ago, my friend Othmar Tobisch took me to an introductory meeting of Transcendental Meditation. I was pregnant, and I wanted to be calmer and create a better experience for my child. On the way there, I told him I was too busy to meditate. His answer has come to me many times: "If you don't have time to meditate, then there's something wrong with your life." Othmar went on to say that my life was out of balance and too consumed with work, and he was right. I went on to do the TM training and to graduate with my own mantra or sound to use during meditation. Not only was my pregnancy and birth relaxed, but I have a spiritual relationship with my daughter that began in the womb. Over the years, my family could tell whether or not I had meditated before breakfast by the way I moved in the kitchen and talked to them. If I had meditated, I seemed more fluid and the work looked effortless; nothing seemed to bother me and I was cheerful and philosophical. However, if I hadn't meditated, I was rushed and even panicky, darting around and snapping at everyone.

What has worked for me for twenty-five years is waking half an hour early, propping pillows behind me, and meditating for twenty minutes or so. Then, before dinner each night, I take another twenty minutes to sit in a chair or on the bed and meditate again. Othmar Tobisch says you needn't be so narrow about meditating for exactly twenty minutes. "I will use whatever time I have, whether it is five minutes or thirty. The important thing is that I meditate."

Transcendental Meditation has relaxed not only my mind, but my body as well, slowing my breath and my pulse. During my pregnancy my blood pressure was low, and it has remained low ever since. I found I could slow my pulse by slowing my breathing during meditation. Doctors always ask me about my diet and exercise, never realizing it is meditation that is responsible for my slow pulse and low blood pressure. My mother-in-law decided to try Transcendental Meditation when her doctor put her on medication for hypertension. Her blood pressure was abnormally high, and she felt dizzy and disoriented. After a few months, the doctor told her how pleased he was that the pills had lowered her blood pressure to normal. She just smiled and thanked him, but didn't add that she had thrown the prescription away.

In doing TM, each person sits in a comfortable position and begins to relax, breathing normally and settling into the chair. It's not a good idea to lie down because most people will go to sleep, but TM practitioners say if you do go to sleep, it will be deeper and more restful than regular naps. After sitting for a few moments and feeling more and more relaxed, you begin to say the mantra, which is a sound from Sanskrit chosen by TM teachers just for you. They ask that you not share this sound with others because it is yours and it may not work for them, or may cause a negative experience. Then you begin saying the mantra in your mind, silently, over and over, letting thoughts come and go, and then saying the mantra again. At first I set an alarm clock so I knew when twenty minutes was up, but in a short time my internal clock let me know the time. Toward the end of the meditation, you stop saying the mantra and feel the peace and centeredness inside you. When you're ready, after one or two minutes, you open your eyes. Some people take longer to "resurface" than others, and may feel dizzy or disoriented if they come back too soon. Each individual must time his or her re-entry based on his or her own needs.

At the beginning you may need to meditate in the same place every day where it is quiet and comfortable. I found that after a while I could meditate anywhere, in train stations, airports, hotels, even with hundreds of people talking. I could shut them all out and exist for twenty minutes in a relaxed, calm sphere of peace. The teachers of TM say that meditating will help you feel less aggressive and less angry, whether on the highway surrounded by honking cars, or in a grocery store line when someone cuts in front of you. Meditation will help you let things go, things that aren't that important and that you can't control anyway. Over time you'll notice you aren't as easily irritated, and you can interact more neutrally with people who used to irritate you.

During your divorce, meditating would be an excellent way to alleviate stress, to put everything in perspective, including your interactions with your ex-spouse and children. Meditation supports the premise of this book, that you can create a conscious and peaceful divorce by being a conscious and peaceful person. I recommend TM because of its success in my life, but many other excellent meditation techniques exist. One of my teachers suggested trying a "universal mantra," the Sanskrit sound "naddam," which she says anyone can use successfully. You might want to try it while following the meditation technique suggested above. It's good to find a reputable teacher of the method you prefer who can personally train you, answer all your questions, and model the method for you. Learning to meditate is a lifelong gift of self-love.

TRY HYPNOTHERAPY OR SELF-HYPNOSIS

You may have some concerns or skepticism about hypnosis. This probably comes from your image of stage hypnotists who make people laugh uncontrollably or bark like dogs. It seems as if the person being hypnotized has no control but is being made to do things against his or her will. This can seem very scary to people, and it has given hypnotherapy a bad name. I studied hypnotherapy because it is the most effective counseling technique I have ever experienced, and it's incredibly helpful as a method of relaxation. My own hypnotherapist helped me to resolve lifelong issues by teaching me to relax and access my unconscious mind, the deeper part of me that knows what is true. Frankly, traditional cognitive therapy has never worked very well for me. Just sitting in an office, chatting with a therapist, was supportive, yet the deeper issues remained unresolved. During graduate school I read the works of Brian Weiss, who began as a traditional psychotherapist. When treating one client who was not improving, he began using hypnotherapy and past-life regression, which ultimately cured her of all presenting problems.

In a hypnotherapy session, the client sits or lies down. The practitioner calmly begins to relax the client by doing a "body tour," mentioning each body part and suggesting that it fully relax. Some experts in stress management call this "progressive relaxation." Beginning at one end, such as the feet or head, and moving up or down the body, the therapist's voice soothingly relaxes the client. This can be the entire session if your goal is to feel more relaxed. A hypnotherapist can make a tape of the session that you can play at home to help you relax or go to sleep. In fact, you can go to a session for problems such as insomnia, tension headaches, smoking, overeating, and other stress-related issues. You can ask that a tape be made for each session or each problem, and then play it at home, where you can do self-hypnosis. Recently, I did a two-hour session with a doctor, whose original symptoms of tightness in his chest and an inability to breathe deeply were gone at the end of the visit and have not recurred. I highly recommend seeing a certified hypnotherapist who has been suggested by someone you trust, or whom you've found by calling a local training facility or the state or local association. Also, you might want to try the following exercise, which can help you relax mentally and physically. If you have any health concerns, check with your physician first before attempting this technique, but it's designed to be beneficial for anyone in normal health.

Progressive Relaxation Exercise

Find a comfortable position, either sitting or lying down, whichever position would help you completely relax. Make sure your feet aren't dangling and your head is fully supported. Adjust the light in the room so it is soothing; make sure you are alone and will not be disturbed. Unplug the phones and turn down the answering machine. You want the space to be as quiet as possible. If people are going to be arriving or walking by the room, put up a sign that says DO NOT DISTURB or something similar. Close your eyes and begin to sink into the furniture, letting it support you completely.

Read this ahead of time, or better yet, make a tape of this passage to listen to as you relax. Be sure to read slowly with lots of pauses. You can do this exercise whenever you feel tense and need to relax.

Just begin to settle in, to feel yourself sink down into the comfort of the space, adjusting your body until everything is just right. Feel supported, every part of your body from your head to your feet. Let yourself be held completely. There's nothing you have to do. Let yourself go. Notice if you hear anything in the room or outside; let the sounds come and go and let them help you relax even more. You might notice that your body feels lighter, each part sinking down, down into the chair/couch/bed. Feel your breath come in and out, in and out. Your chest and stomach rising and falling so softly, so quietly. Just continue to feel and listen to your breath, to follow it inside you, deeper and deeper as you breathe. Focus for a moment on your feet just lying there being held and nurtured, and let them relax even more. Let all the tension leave your feet and ankles, as the toes, the insteps, the heels let themselves unwind. This calm sensation travels up to your calves and knees, undoing knots, unlocking joints, warming muscles. Now this feeling of relaxation reaches your thighs, allowing them to release and soften; it spreads to your hips, letting the bones, the muscles open, the buttocks and hips dropping even farther into the chair/couch/bed. Your arms are limp at your sides, gently resting, the elbows unwound, the wrists flexed, the hands open, fingers apart. Feel the arms loosen and sink even farther, even deeper. As you continue to breathe slowly, let your stomach and chest open and fill with the breath of life.

As you inhale, take in all positive energy; let it flow inside every pore, every vein, every bone. Then exhale all negativity, all tension, all darkness. Let your body be filled with light and life. Feel this nourishment in your shoulders as they lower and let go of what they are carrying. Feel the release. Feel the lightness and warmth in your shoulders and neck. Swallow slowly and notice that your throat is smooth and moist, that it is open and loose. Feel yourself let go of the weight of your head as it settles even more deeply, is held completely for you.

Notice any tension in your face and let it go, lips parted, cheeks soft, eyes heavy-lidded and resting, brow and scalp smooth, mind drifting and at peace. See white light surround you from head to feet, encircling you in sweetness and joy. Take in this feeling of complete peace. Your body thanks you for letting it rest and relax. For letting it heal.

Sit or lie there for one or two minutes, just taking in the healing energy of the light. As you begin to come back, moving up from 1 to 5, notice your breathing, in and out, in and out. As you focus on your breath, you are, 1, becoming even more grounded and aware of your chest and stomach rising, 2, of your torso, arms, hips, and legs resting there, 3, beginning to move your arms and legs slightly, stretching and becoming even more aware of the support under you, 4, moving your head and feeling the solid furniture beneath it. Becoming even more aware of where you are sitting or lying, knowing that you are in a room, that you feel very refreshed. When you are ready, 5, taking one or two deep breaths and opening your eyes. Slowly adjusting to the light and the room, looking around and moving your body even more. Now, all the way back. Noticing that you feel calm and ready for the rest of your day.

Let Nature Help You

The final suggestion to help you relax mentally, to slow yourself down, is to spend time in nature. This was suggested previously for physical relaxation, but nature also benefits the mind. Being in a pristine, beautiful setting can clear your head, make you forget civilization and all the problems there. You can sit by a river or climb to the top of a mountain and get a whole new perspective on your life. However, if you love cities and luxury, being in an elegant suite with room service and a pool to swim in may be relaxing for you. To be honest, though, the constant input from people, TV, and phones is not as mentally relaxing as being in the middle of the wilderness without these distractions. If you have never been a "nature person," find a group excursion that allows for plenty of solitude, too. Then you would have the support of guides, but also the chance to be alone to cleanse your mind.

During a divorce, time in nature also helps you to release negative emotions. If you're frustrated, resentful, or angry, walking briskly, swimming, kayaking, or any energetic activity can help you release your pent-up emotions and feel healthier in the process. If you are sad or depressed, it might feel like an effort to move, but a walk outdoors in a beautiful place can do wonders for your attitude. During my divorce, I remember going on gentle bike rides to my favorite cliff by the ocean; on the way, I could feel the wind on my face, breathe deeply, and let go of my pain. Once at the cliff, I would settle against its bank, write in my journal, look out at the sea, and cry. By the end of the ride, I felt a million times better.

While you're in the wilderness, ideally overnight, follow your natural rhythms. Sleep when you feel like it, or take a walk, sketch, write, eat when you're hungry, or do nothing. If you retreat for a few days, you'll return home with a clearer perspective. Turner, quoted several times, went to a meditation center during his separation from his wife. He slept in a tent, helped cook and clean up, and ate with others. During the day, he walked by a stream and into thick forests, meditated, wrote, slept, and just did whatever he felt like. By the time he returned home after just three days, he felt like a new person, clear about his life and what he needed to do.

Nature is a healing force in itself. During your separation and divorce, you'll have times when you feel overwhelmed, indecisive, or in some way impaired by stress. One month after I left my husband, I needed to get away alone. Camping in the California desert for ten days, I slept out in the open, fasted, walked, and prayed. It was the most transformative time of my life, and I came home clearer about my choices and my identity. With nothing but the expanse of blue sky, wind in the Joshua trees, and my own thoughts, I realized the truth about so many things. It also was a time for my mind to rest, to stop thinking so much and be as still as the desert at nightfall. You don't have to go camping for ten days in the desert. It can be a simple retreat into the natural world for an hour or a weekend, enough time to help you return refreshed and able to face your life.

Feeling High Esteem During Self-Care

During your divorce, high self-esteem, or self-love, helps you take care of yourself, in order to be physically and mentally healthy and relaxed. Those of you with low esteem may not feel that you deserve such loving treatment from yourselves or others. Most of us developed our self-esteem from the comments and treatment in our families and neighborhoods, in schools, and later in our places of work. Parents, siblings, peers, teachers, coworkers, and bosses treated us in ways we internalized as "the truth." These beliefs then became the basis of our self-esteem. If your brother always said you were annoying, slow, smelly, stupid, fat, or useless, you could have ignored these insults or believed them. Sometimes parents label one child "the smart one," another "the athlete," and one "the artist," or other names that can become limiting and self-fulfilling prophecies. Over a lifetime, after millions of positive and negative comments, we have a lot of voices in our heads telling us who we are.

If you believe you're too busy to relax, exercise, take time alone, meditate, go out with friends, or other pleasurable things, then take another look at your priorities. You are putting other people and work above you in the Hierarchy of Love mentioned in chapter 1, and putting yourself at risk for stress-related maladies. Consider that the development and nurturing of self-esteem is essential to your continued well-being. It is what causes you to take action, to set in motion an exercise or eating plan, a visit to a therapist, or a vacation to a mineral spa. High self-esteem is self-love, a positive regard for ourselves, based on the belief that we are deserving of kindness and care. For a moment, think of someone you love very much. Envision what you would do to ensure this person's safety and happiness. Would you do this much for yourself?

This would be a good time to open your journal and answer the question, "How much do I like myself?" Begin with positive qualities, using the phrase, "I like . . . ," and list everything you can think of, even little things about your appearance or personality, treatment of others, skills, and abilities. See how many "likes" you can find. Fill the page. Now answer, "What do I dislike about myself?" beginning with "I dislike . . ." Write until you feel finished and reread both lists. Which one is longer? Mark or star the statements that you most believe, positive and negative. The favorable ones can become affirmations, making firm what you already believe about yourself and want to continue to believe. The more critical statements can be turned into affirmations by changing the language. For instance, if you say that you hate your height, there's nothing much you can do about this but accept your size. You can say, "I accept the size I am." If you wrote, "I dislike my tendency to gossip," you can say the affirmation, "I only say neutral or positive things about others," and then take action by refraining from gossip.

Do you have any beliefs keeping you from taking care of yourself during your divorce? If so, what are they? Write them in your journal. An example is, "I am an irresponsible person in wanting a divorce, so I don't deserve financial security." One of my limiting beliefs until recently has been, "I am undeserving of an ideal life because I was a bad wife who deserted her husband." Listen to the language: "undeserving," "bad," and "deserted," which reflect exaggerated feelings of guilt. I have now changed this "message tape" in my head to, "I deserve an ideal life, including good health, happy relationships, a beautiful home, and a fulfilling profession. My life is getting better and better." You can change your negative beliefs by replacing them with positive ones that support your desire for high esteem. Just alter the wording of statements in your journal, say them over to yourself until they feel anchored, and begin to live your life based on these affirming truths.

SUGGESTED AFFIRMATIONS

The following affirmations or positive statements will "make firm" the many suggestions offered in this chapter. Feel free to change any of the wording to fit your specific needs. To review, it's best to write affirmations in the present tense, using "I," your name, and language that is positive. For ultimate success, write affirmations, say them aloud, and post them on your mirror, wall, car visor, or anywhere you will see them daily. You may want to write your desires or affirmations, carry this list with you each day, look at it when you get up, when you have a break, and before bed. I've also known clients who wrote affirmations and goals, put them in a desk drawer, and still had them come true. This is because they deeply believed in these values, turned them over to the universe, and then relaxed.

1. I, (your name), love myself unconditionally.
2. I, _____, want only what is best for me.
3. I, _____, do whatever is necessary to be healthy physically and mentally.
4. I, _____, exercise by taking my body out to play.
5. I, _____, love how my body feels when exercising.
6. I, _____, follow my intuition about what exercise to do and how often, treating my body with great kindness.

7. I, _____, rest or sleep when I am tired.

8. I, _____, go to sleep easily and sleep through the night.

9. I, _____, have a loose and relaxed body.

10. I, _____, listen to my body and eat what it wants when I am hungry. I stop eating when my stomach feels comfortable.

11. I, _____, am a sensual and sexual being and take care of my needs.

12. I, _____, have a positive attitude.

13. I, _____, know and express what I want, set my boundaries, and say "no" when necessary.

14. I, _____, can ask for help and companionship from friends and family.

15. I, _____, see a therapist or other professional when necessary.

16. I, _____, know how to relax by sitting quietly, closing my eyes, and meditating for whatever time I have.

17. I, _____, can relax my body and mind using visualization or self-hypnosis.

18. I, _____, feel confident.

19. I, _____, know how to take care of my needs and feel great.

20. I, _____, trust that my life is getting better and better.

Some of you may not feel as positive as these affirmations indicate. This is perfectly normal. The point is to act as if these affirmations are already true by writing, saying, and reading them daily. You will begin to notice you feel more confident and able to take action, and as you do this, your life will begin to change for the better. The key steps are having positive thoughts and goals and taking action based on these desires, creating increased confidence and a richer life.

DEVELOP A PLAN AND TAKE ACTION

After reading the above information about self-care, you may need some time to decide which suggestions to implement. When you're ready, create a realistic plan based on your lifestyle and preferences. This may look a bit like the formula presented earlier in the chapter, but now you have additional choices to select. Look at each category of maintaining good physical and mental health and find the specific tools that appeal to you. Then take action. Perhaps open your journal and write an answer to the question, "What am I *willing* to do to reduce stress and be physically and mentally healthy?" Then write what it is you will do and when. The word "willing" is the key because you will only do what you truly want to. Don't write that you will jog five days a week if you're doing this from a place of "should" or from what others might be doing. You won't really follow through for very long, if at all. Remember to choose from intuition, from that deep place inside you that knows what you want and what you will actually *do*.

Next, write down your plan of action and when you will do it. An example might be:

> *I'll go rollerblading after work Tuesdays or Thursdays, beginning next week on the sixth, and I'll take a yoga class at noon on Sundays, beginning on the eleventh of the month. I promise to set aside thirty minutes a day to relax, and to schedule a massage at least once a month.*

Ask yourself if this schedule is realistic or if it's too ambitious. If an idea is less appealing, then omit it. It's better to start simply and slowly than to set up a plan that will fail.

Next, write a plan for the rest of the categories, such as rest, food, sexuality, attitude, meditation, being in nature, and so on. The more realistic and specific you are, the more you'll follow through. Keep your self-esteem high by being accountable. Say what you'll do and do what you say.

RITUALS FOR SELF-CARE

All the exercises and suggestions in this chapter are rituals of self-healing. By doing the journal exercises and treating yourself to abundant self-care, you are ritualizing the experience and accepting that you deserve everything pleasurable and nurturing. The underlying message in any ritual, especially in this chapter, is "Love yourself to wholeness." You can and you will.

8

Healing the Heart

Yesterday
I fell through
the looking glass
not to cheshire cats
and tea parties
but to fear
that made me
curl knees to chest
beneath dark quilts.

Today
I'm more in love
than fear
can see the croquet match
red and white rose trees
and the caterpillar asking
'Who are you?'
I'm not quite sure
but the queen doesn't scare me
and I'm on my way home.

Following Alice

The final stage in a conscious divorce is the process of healing yourself and moving confidently into your future. This recovery is accomplished by trusting the passage of time, focusing on your own life, releasing any remaining resentments, and forgiving yourself and your spouse. There's no magic wand for such transformation. Forgiveness is work, and only you can do it. The reward, however, is the miracle of a healed and peaceful heart. For those of you who have been hurt by divorce—and on some level, this is all of us—the process of recovery begins when you are tired of suffering. It begins when you decide to give up the game of blame and punishment, when you choose to let go of fear, anger, and martyrdom, and decide to forgive the past. Only then can you completely move on.

Once you decide you want to heal, you can begin the process of forgiveness, which clears the slate of old hurts and allows each person to write a new script. This clearing through forgiveness is not a whitewash, not a message that the other person was justified in hurting you. But the act of forgiveness allows you to move out of the past, out of the place of guilt and blame, into a new realm in the present moment. Here, you can relax, breathe more deeply, and feel the relief of a clear conscience. It is not your job to play God, to police the universe, doling out justice to others. If your partner has hurt you, then know that his own higher consciousness will eventually show him his part in creating this divorce. Your job is to focus on your own words and actions, on your own path and its messages. Forgiveness, then, is the answer to your unspoken prayer, "Please, help me heal. Help me feel joy again. Help me feel peace." Many individuals have spoken about the transformative power of forgiveness, from the prophets of God to modern psychologists and physicians. Their specific words may differ, but the message is the same: faith, love, and forgiveness can heal you.

Before reading further, it might be beneficial to sit quietly for a few minutes and discover where you are in the healing process. First, read the questions below so you can recall them in silence. Then get comfortable and close your eyes. When you are ready, ask yourself: "How am I doing emotionally?" "How healed am I right now?" "What would help me recover from this divorce?" Just let feelings and thoughts come and go as you seek answers from Inner Wisdom. When nothing more is coming to you, take another minute to sit quietly; ask Highest Consciousness for assistance in this healing process. Use whatever words feel right to you, but ask for help and know that you will be answered. You might want to write in your journal, recording the thoughts and feelings that come to you during this exercise. Then over the next few weeks, pay attention to any "messages" you receive from other people, from nature, from your own mind, regarding your transformation. You may find it helpful to record these ideas in your journal and then take appropriate action.

HEALING THROUGH THE PASSAGE OF TIME

For many of us at the beginning of a divorce, the pain seems huge and infinite. It may feel as if we're dying, and, in a sense, we are; but we're also shedding our old selves and being born anew. The birth process is often messy and painful, overwhelming, and disorienting. It takes time to adjust to the intense changes that bombard us. However, if you can be "held" during this birthing, by realizing your feelings and processing them in your journal, or with someone you trust, you will begin to feel better. For those of you who are the initiators of the separation or divorce, it may seem that you will recover more quickly than your spouse. This is true for some of those interviewed. Individuals who have been leaving their relationship emotionally for many years have done much of their grieving ahead of time, and seem to be able to leave with less remorse.

Jade, mentioned previously, who was married for forty-six years, left her relationship very consciously and with a minimum of guilt. The longer she was married, the less attached to her husband she felt. In a sense, she had done her mourning years before, and had already left emotionally. Then for several weeks before she moved out, she took sheets, towels, clothing, and small pieces of furniture over to a friend's house. Finally, she left in the middle of the night, leaving her husband a note. She knew he would object and try to stop her, so she took care of herself by leaving the way she did. Now, a year later, she lives in a mobile home and loves her life, taking trips abroad with friends and family. She and her ex-husband have remained friends who help each other with projects and go to dinner at their daughters' homes. Jade is so happy living alone that she says, "I'm not going to get married again because my closet is full." Her life and heart are full as well.

As the leaver, it has taken me longer than it has Jade to heal from my decision to divorce. I think this is because I hadn't disengaged as much emotionally, and still had work to do on myself and the marriage. It is now, in the sixth year after my divorce, that I feel the most resolved, the most at peace. You will take whatever time you need. Ignore those people who say, "Are you still crying about him? Don't you think you should move on?" Just tell them you're still grieving, and you are taking the necessary time. Better yet, surround yourself with people who lovingly support you to recover at your own pace. If you're being honest with yourself, you can tell if you are staying stuck in the past, and are afraid to move on. Some of my clients have admitted that they enjoy the attention they get from being the "victim"; they experience special treatment by being in grief and pain, and it somehow feels safer than moving into the unknown future. A therapist can help you discover if you're truly grieving the loss of your marriage, or are prolonging the process out of fear or a desire for attention.

For those of you whose spouses initiated the divorce, the time it takes to recover also varies. Madeline, whose husband left the relationship, says, "I can't believe it's taken me fifteen years to feel resolved about my divorce. I spent so long blaming him and feeling victimized. Even after years of therapy I still have chosen men who don't treat me well. Now I'm not with anyone and it's all becoming clear." Not everyone needs fifteen years to heal from a divorce, but it does take everyone different amounts of time. Crystal says she still has days of deep sadness, and isn't completely recovered from her divorce, after eight years. "I just really miss my family, our family, and wish we were all still together. I guess I'm still holding on to that dream."

It's often difficult to determine how much time it will take to heal. Rhonda, married nearly thirty years, says of her recovery, "I thought it would only take eight months or so, but it's taken me three years to recover from the years of abuse. I was so emotionally beaten up and verbally abused that I was a wreck by the time he left. I was so codependent that even though the marriage was rotten, I stayed. On the day he left, I ran out onto the driveway crying and crying when suddenly I said to myself, 'Oh thank God.'" Rhonda, who is still in therapy, loves supporting herself financially and living alone, and says, "I feel reborn." Ronnie, whose wife left him after thirty-two years of marriage, admits he was mad and hurt at first, but he says he knew it was coming, and now after two years, he's philosophical. "She took a trip and when she left I kind of had a feeling things would be different when she got back. I didn't know she'd leave, but I wasn't really so surprised. It'd be harder if we never saw each other, but I see her several times a week and things haven't changed that much except we live in separate places. We get along better that way."

It's important to take enough time to deal with your feelings about your former marriage and spouse before beginning a new relationship. Many clinicians believe that second marriages are less successful if there hasn't been adequate closure in the first relationship. Spouses may still love each other or are still resolving issues with the former partner. I vividly remember a conversation with an old friend that happened more than twenty years ago, just before her second marriage. Tess told me she still loved Russ, her first husband, and that she would always love him. I suggested that she not remarry right away, but she felt it was too late to change the wedding plans. Peter, who has been married and divorced three times, waited just until each divorce was final to marry again. He never went to therapy, never looked at his part in the dissolution of each marriage, and practiced "serial monogamy" unsuccessfully. Now, he's decided not to marry again, but he has had a girlfriend since the third divorce was final. His second wife says, "I hope he never marries again. There should be a law against it."

We have a tendency in this highly addictive culture to use relationships to avoid our inner turmoil and confusion. Rather than trying to sort out our own feelings and change our behavior, we immerse ourselves in another relationship to mask what is going on within us. It's best to get to know yourself and the part you played in the ending of your marriage before finding someone new. Otherwise, you risk making the same mistakes all over again. I remarried two years after my divorce was final. Although I saw a therapist regularly and dealt with my feelings about the divorce, I still grieved the loss of my former marriage and family for at least another year, while married to someone new. This was difficult for me and for my second husband.

Hannah says she cried for over a year, grieving for her former husband and their marriage, while living with someone new. She says, "My first year with my new husband, Marshall, I was in so much pain that I cried every night in his arms, and he understood." Not every spouse would be so patient and understanding. If possible, do your closure and grieving before you remarry. Work on your own issues, and then be ready to contribute fully to a healthy, new relationship. Be good to yourself and take the time you need.

You'll know when you've recovered from your divorce by

how you feel and how you respond to your ex-partner, to family and friends' comments, and to being in an environment that could trigger memories and feelings. You have reached the final stage of acceptance when you feel neutral at these times, when you are happy for your ex-spouse's success, or even uninterested in his or her life. You can go on vacation to a place you once visited with your former partner and enjoy yourself thoroughly. These are all signs that the passage of time has helped to heal you. You are ready to move on.

HEALING THROUGH FOCUSING ON YOUR OWN LIFE

It's tempting for some of us at the beginning of a divorce to focus on our ex-spouse's life, driving by the house, asking friends about him or her, calling about anything just to talk, still wanting to connect in some way. This is normal in the disengaging process, but if overdone, it can prolong the pain and postpone the healing. You can probably remember the ending of a love relationship when you were much younger, how hard it was to see the person, how you "nearly died" when you did. I remember a breakup in college in which I avoided going to the library because I knew where my former boyfriend sat, and feared he would be sitting with "her." And yet, inevitably, I walked by the tables, through the aisles of books, to spy on him, which deepened my grief and pain. What self-torture; and yet for some strange reason, it helped me recover. Perhaps it was the immersion in reality, facing the fact that he was now with someone else. After my divorce, I had to drive by my old house daily on the way to work, and weekly I stopped to see my children, who still lived there. But, in all honesty, I wanted to go there to catch a glimpse of my ex-husband and to see the house and animals, even though I felt sad each time. Perhaps because I'd left my marriage so quickly, I needed to desensitize myself, to wean myself of home and loved ones by actually visiting the house and grieving my loss.

If this process sounds familiar, you may be disengaging from your partner and the marriage. This is normal as long as it doesn't become obsessive and keep you from focusing on your own life. At times, staying stuck in the past is comforting because it is less scary than moving into the future. But it can actually keep us from facing ourselves, learning from our mistakes, and beginning a new life. Are you living in the past with your ex-spouse? This could be anything from keeping romantic mementos, to wanting to see him or her, to playing old songs, to frequently calling your ex-partner. You may wish to write this question in your journal: "Am I living in the past or preoccupied with my ex-partner?" If the answer is "yes," write how you are doing this. Next, answer this question: "What could I do to change my behavior?" For instance, if you call your ex-wife or husband every day at dinnertime, what could you do at that time instead? If you find yourself looking through old photos quite often, and it feels compulsive, then you could box them up and put them in the garage for a while. Perhaps make an agreement with yourself, a friend, or a therapist to talk only to your former partner about essential issues such as the children and their needs. With honest reflection and feedback from others, you can decide if your behavior is obsessive, or normal. Is it keeping you immobile, or helping you to move on? Listen to your intuition, which always tells you the truth.

One of the most successful ways to heal from a divorce is to focus on your own life. For the first time in years—or, for some of you, the first time ever—you can explore your own spirituality, relationships, work, and leisure. Being on your own means you can delve into areas of yourself that have long been dormant. Aaron, divorced for eighteen months after two years of marriage, remarks, "Being with another person can be pretty stifling; you find yourself so consumed with them that you forget what you love to do. I've now gone back to surfing every day and I feel great physically and inside my head." June, separated from her partner for six months, comments, "I'm reading again for pleasure and walking every day on the beach. I don't miss the fighting and the tension. It feels good to be free to do what I love." Rhonda says about her new life, "I'm free of fear for the first time in decades. My health problems have disappeared, and I feel so much energy. It's not too late for me to live." So, ideally, what would you like to be doing with your life?

Open your journal and write first about the spiritual life or practice you would like, beginning with the words, "I'd like to . . ." A spiritual life can be anything that uplifts you, that enriches and makes you more of your ideal self. It could involve meditating and praying, walking in nature, going to a place of worship, sitting quietly, listening to music, listening to inspirational tapes, reading spiritual books, going to sermons or talks, or anything at all that supports the unfolding of your highest self. Remember, you can do anything. Let go of limiting thoughts, and just for now release the restrictions around time and money. Trust your intuition, your inner voice, which knows who you truly are and what you want. Just write a wish list having to do with your spiritual life. Perhaps you would like to go to Nepal and study with a Tibetan shaman, as one of my friends is doing. Maybe you could use a retreat or time at a spa.

For some of you it might be comforting to return to the church of your childhood, or to explore what feels most spiritual to you. Leah, divorced for five years, who was raised in the Jewish faith, has begun to go to temple as she did as a child, finding in it the wholesome focus on family that she needs after her divorce. Monte, divorced for two and a half years, has decided to take this time after his divorce to explore various spiritual paths. He is attending his first Buddhist retreat, a Haiku weekend. Miranda, divorced for less than a year, is a member of the Baha'i faith; she is attending a weekend at a Baha'i school to discuss marriage from a spiritual perspective. Kevin, separated for three months, doesn't believe in traditional religion but finds peace and inspiration while fly fishing.

When your journal list of spiritual choices feels complete, reread what you've written. What are the things that stand out, that say, "Do me soon"? Put stars by these and then a date indicating when you will actually do them. For example, if you wrote, "Learn to do T'ai Chi" and it is starred, then think about when you are free and find a teacher. Next, put the date, place, and time next to your "wish" in order to make a commitment and follow through. You may have listed others, such as, "Go to church," "Walk alone in nature," "Plant a healing garden," or "Say prayers each morning." It doesn't matter what you wrote. What matters is that it fulfills your quest as a spiritual seeker. It helps you feel more whole, more comforted, and uplifted.

Next, focus on the area of relationships. Answer the question in your journal, "What relationships do I want in my life and with whom?" You can begin with a phrase like, "I'd like these relationships. . . ." Perhaps you want old friendships with certain people, and you can say this. You might want to develop a new friendship with one or two people, and you can write down their names. If you want a romantic connection, write the person's name, if you know, and what you want in this relationship. If you don't have a specific person in mind, but know what qualities you would like, list them now. Shelley, divorced for eighteen years and unmarried, wants another marital relationship and has begun to ask for what she wants. She explains, "Every night before I go to sleep I read over my list of qualities I want in a man. It's a really specific list, down to the color of his hair and eyes, his habits and dress. I read it all out loud and then offer it as a prayer to the Cosmos. Then I go to sleep knowing my request is out there working its magic." You may want to be less specific, because a request as specific as Shelley's may actually limit your potential. Instead, just ask for love to come into your life, ask that you have the opportunity to give and receive love. Then you can turn over this request to God or Highest Consciousness, and let the future unfold. If you don't want a romantic partner, but want to strengthen your relationship with your parents, siblings, or children, you can say this.

Next, answer the question, "Who are the people I may not want in my life?" Then list the individuals who, perhaps, are no longer supportive, or who have become distant. You may have been drifting from them for some time, or perhaps the divorce has caused estrangement. Next to each name, write whether you wish to work on this relationship or let it go. Decide how you will improve some of these friendships, and how you will end others, and when. Write down these decisions next to the names. Ralph Waldo Emerson says in his essay "Self-Reliance" that we should sever any relationships that no longer serve us, that we have outgrown, that do not help us grow into better people. This severance may seem harsh, but remember to follow your intuition and do what your inner wisdom suggests for your ultimate good.

What do *you* need to do to make your relationships healthy ones? Notice what it is about yourself you need to work on or change. How and when will you do this? In your journal, write what you need to do to improve your friendships, and put the date you will begin. This is a specific way to be accountable to yourself, so the changes you need to make will really happen. The more you look at your behavior with others, the better chance you will have of creating thriving, lasting relationships.

During and following a divorce, it is helpful to have a profession to focus on instead of the drama—preferably work that you love, that makes you feel competent and successful. If you love your job, read no further. If it is your life's work, if it fulfills you and allows you to serve others, then just close your eyes and whisper, "Thank you." If, however, you are not currently doing what you love, waking effortlessly in the morning excited to go to work, then read on. Having work that writer Kahlil Gibran calls ". . . love made visible" is an incredible gift that we can give to ourselves. Again, it takes turning inward and asking what is the "right work" for you. Open your journal and answer the question, "What do I want to do for my life's work?" Do not let thoughts of money, responsibility, or any "shoulds" cloud your thinking at this time. Just write down what you would love to do. The key word here is *love*. Maybe it has been so long since you "checked in," that you aren't sure anymore what you want. You may need to go back to a more carefree time and reminisce about what you enjoyed doing. If something general comes to mind, such as "be a healer," that's fine, even preferable. You can say to your higher self, to the universe, or Highest Consciousness, "I want to be a healer. I don't know what this will look like. Please guide me to find and do my life's work." Then, you aren't limiting yourself, but being open to all possibility.

Randi, who just turned thirty-five, took a summer job at eighteen in a local candy factory. At the time, she planned to go to college to become a girls' basketball coach. The money was so good that she bought a car, worked overtime, and got raises and bonuses. Then she got married, bought a house, had a mortgage, and you can guess the rest. Randi's still there, at a better job and salary, but she never fulfilled her dream. Henry David Thoreau, in his book *Walden,* says to do whatever you dream of doing right now. Don't defer it. Don't wait until retirement to do what you love. Do it now.

So, what are your dreams and how can you manifest them? Several months ago, I signed up for a five-day workshop in the

California desert. When I told the facilitator I was a therapist and teacher, but really wanted to stay home, be a writer, and lead workshops, she remarked, "Oh, you're beginning your true life's work. Great!" You, too, can begin your life's work today. The first step is to decide what this is. Now, look at what you've listed in your journal as potential professions and star the one or two that say "star me," that reflect your heart's desire. Take one at a time and begin writing the steps necessary to achieve this goal. If, for instance, you put down "being a graphic designer," then list what you need to do for this profession. You may need to do research, but for now just list what you know. Then write down how long it would take to prepare, how long you would need to continue at your current job, how much retraining would cost, and so on. It would help to make an appointment with a career counselor to find out the current requirements, job market, salary, and other information. If the path seems too difficult and too long, then just take it one step at a time. Enroll in a graphic-design class just for fun and inspiration. Do it for a hobby now and then see how you feel.

What is the point of making a lot of money if you hate what you do? Why not find something that gives you joy, a sense of fulfillment and esteem, and brings in a decent salary? Especially while divorcing, it's important to have something that sustains you, makes you feel good about yourself, even brings recognition. The only danger in loving your work is loving it to the exclusion of health and relationships, loving it so much that you are consumed and "hiding out" emotionally. A friend, Karinn, newly separated after three years of marriage, says, "Thank God for my work. I commute for forty minutes with the stereo blasting and then sit at my computer all day and never think of him." Karinn has had enough therapy to know when she is using her work as an addictive substance. Most of the time, she "feels her feelings" and processes these emotions, writing in her journal and talking to friends and a counselor. She admits to "escaping" into her work in the evenings to avoid depression, but she believes that for now, it's "better than being on Prozac." Madeline laughs when she talks of attending Workaholics Anonymous meetings in a university town inhabited by thousands of work-addicts and having three people at the meetings. She feels that excessive working is one of our society's major addictions but it is condoned and even encouraged. Just be aware of your own patterns with work, especially during the stress of divorce. Be as balanced as you can.

During a time of enormous change, it is good to create ways to play. As mentioned in the previous chapter, playing is a great way to relax. Leisure activities also keep the focus on *you* where it should be, instead of on your ex-wife or ex-husband and the upheaval of divorce. Open your journal and answer the question, "What would I enjoy doing in my leisure time just for me?" Then list fun activities that you can do right away or that need a class and a teacher. Star the ones that most appeal to you and put a date when you will begin. Crystal took a pottery class during her divorce to help her work out her anger and relax her shoulders and her mind. She practiced hand building, working the clay again and again, the lumps and bubbles becoming problems that she smoothed out with her hands. Then when she pounded the clay and threw it on the wheel, she could get out her aggression and frustration and feel much calmer as she centered her pot.

Writing ideas down and then acting on them will help you to feel empowered and firmly planted in your own life. If you have always wanted to take a sculpture class, take one. If you want to write poetry, buy a journal and begin. You are only limited by your own fear, which is the ego's way to block and suppress you. Break free of self-imposed limitations and take a risk. Go dancing, cut your hair, take up roller-blading, hang-gliding, parachuting, Zen meditation. Sit still, run a marathon, eat only vegetables, get a cat; it doesn't matter, just do what would make you feel whole and happy.

In my own life, shortly after my separation, I began riding my bike to work, planted an herb garden, joined a writing group, finished a poetry manuscript, went dancing on Friday nights, and took up meditating again. I put a hammock in the garden and lay there looking up at ripening apples. It was a magical time, because I listened to my body and mind on a moment-to-moment basis, being spontaneous for the first time in my life. You, too, can listen to your inner voice and find the paths marked with your name. This doesn't mean that the journey after a divorce will always be free of stones and brambles. You may still stumble occasionally, but being on your *own* path will bring you a sense of confidence and fulfillment.

HEALING THROUGH RELEASING RESENTMENTS

The first time I worked on my resentments and need to forgive, I found it difficult. This was because the person had hurt me, and I refused to excuse what he had done. At this point in my life, it was my father I hated and blamed for my unhappiness. It took me several weeks in a course taught by Judy Wardell-Halliday to realize that the forgiveness was not for the other person. It was for me. You may remember the question from a previous chapter, "Do you want to be right, or do you want to be happy?" Here, this can be changed slightly to, "Do you want to be bitter, or do you want to forgive?" Forgiveness begins with a conscious choice: to cling to the ego's attachment to sin, blame, and guilt, or to replace the ego-voice with one of love and forgiveness.

In order to forgive, you must first search your mind for any hatred or unloving thoughts. The next step is to bring these thoughts into the light by admitting them, preferably in writing, and then letting them go through the process of forgiveness. It is only by loving and forgiving that we can we be happy and whole, in "heaven." When you project fear and hatred onto others, you block the love inside your heart, and this place filled with ego feels like "hell." So, emptying the anger and filling your heart with love and forgiveness is the key to feeling joy inside. It is the key to healing your mind of the negative, destructive view of the other person. Then you can truly love that person. Not only does forgiveness heal you, but it heals the other individual as well. Each time you think of her and see her, she can feel this change of heart; she can feel your love and peace. The healing power of forgiveness extends beyond the individuals involved; each act of forgiveness reverberates through the entire universe, healing everything and everyone it touches.

The question, then, is how soon do you want relief? Sadly, some people never do. They stubbornly cling to self-righteous anger for years, even to their deaths, even though they are in emotional pain and are creating physical suffering. My father, for instance, refused to forgive an elementary teacher and principal for how they treated him; he detested his own father and cut off all contact, and he never forgave himself for being insensitive to his mother just before her death. He carried this unforgiveness with him to the grave. I hope you are not as stubborn, filled with pride, and addicted to suffering. An attorney told me a tragic story of a father who divorced his wife and modeled a stance of animosity and unforgiveness for his son. Then, twenty years later, his son divorced his wife and behaved in the same manner. The attorney observed both men in court, the father supporting his son to "go for the jugular" and "take her to the cleaners," and he said of this scene, "I could hardly stay seated while the two of them ranted and raved; they looked so twisted and bitter, the father so venomous and hateful and the son just a younger version of his dad. What a terrible legacy to pass on: lifelong resentment."

Your readiness to forgive depends on your readiness to let go of the past and move into the future. Resentment, anger, and unforgiveness live in the past where they were created, but sometimes we keep the events alive, the wounds fresh, and we remain stuck in what was. The only way out is to tell the truth about what happened, including our feelings. Also, we must admit that on some level we enjoy keeping the self-righteous anger alive; it feeds our ego and our victim stance. We can be the one who is "right" and has been "wronged," a "one up and one down" perspective that just keeps us from accepting what has happened, letting go, and getting on with our life. For some people, staying resentful is an unconscious way not to move on; change is too scary, the unknown too unpredictable, and so, remaining angry is a way to feel safe. Unfortunately, we are miserable in the process, and we will continue to be unhappy until we admit how we feel and begin the process of releasing our fear and our pain. This truth-telling must happen before we are ready to forgive.

If you have been working on releasing your fear, anger, and resentment, and feel that this piece is finished, then proceed to the section on forgiveness. One word of caution. Many of us *want* to be good, forgiving people. We hate the idea that we might have negative feelings about others. At times, especially if we've been raised in a religious household, we think in order to be "good" we always must be loving and forgiving, that to feel resentful or angry is "bad." The truth is, as humans we have feelings, lots of them, and they change from moment to moment. We are not our feelings; we just have them. It is better for our health, and for our relationship with ourselves and others, to tell the truth about how we feel. If you are still upset with your ex-spouse, then say so, get the feelings out of your body so you can feel better and move into the future. For those of you who have done Twelve-Step work, this exercise is somewhat like doing a fourth step, an inventory of resentments.

RESENTMENT LIST 1

First, open your journal and write "Resentment List." Begin not with your ex-partner, but with yourself. Does this surprise you? Often, the person you most need to forgive is you. It helps to empty all the negative feelings that we are holding about ourselves, to clean the inner slate and become ready to forgive others. You might begin with the phrase, "I resent myself for . . ." and list whatever comes up. Another way to say this is, "I can't forgive myself for . . ." Write quickly from "the gut" rather than the mind. The only rule is to be completely honest. When you are finished and nothing else is surfacing, reread your list. Have you been fair or too hard on yourself? Rewrite or omit those that are too harsh or too one-sided. Change the wording to reflect fairness. For instance, if you wrote, "I can't forgive myself for leaving my son with my ex," you might be closer to the truth if you wrote, "I feel sad that I left my son with my ex. I had no place for him to sleep for the first few months." Tell the truth, but don't crucify yourself.

An example of an honest resentment is, "I resent myself for being so quiet during mediation and not standing up for myself." Then, later you can write a forgiveness for yourself. After all, you did the best you could at the time. It is interesting that my mediator called me up after our sessions and asked why I was so quiet, and told me I seemed like a victim. This shocked me, as I didn't remember the sessions this way. At first, I was mad at myself and felt some shame, but I realized I just wanted the divorce to be over, with as little conflict as possible. I felt guilty for leaving and didn't think I had a right to ask for much. Thankfully, my mediator made me realize I did deserve a great deal. The point is, you may be angry at yourself for a good many things, but be compassionate, too, in understanding *why* you did what you did. Just keep writing personal resentments, relieving yourself of guilt and remorse in the process. It will feel good when you have emptied your mind of this list. If you decide you need to change some of your character traits and behavior, you can. If you feel the urge to forgive yourself or to apologize to your spouse, you can do this, too. For now, though, let's release more resentments.

RESENTMENT LIST 2

Next, focus on any anger or resentment toward your ex-spouse. You looked at this anger in a previous chapter, but notice if there is any left. How can you tell if you are purged of all resentment? If you think you're free of anger and spite, you've reached the level of detachment in the divorcing process. This means that no matter how successful and happy your ex-spouse is, you aren't jealous or hurt or even that interested; you have your own life to live and you are doing great. At this stage, no one blames or even misses the other person; in fact, your former partner is irrelevant to your sense of self, is not necessary to your esteem or happiness. If you feel this way on a consistent basis, you have truly healed from your divorce. Rhonda illustrates this stage. "It's been over three years and now I'm finally free. I couldn't have had the courage to leave him, so his leaving me was really a gift. He's with someone else and I gave him a lot of the things from the house, but I don't even care. I'm free." Those of you who are no longer angry or resentful can turn to the forgiveness section and do the exercises, or to other parts of the chapter. You can probably find some work to do on yourself if the process with your former spouse is complete.

This section is for those of you who are still upset with your former partner. Some of this is about what he or she did to you; most of it is about your unhealed perspective of what he or she did. In any case, if you're angry, it's a good sign. It means you are acknowledging the truth about how you really feel and are closer to expressing your honest emotions. You are closer to relief and empowerment. First, open your journal and write your ex-wife's or ex-husband's name at the top, and under this heading, the phrase, "I resent/hate/or do not forgive you for . . ." and begin to make your list. Leave a blank line underneath each and some space to the right for an additional exercise that follows. Write until your hand is limp or until you can't think of any more. If you need a break, take one, and begin again. It's best to do this exercise in one sitting, while you are "fired up." Be prepared for emotions to surface, everything from rage to frustration, and jealousy to sadness. Keep breathing and making sure your neck and shoulders are not getting too tense. If they are, stop and take at least three deep breaths, stretch your upper body, and perhaps drink some water. Then with one more breath, pick up your pen and begin again.

You're finished when you write the words, "I resent you for . . ." and nothing comes up. Write this phrase three times and if it still is blank, you are probably finished . . . for now. Be assured that more will come up from time to time, especially if the two of you are still in contact. If not, this may or may not be your final resentment list. What I like to do next is read them over, and in the space next to each sentence I write what my part is in this resentment. For instance, recently I wrote a resentment list and said, "I hate you _____" about one of my son's ex-girlfriends who hurt him. Next to this, I wrote, "This isn't any of my business and I need to stop being so nosy and overinvolved. I need to realize that he did something, too, to cause the relationship to end. He is on his own path and I need to let go." Then, I wrote a forgiveness for the girl and for myself and could let go of it all.

If a goal for you is not just getting out your anger toward your ex-spouse, but looking at your own part, then do the second part of this exercise just described. If there are any resentments that seem trivial or can be released now, do so by crossing them out, or writing "I forgive you for . . ." under the sentence in the blank space. After you "let go" of these resentments, look at the ones that remain. You will be writing forgivenesses for these resentments later.

RESENTMENT LIST 3

Keep in mind that you could write resentments and forgivenesses for many people in your life, from your parents, siblings, and peers from childhood, to anyone in your life now. Because this is a book on divorce, we will focus on the resentment of ourselves and our spouses. If, however, you feel angry at others involved in your divorce, then you can include them here. During my divorce, I resented my former husband's new partner, which may sound ridiculous since I chose to leave and did not want to return. However, unconsciously I held a fantasy that he would always love me and keep me on a pedestal etched in gold. He'd live alone for the rest of his life and feast on my memory. I know this sounds pathetic, but it shows the power of the ego. Even recently, I wrote his new wife's name on my resentment list, and when I was honest, the indignant anger was at my ex for ever marrying again, and at her for accepting. Didn't he want a deep unrequited love, and didn't she know the depth of his devotion to me?

My part, and what I wrote next, was about how selfish and egocentric I was to be angry at them, given that I initiated the leaving process. At times, because of our wounded pride, it's easier to be mad at our former spouse's new partner than to be angry with our ex. After all, they were stolen away from us, weren't they? How many times have you heard these phrases, "She stole my husband," or "He took her away from me," or "She tempted him and he couldn't resist," or "He made her do it"? When you aren't in the middle of a divorce, these statements sound idiotic. Who could make a grown woman or man leave a spouse and family unless they wanted to? I do understand the lunacy that causes us to blame the new partner. It's less painful to blame the "other" man or woman, than to realize our mate no longer wants to be with us. To defend our crushed egos, we lash out.

When my ex-husband met someone else, I was upset, but now I bless her for holding him during those lonely times after I left. He deserves to be loved and treated well, and I am thankful for this woman who now is his wife. Six years ago, however, I hated her. If this is where you are, in anger or resentment toward your ex's new partner, then write about it now. Open your journal and put the person's name at the top. Then write whichever phrase works best for you, such as "I hate you for . . ." or "I resent you for . . ." or another statement that feels right. Then save space to the right to include your part. Skip a line after each resentment in order to write a forgiveness at the end of the exercise. When you feel complete, reread the list, add your part to the right, and add any forgivenesses you feel ready to include. Finally, what you have left is a list of resentments that you aren't ready to forgive at this time.

You also have the opportunity to make a resentment list for anyone else involved in the divorcing process with whom you are angry. For example, at first I was upset with my best friend, who didn't think I should leave my husband and gave me endless advice. I was able to talk with her and we worked it out. I did use my journal to write forgivenesses for what she did then and at other times. It helped to keep our friendship clear and strong. Go ahead and write the names of anyone involved in your divorce that you resent. Proceed with the same method of writing the list. Now ask yourself if you are finished with all the people immediately connected to you and your spouse during your divorce. If so, you are ready to move on to the first stage of forgiveness.

FORGIVENESS WITH RESISTANCE

I first learned this technique fifteen years ago from Judy Wardell-Halliday. It is an excellent pre-forgiveness journal exercise to "test the waters," to see if you are truly ready to forgive the person and what he or she did. Open your journal to a clean page and write the above title. Begin with yourself, then proceed to your ex-partner and the others in your life. Look at the list of resentments about yourself. Begin with the first one. Let's say it is, "I am angry at myself for ever marrying _____ in the first place," or "I'm mad at myself for not leaving sooner." Then take the phrase and change the words to, "I forgive myself for marrying _____." If a voice of resistance comes into your mind, just write it down; it might be something like, "I am such an idiot," or "No, I don't." Then write the forgiveness again for the same item. The goal is to write the forgiveness and feel complete with it, without any argument in your head. At this point, the anger might change to sadness or to a calmer, more accepting feeling. You may realize you were doing the best you could, and feel less judgment and more compassion for yourself. This is the point of the exercise—to be merciful and understanding.

Then with a bit more self-forgiveness will come a willingness to forgive others. If no resistance comes up, go on to the next resentment on the list. You might want to write what you could have done differently, or what you could do if such a situation ever occurs again. For instance, I was too passive in my marriage at times, and went along with things I didn't want to do. Over the years, I had stored a large number of resentments toward my husband for being so dominant, when, quite frankly, all I had to do was speak up and say, "No." The reason I didn't was I feared he would leave me, and then, ironically, I finally left him. In looking at my part, I know that my passivity allowed him to move in and take charge. Each time I said, "I don't care," I perpetuated the inequality. So, be honest in this exercise and realize what you did and what you can change. Follow this process until you are finished with yourself and are ready to move on to your ex-partner.

Use the above directions to begin forgiving your spouse. Start with the first resentment, change it to a forgiveness, and then see if any resistance comes up. An example might be, "I hate you for being gone so much traveling and working." Then change it to, "I forgive you for traveling and working long hours." Resistance might sound like, "You jerk, I don't forgive you for leaving me and the children alone for three months." Then write the forgiveness again and again with whatever resistance comes up. You are finished when nothing surfaces after you write the forgiveness and you can calmly write, "I feel sad you were gone so much, and I forgive you." Sometimes the form of it changes as you let go of the specific aspects. You are emptying yourself of poison. Each resentment is full of toxic emotion that triggers a reaction in your body. Why do you think people get headaches and stomachaches when they are angry, tense, and volatile? Let these toxins go. Let these stored-up resentments disappear with the stroke of a pen. The antidote is forgiveness.

Ward has been storing his anger and hurt for at least five years and this is taking its toll on his health. He has still not gotten over Julie, his ex-wife, even though she is with someone else. His life is in a rut of work, playing music, and drinking heavily. He hasn't dated anyone else, and it is difficult for friends to get him out of the house. His closest friends worry that it will take an illness or accident to make him wake up and begin the process of healing through forgiveness. He needs to move on but he just can't seem to budge.

Stuffing down anger and resentment also causes emotional "eruptions" to occur. Carey, divorced from Serena for three years after twenty years of marriage, has never dealt with his anger toward her. Now when they talk on the phone about the children, he often ends up yelling about something trivial. Recently, he got mad about a bed frame in his garage that she stored there. "This isn't a goddamn storage facility; do you want the bed or not? Either come and get it or I'm keeping it." At this point, Serena said she was hanging up, that it wasn't possible to talk. When he called back, he apologized, but the root of the anger has never been discussed. When she tries to talk about feelings, he changes the subject. Carey often yells at his children over minor issues, and these outbursts really stem from unresolved anger toward Serena. Other people see this, but Carey gets upset if it's brought to his attention. Ignoring unpleasant feelings has always been his coping mechanism, but they are getting more difficult to mask.

Forgiveness, then, is not just for the other person, but for you. It is the ointment for your painful burn. The injury will heal in time; it might leave a scar, but it will no longer hurt when touched. Continue to write your "forgiveness with resistance" list until it feels complete, when you can write each forgiveness alone without any objections. Proceed to the list of others, or save this for another time. Just completing this process for yourself and your ex-partner is an undertaking. Anytime you feel angry at someone in your present life, you can use this technique to release the feelings of anger, and then forgive. If you have addictive tendencies, this method of emptying your resentment and then forgiving can keep you from acting on your addiction of choice. Instead, you can feel resolved and at peace and not need anything outside yourself to help you cope.

FORGIVENESS

If you are ready to forgive the people in your life for whatever they have done, you can write a final statement, beginning with yourself: "I forgive myself for the mistakes I've made, realizing I am human and deserving of compassion. I know I'm doing the very best I can." That felt wonderful to say. You can write a similar statement of self-forgiveness. Write it boldly in large print. Put the words on your mirror. You deserve your own forgiveness for being yourself. This doesn't mean you can do things that hurt you and others on a consistent basis and then say, "It's okay." You do need to clean up your act and be honest when you're not being a conscious or responsible person. You have an obligation to yourself and to others to keep growing and improving, to keep perfecting that being that is you. When it comes to forgiving your ex-partner and the others in your life, write a similar forgiveness statement when you feel ready. It may not be this minute, but realize that the sooner you forgive completely, the sooner you can be free. For your ex-spouse you might write something like, "I forgive you, _____, for anything you did or said that harmed me. I bless you and release you to your own higher power, to your own path and journey. I wish you peace." You can write a forgiveness statement for anyone on your list when it feels right.

AMENDS AND OTHERS' FORGIVENESS OF YOU

A piece of the forgiveness package that has worked miracles in my life is the making of amends and the asking for forgiveness.

You don't have to do this directly with the persons involved, but it is very powerful if you do. Anyone who does Twelve-Step work is familiar with the ninth step and the making of amends; all of us have said "I'm sorry" to at least one person in our lives and this is basically, but not completely, what it means to make amends. The first thing to do is to look at the people we have harmed in some way and list them and what it is we did to them. Next, you can write letters stating what you did and saying you're sorry. All you are responsible for is the realization of the error and the willingness to make amends and take action. You cannot control the response of the other people or the outcome, whether or not they forgive you. The healing comes in the action you take in being honest with yourself and with others. The best part is cleansing your conscience of all guilt. Begin with a clean page in your journal and list the people you have harmed in some way and what you did to them.

On one of my amends lists, I put my ex-husband and stated that I had been very selfish and thoughtless before I left. I did many things to show how happy I was to go and didn't think about how my actions must have felt to him. Now, nearly seven years later, I feel remorse and want to make amends. If contact from you would be harmful, either to the person or to his or her new partner and family, just write a letter for yourself, perhaps read it aloud, and then burn it in a ritual. Sending the letters is a bit more effective in the courage it takes, the honesty on your part, and the clearing of your conscience, but do whatever is best for the other person first and then for you. Within a year after I left, I wrote amends to my children and to my ex-husband. They all thanked me for writing them but didn't discuss the content specifically. You might prefer to call the person on the phone or make an appointment to meet. Do whatever will truly help you to clean the slate and begin anew, as long as your contact is respectful of everyone.

Another idea is to write amends and forgivenesses for yourself in your journal. First, you can write letters to individuals saying you're sorry for harming them and include the specifics of what you did. Then, write forgivenesses as if from them to you, in order to remove the error and absolve you of wrongdoing. The point is to get the guilt and remorse out of your system, and how you do it is less important than the fact that you accomplish it. Your honesty in admitting what you did is character-building. You can clearly see your errors and then work on improving how you treat everyone in your life. Here is a sample letter to my ex-husband.

Dear _____:
I am writing this letter to make amends to you for anything I have done that may have harmed you. Specifically, I am sorry for blaming you for being controlling during our marriage, when I was too passive and didn't make my feelings clear. I'm sorry for being judgmental of you, especially spiritually, and for being critical of you in front of the children. In general, I wish I had been more honest about my feelings, especially my hurt and anger. Instead, I stuffed it inside where it festered for many years. Also, I apologize for ignoring your feelings while moving out and during our separation. If I seemed callous and insensitive, it was because I needed to be strong in order to leave. I know this was difficult for you and I'm sorry for that. I didn't want to hurt you. I didn't know how to do it differently at the time. I hope you can forgive me and we can continue to be friends and supportive coparents. I wish you every goodness.

Here is a sample letter to a friend.

Dear _____,
I'm sorry that during my divorce I didn't have much time for our friendship. At least twice I forgot to meet you and left you waiting there. If my behavior hurt you, I am deeply sorry. At one point, you

cut off contact with me, and I don't blame you. I hope you can forgive me for being so preoccupied with my own life. I love you and
never want distance to come between us again. I value your friendship so very much.

Even if you send your amends letters, there is no guarantee
you will receive direct forgiveness from the recipients. So,
give yourself a blessing, by writing in your journal something
like, "I forgive you, Sue, for focusing on your divorce and personal life at a time that was very complex for you. I love you
and appreciate your apology." Then, the cycle is complete. You
admit any unresolved resentment toward yourself or others;
you forgive each person and each act; you make amends for
your actions; you accept forgiveness for any harm you have
done. It's like cleaning house, only the house is your own body
and mind, and instead of powdered cleanser, you are using the
healing power of unconditional love and honest forgiveness.
The ingredients are foolproof.

THE POST-DIVORCE RELATIONSHIP
WITH YOUR FORMER SPOUSE

After your divorce is final, you may think that the relationship
is over, the grief is over, the person is no longer in your life. In
terms of my own experience and based on my interviews,
nothing could be farther from the truth. If you have children
that you are co-parenting, the relationship will just keep trans-
forming. Even if you don't have children, you may have your
ex-partner in your life in some way. This is, of course, unless it
has been an abusive marriage and you fear that your ex-spouse
will harm you. In this case, do not contact or accept contact
from your wife or husband. Perhaps the individual has been in
counseling and is recovering from an addiction. This is good
for her or him and for your children if you have any. But I

would be very cautious about seeing the person unless a therapist or other support person is present. Be careful.

For those of you not in an abusive situation, the prognosis for your relationship is good, if you want to maintain a connection with your "ex." Usually, one person is angrier than the other, and it takes more time for him or her to forgive. It helps if one partner reaches out and, if appropriate, makes amends. This clears the way for the other spouse to get over the hurt feelings and become open to a reconnection. It feels good to have a friendship or at least a respectful partnership with your ex-spouse, especially if you have children. Hannah speaks of her healed relationship with her ex-husband: "At our son's college graduation we sat together with our new partners, and when Harrison walked across the stage, we grabbed hands and Randall cried, 'Look at our son, Hannah! Isn't he magnificent!' It was then that I knew it all was healed in love."

Recently, my daughter took me to breakfast for my birthday. I told her how much I loved her father's gift. She beamed from ear to ear and said, "Dad's a good guy. He was so worried you wouldn't like it. I knew you would. Wasn't it sweet of him?" My grown children would like nothing more than for their parents to get back together. This isn't going to happen, and so the next best thing is that we still care about each other, speak of one another with respect, and show a united front when our children need us. Each year that passes since the divorce brings us closer to the friendship we had before we married. For this I am very grateful. It has taken effort on both our parts, but the result feels very good. What can you do to create and maintain a respectful relationship with your ex-partner?

First of all, do the resentment and forgiveness exercises listed above. Be sure to own your part in the problems in the marriage and the cause of the divorce. Be honest, at least to yourself, and if possible, deliver the forgivenesses to him or her. Making amends for any harm you have done will help heal the rift in the relationship and create the possibility for renewed friendship. Recently, I called my former husband to make amends for things I could not say earlier, and since then our friendship has deepened. I hope you have an ex-spouse who is as conscious as you are, who wants to let go of any negativity between you, who wants to forgive and wants you both to heal. If, however, your ex-partner refuses to see his or her part, will not talk with you about issues, and would not be open to forgiveness exercises or amends, then there is not much you can do. For your own healing, you can empty yourself of all resentment, forgive him or her and yourself, and do a final ritual of release, included below.

CEREMONIES OF BLESSING AND RELEASE

If I could do one thing over or add something to my divorcing process, it would be to have a meaningful closure with my ex-husband. I did suggest we perform a ceremony or ritual to acknowledge our years together and mark this new phase, but he wasn't ready. So I did my own rituals to mark this important rite of passage. If possible, perform a ceremony together to honor the marriage and one another as you walk your own paths. What follows are ceremonies to do as a couple, alone, or both. Your ex-spouse will benefit if he or she is willing to feel the feelings that will inevitably arise. It is incredibly poignant and expansive to share this moment of closure together. Turner was not afraid of crying and talking about his regret and sadness with his wife as they prepared to separate and divorce. They set aside time to cry together and process their feelings, to discuss the good times in the marriage and what they had accomplished together. At this point, they had become two close friends who knew each other intimately and needed reassurance as they began new lives apart. This is a blessing, to be two conscious people valuing the years together while honoring the decision to separate.

Perhaps because of society's critical view of divorce, and the difficult emotions experienced by those divorcing, few ceremonies or rituals exist to mark this passage. When couples are still upset with one another, or are still grieving the marriage, it might seem impossible to "celebrate" the years together in a divorce ritual. Ideally, such a ceremony comes after you have forgiven one another and made amends. Much or all of the rancor is gone. What remains is a poignant, wistful feeling, some nostalgia, more sweetness than bitterness. If you are still hurt from the divorce, but want to have a ceremony of closure, it is possible. Most people grieve for years, and the feelings of sadness come in waves, usually set in motion by a holiday, a birthday, an anniversary, a gift, or a vacation spot you once visited together. There might not be a time to hold such a ritual when you would be free of feelings. It's normal and expected that a ritual would evoke deep emotion, and that the two of you would express it.

Such a ceremony is a cross between a wedding and a funeral; it isn't as joyous and uplifting as a wedding, nor as final as a memorial. A divorce ceremony marks the end of one phase of your relationship and the beginning of another. No union of body, mind, and spirit ever ends. It is just transformed. The invisible cords of love and union connect the two of you on the spiritual plane. These cords will always connect you, especially if you have children who are the tangible evidence of your original commitment and your love.

You can write and speak your own vows to one another or have a minister or good friend officiate, using one of the suggested ceremonies that follow. It's completely up to you how many people to invite, from just the two of you, to close family and friends, to everyone invited to your wedding. The reason to invite people at all is for acknowledgment and support; they are witnessing and honoring your years together and offering their compassion, understanding, and acceptance of your decision. If you have children, they can be invited to be part of this passage and new beginning. Having children present is incredibly emotional for everyone, yet it serves as a reminder that the family still exists and must be protected and cherished. A ceremony will help your children heal by normalizing the experience of divorce; they will witness your commitment to be good coparents, honoring the years of marriage by being respectful of one another now. If you do not have children, a divorce ceremony can be an important way to bless and release one another, to close one gate gently before opening the next one. Just delete the references to children from the following ceremony in order for it to meet your needs. If your spouse will not participate in a ceremony with you, then do the second ritual on your own, to create closure and the freedom to move on.

CEREMONY FOR COUPLES WITH AN OFFICIANT OR MINISTER

We have come here today to honor _____ *and* _____ *for their years of marriage, for their love and commitment during those years, for all the joys and sorrows, and for the times of celebration and mourning. We are here in compassion, understanding, and acceptance of their decision to divorce. We know it has been a difficult decision but one made with conscious thought and heartfelt emotion. During their years of marriage, they have built a strong union and a stable home for their children. This dedication to their family will continue as they now become supportive and respectful coparents.*

We ask Spirit to bless _____ *and* _____ *as they remember only the good in the marriage and in one another, as they forgive one another, and become ready to begin new lives. May they feel Spirit's love within them; may they see innocence and purity in each other's eyes, the soul's light shining through. To their children: we ask that you forgive your parents, realizing that they have done their best to preserve the marriage and remain devoted parents to you. May you be healed of pain, your spirit cleansed. May you accept your parents' decision and feel at peace.*

Let us all support _____ *and* _____ *now and in the future, knowing that they are still joined by Spirit to their families and to us. Their relationship to one another is changed; it will continue to transform in the years to come as they each take new paths into the future. Now, each of them will offer a blessing for the other and follow these words with a ritual of release.*

ONE PARTNER: *Thank you for being my mate, for loving me and teaching me so much. I forgive you and ask for your forgiveness. I will always hold you in my heart. I wish you only goodness, and release you to your own inner wisdom and highest destiny.*

OTHER PARTNER: *Thank you for being my mate, for loving me and teaching me so much. I forgive you and ask for your forgiveness. I will always hold you in my heart. I wish you only goodness, and release you to your own inner wisdom and highest destiny.*

With this symbolic gesture of blessing and release, let them begin new lives.

At this point, you could cut golden cords, each taking half; you can put your wedding rings into a special box or place; you can let doves go into the sky, or light two separate candles from one; you could each take a rose from the altar or table, or each take identical plants; you can kiss children and family, rededicating yourselves to them. You could even take separate hot air balloons, to represent a new direction into the universe.

The gesture of release should be meaningful to the two of you based on your marriage. You can do whatever fits.

After this symbolic event, the officiant prays:

Please bless _____ *and* _____ *as they honor one another, their years of marriage, and their continued commitment to their children, family, and friends. Please heal the past from all suffering, and endow the future with abundant joy. May* _____ *and* _____ *be healed of all pain, remembering only the beauty of their union, the love they gave to one another and to their children. Support these two souls as they begin their newest journeys. With this prayer, let all be forgiven, let love be remembered, let only peace fill their hearts. Amen.*

The officiant says to the group assembled, if more than just the couple:

In the months and years to come, offer support and friendship to _____ *and* _____. *Your presence here is a blessing to them and to yourselves. Remember that love never ends. The forms may change, but the energy of love remains. And so it is. If you would like to send a silent blessing to* _____ *and* _____, *you may do so at this time. Thank you all for coming.*

RITUAL OF RELEASE FOR ONE PERSON

If your partner doesn't want to participate in a joint ceremony, then you can perform a ritual anyway. After all, a ceremony is to help you lovingly release the other person, feel cleansed, and be able to get on with your life. There is no guarantee that our spouses will forgive us, will want a continuing friendship, or even be good coparents. Remember, we can ask for what we want, but there is no guarantee we'll get it. In the meantime, we need to take care of ourselves. And this means healing from the past and embracing the future.

I went alone to a favorite beach, carrying my ex-husband's letters and one of his sweaters. I left the sweater on a steep cliff, burned the letters, buried the ashes, said prayers of release and blessing, and dove into the water. You can do whatever supports you to let go of the marriage and your partner, whatever helps you feel lighter and clearer about your divorce. If you feel silly performing a ceremony or ritual alone, this is natural. Just feel self-conscious for the time it takes, looking at the feelings lurking beneath the doubt. Do whatever you need to in order to prepare for your ritual. Then, just do it. Trust me. You'll feel so much more resolved afterward.

The following is a sample ceremony using my words. Please change whatever you wish to fit your feelings and situation, changing husband to wife where necessary and adding your partner's name in the appropriate places. Address this invocation to whatever you believe in, from your own inner wisdom, to God, to anything in between. When doing the symbolic ritual, choose whatever would be representative of the two of you or the marriage. It also depends on where you live. I like the idea of doing the ritual in nature, but this may not be possible for you. Some ways to express release might be: letting go of an object that symbolizes the marriage for you, burning it, letting it fly away, burying it, giving it away. You could use objects such as letters, photographs, jewelry, clothing, or whatever is symbolic. You can write a poem about your separation and read it. You could draw or sculpt something. You could give your ring back to your spouse or have it made into another piece of jewelry so it is transformed. If the love between you is still strong, you can plant a rose or jasmine bush to represent the continuation of this love on the spiritual plane. Perhaps sit quietly for a few moments and think about what would be the best place and means of conducting a ceremony. Then create a meaningful rite of passage. This is mine.

Great Spirit / Goddess-God / Highest Consciousness / Spirit / Source: Thank you for this day. Thank you for my life. Thank you for all my many blessings. I am extremely grateful. Great Spirit, please help me release my marriage to you; help me let go of my husband, my home, my dream of what this marriage could be. Oh, Great Spirit, please heal me of this pain, this grief and sorrow. Free me of fear and anger, cleansed of all ego. Let only love and forgiveness fill my heart. Help me release the past and live only in the present moment. Help me let go of my attempt to control people and things. Help me trust that all will be well, all will be exactly what I need. Great Spirit, bless my former husband and help him to heal. Guide him to choose what will bring fulfillment and peace.

With this symbolic ritual (whatever you choose to do to represent the release of your marriage and partner), I let the past go. I release my partner, my marriage, my expectations of this relationship. I return to my former husband all his power; I release the energy I have held of his. In turn, I draw into myself all the power I gave away to him. I feel the return of my energy and spirit. With this symbolic gesture, all is released, all is forgiven, all is healed. What remains is the love in my heart for my former husband and our children, love that is eternal. Thank you, Great Spirit, for all the gifts in my life. Thank you for teaching me so many important lessons. Thank you for helping me to grow into a better person. Ho / Blessed be / And so it is / Amen.

THE END IS NEVER THE END

Just as divorce is another stage in a marriage that continues to evolve, the last chapter of this book is just a part of the divorcing process. And my wish is that you continue to add chapters to this book as you need them. Perhaps the next ones for you might be: Loving Myself Fully, Optimum Health, Finding My Life's Work, Traveling the World, or Conscious Remarriage.

It is my hope that this book has helped you. I've written my life in every chapter, reliving my marriage and divorce and sharing the stories of clients, colleagues, family, and friends. At times this has been challenging emotionally, and yet, extremely empowering. You, too, have been through a great deal during the divorcing process, or are beginning this challenging work. Just remember that the suffering ends; the grief lessens. You will feel joy again. You will forget what hurt you, and remember what you loved most. You will survive and flourish.

May you always be conscious of the decisions you make, knowing your words and actions affect everyone and everything in life's web. Lovingly follow your intuition. Then step confidently from silken strand to silken strand.

Bibliography

Adler, Robert E. *Sharing the Children: How to Resolve Custody Problems and Get On with Your Life.* Chevy Chase, Md.:Adler & Adler Publishers, 1988.

Ahrons, Constance R. *The Good Divorce.* New York: HarperCollins, 1994.

Ahrons, Constance R., and Roy Rodgers. *Divorced Families: A Multi-Disciplinary Developmental View.* New York: W.W. Norton, 1988.

Allison, Susan. "Body Love." In Janet M. McEwan, ed., *Writing For Our Lives.* Los Gatos, Calif.: Running Deer Press, 1997.

Applewhite, Ashton. *Cutting Loose: Why Women Who End Their Marriages Do So Well.* New York: HarperPerennial, 1997.

Barbach, Lonnie Garfield. *For Each Other: Sharing Sexual Intimacy.* New York: NAL Penguin, Inc., 1984.

———. *For Yourself: The Fulfillment of Female Sexuality.* New York: NAL Penguin, Inc.,1975.

Berry, Dawn Bradley. *The Divorce Sourcebook.* Los Angeles. Lowell House, 1996.

Bloomfield, Harold, and Peter McWilliams. *How to Heal Depression.* Los Angeles: Prelude Press, 1994.

Bloomfield, Harold H., with Leonard Felder. *Making Peace With Your Parents.* New York: Random House, 1983.

———. *Making Peace With Yourself.* New York: Ballantine Books, 1986.

Bohannan, Paul. "The Six Stations of Divorce." In *Divorce and After,* edited by Paul P. Bohannan. New York: Doubleday, 1970.

Brown, Laurie Krasny, and Marc Brown. *Dinosaurs Divorce.* Boston: Little, Brown, 1988. (For children.)

Carlson, Linda. *Everything You Need to Know About Your Parents' Divorce.* New York: Rosen Publishing, 1992.

Chopra, Deepak, M.D., *Perfect Health.* New York: Harmony Books, 1991.

———. *The Seven Spiritual Laws of Success.* San Rafael, Calif.: Amber-Allen Publishing, 1994.

Clapp, Genevieve. *Divorce and New Beginnings.* New York: John Wiley & Sons, 1992.

Colgrove, Melba, Harold H. Bloomfield, and Peter McWilliams. *How to Survive the Loss of a Love.* New York: Bantam, 1977.

Coontz, Stephanie. *The Way We Never Were: American Families and the Nostalgia Trap.* New York: Basic Books, 1992.

A Course in Miracles. Glen Ellen, Calif.: The Foundation for Inner Peace, 1992.

Emerick-Cayton, Tim. *Divorcing with Dignity: Mediation—The Sensible Alternative*. Louisville, Ky.: John Knox Press, 1993.

Emery, Marcia. *Intuition Workbook: An Expert's Guide to Unlocking the Wisdom of Your Unconscious Mind*. Englewood Cliffs, N.J.: Prentice Hall, 1994.

Forward, Susan. *When Your Lover Is a Liar: Healing the Wounds of Deception and Betrayal*. New York: HarperPerennial, 1999.

Gold, Lois. *Between Love and Hate: A Guide to Civilized Divorce*. New York: Plenum Publishing, 1992.

Gray, John. *How to Get What You Want and Want What You Have*. New York: HarperCollins, 1999.

————. *Mars and Venus Starting Over*. New York: HarperCollins, 1998.

————. *Men Are from Mars, Women Are from Venus*. New York: Harper-Collins, 1992.

————. *What You Feel You Can Heal*. Calif.: Hearst Publishing, 1984.

Hay, Louise. *You Can Heal Your Life*. Santa Monica, Calif.: Hay House, Inc., 1984.

Hill, Gerald. *Divorced Fathers: Coping with Problems, Creating Solutions*. Cincinnati: Betterway Publications, 1989.

Ives, Sally B., David Fassler, and Michele Lash. *The Divorce Workbook: A Guide for Kids and Families*. Burlington, Vt.: Waterfront Books, 1992.

James, Paula. *The Divorce Mediation Handbook*. San Francisco: Jossey-Bass Publishers, 1997.

Kirshenbaum, Mira. *Too Good to Leave, Too Bad to Stay*. New York: Dutton, 1996.

Kingma, Daphne Rose. *Coming Apart: Why Relationships End and How to Live Through the Ending of Yours*. New York: Fawcett Crest, 1987.

Krantzler, Mel. *Creative Divorce*. New York: The New American Library, Inc., 1973.

Kubler-Ross, Elisabeth, M.D.. *On Death and Dying*. New York: Simon & Schuster, 1969.

Lansky, Vicki. *Divorce Book for Parents*. New York: New American Library, 1989.

Lerner, Harriet Goldhor. *The Dance of Anger*. New York: Harper & Row Publishers, 1985.

Leshan, Lawrence. *How to Meditate*. Boston: Little, Brown and Co., 1974.

Lucas, John C. *Conscious Marriage: From Chemistry to Communication*. Freedom, Calif.: The Crossing Press, 1998.

Marston, Stephanie. *The Divorced Parent: Success Strategies for Raising Your Children After Separation*. New York: William Morrow, 1994.

Nichols, J. Randall. *Ending Marriage, Keeping Faith: A New Guide Through the Spiritual Journey of Divorce*. New York: Crossroad Publishing, 1993.

Norwood, Robin. *Women Who Love Too Much.* New York: Pocket Books, 1985.

Pitzele, Sefra K. *Surviving Divorce: Daily Affirmations.* Deerfield Beach, Fl.: Health Communications, 1991.

Quick, Barbara. *Still Friends: Living Happily Ever After Even If Your Marriage Falls Apart.* Berkeley, Calif.: Wildcat Canyon Press, 1999.

Raschke, Helen. "Divorce." In *Handbook of Marriage and the Family,* edited by Marvin Sussman and Suzanne Steinmetz. New York: Plenum Press, 1987.

Reisman, C. *Divorce Talk: Women and Men Make Sense of Personal Relationships.* New Brunswick, N.J.: Rutgers University Press, 1990.

Reisman, C. K., and N. Gerstel. "Marital Dissolution and Health: Do Males or Females Have Greater Risk?" *Social Science and Medicine* 20 (1985): 627–635.

Ricci, Isolina. *Mom's House, Dad's House: Making Shared Custody Work.* New York: Collier MacMillan, 1982.

Roth, Robert. *Maharishi Mahesh Yogi's TM: Transcendental Meditation.* New York: Primus, 1994.

Saposnek, Donald. T. *Mediating Child Custody Disputes: A Strategic Approach.* Revised Edition. San Francisco: Jossey-Bass, 1998.

Saposnek, Donald T., and Chip Rose. "The Psychology of Divorce." In *Handbook of Financial Planning for Divorce and Separation,* by D. L. Crumbley and N. G. Apostolou (eds.). New York: John Wiley & Sons, 1990.

Seligman, E. P. *Learned Optimism.* New York: Pocket Books, 1998.

Sitarz, Daniel. *Divorce Yourself.* Illinois: Nova Publishing, 1998.

Smith, Gayle Rosenwald, and Sally Abrahms. *What Every Woman Should Know About Divorce & Custody.* New York: A Perigee Book, 1998.

Tannen, Deborah. *You Just Don't Understand: Women and Men in Conversation.* New York: Ballantine Books, 1990.

Trafford, Abigail. *Crazy Time: Surviving Divorce and Building a New Life.* New York: HarperPerennial, 1992.

Triere, Lynette, with Richard Peacock. *Learning to Leave.* New York: Warner Books, 1982. (Out of print, but worth finding used.)

Vaughan, Diane. *Uncoupling: Turning Points in Intimate Relationships.* New York: Oxford University Press, 1986.

Viorst, Judith. *Necessary Losses.* New York: Simon & Schuster, 1986.

Wallerstein, Judith S., and Sandra Blakeslee. *Second Chances: Men, Women, and Children a Decade After Divorce.* New York: Houghton Mifflin, 1989.

Wardell-Halliday, Judy. *How to Eat and Live Like a Thin Person.* Maine: Hazelden, 2000.

————. *Thin Within.* New York: Random House, 1996.

Watrous, Angela, and Carole Honeychurch. *After the Breakup.* Oakland, Calif.: New Harbinger Publishing, 1999.

Weil, Andrew, M.D. *Natural Health, Natural Medicine.* New York: Houghton Mifflin Company, 1995.

Weiss, Robert. *Marital Separation.* New York: Basic Books, 1975.

Weitzman, Lenore J. *The Divorce Revolution: The Unexpected Social and Economic Consequences for Women and Children in America.* New York: The Free Press, 1985.

Whitmore-Hickman, Martha. *Healing After Loss: Daily Meditations for Working Through Grief.* New York: Avon Books, 1994.

Wilcox, Adele. *Mending Broken Hearts: Meditations for Finding Peace and Hope After Heartbreak.* New York: Berkley Books, 1999.

Williamson, Marianne. *A Return to Love.* New York: HarperCollins Publishers, Inc., 1975.

———. *Illuminata.* New York: Riverhead Books, 1994.

Woodhouse, Violet, and Victoria Felton-Collins. *Divorce and Money.* Berkeley, Calif.: Nolo Press, 1993.

Resources

Organizations

Academy of Guided Imagery
P.O. Box 2070
Mill Valley, CA 94942
(415) 389-9324

Al-Anon World Service
1372 Broadway
New York, NY 10018
1-800-356-9996
Monday–Friday 8–5

Alcoholics Anonymous (AA)
475 Riverside Drive
New York, NY 10163
(212) 870-3400

American Association for Marriage and Family Therapy
1100 Seventeenth Street N.W., 10th floor
Washington, D.C. 20036
(202) 452-0109

American Bar Association
Section on Family Law
750 N. Lakeshore Drive
Chicago, IL 60601
1-800-621-6159

Association for Conflict Resolution (ACR)
1527 New Hampshire Avenue, N.W., 3rd floor
Washington, D.C. 20036
(202) 667-9700
spidr@spidr.org

Association of Family and Conciliation Courts
329 W. Wilson Street
Madison, WI 53703
Phone: (608) 251-4001
Fax: (608) 251-2231
afdc@afccnet.org

Children's Rights Council
200 Eye Street
Washington, D.C. 20002
1-800-787-KIDS

Conflict Resolution Center, Inc.
204 37th Street
Pittsburgh, PA 15201-1859
(412) 687-6210
crcii@conflictnet.org

Family Service America
11700 W. Lake Park Drive
Milwaukee, WI 53224
(414) 359-1040
(To find a mediation service)

The Fatherhood Project
Families and Work Institute
330 Seventh Avenue, 14th floor
New York, NY 10001
(212) 465-2044

Family Pride Coalition International
P.O. Box 50360
Washington, D.C. 20091
(202) 583-8029

The Institute for Human Potential and Mind/Body Medicine
 (Deepak Chopra, Executive Director)
8010 Frost Street, Suite 300
San Diego, CA 92123
1-800-82-SHARP

Joint Custody Association
10606 Wilkins Avenue
Los Angeles, CA 90024
(310) 475-5352

**Maharishi Ayurveda Health Center for Stress Management
and Behavioral Medicine**
P.O. Box 344
Lancaster, MA 01523
(978) 365-4549

National Child Support Enforcement Association
Hall of States
400 N. Capitol Street N.W., No. 372
Washington, D.C. 20001
(202) 624-8180

National Coalition Against Domestic Violence
P.O. Box 18749
Denver, CO 80218-0749
(303) 839-1852

Women Work: The National Network for Women's Employment
1411 K Street N.W., Suite 930
Washington, D.C. 20005
(202) 467-6346

National Organization for Men
11 Park Place
New York, NY 10007
(212) 686-6253

National Organization for Women
99 Hudson Street
New York, NY 10013
(212) 627-9895

Office of Child Support Enforcement
Administration for Children and Families
U.S. Department of Health and Human Services
370 L'Enfant Promenade, S.W., 4th floor
Washington, D.C. 20447

Parents Without Partners (PWP)
401 N. Michigan Avenue
Chicago, IL 60611
1-800-637-7974

Single Parents Association
Hotline: 1-800-704-2102
Monday–Friday 9–6 CST

The Stepfamily Association of America
215 Centennial Mall South, Suite 212
Lincoln, Nebraska 68508
(402) 477-7837
1-800-735-0329

The Stepfamily Foundation
333 West End Avenue
New York, NY 10023
(212) 877-3244
(Phone counseling)

TRW Complimentary Report Request
P.O. Box 2350
Chatsworth, CA 91313-2350
1-800-879-8848
(Free credit report)

National Partnership for Women and Families
1875 Connecticut Avenue N.W., Suite 710
Washington, D.C. 20009
(202) 986-2600

Internet Resources

When using the Internet, just type in the word "divorce" in order to access all the sites. The following are a few of the sources available.

abanet.com
American Bar Association, providing family-law links, public education, and discussion.

acod.net
Adult Children of Divorce.

allexperts.com
Questions and answers on divorce.

divorceasfriends.com
Bill Ferguson's program, including workshops, phone consulting, and other links.

divorcecare.com
Christian-based support network.

divorcecentral.com
A national information service based in Washington, D.C.

divorcedoc.com
Child custody evaluations, laws, and clinical psychology articles.

divorceinfo.com
Negotiation tactics and legal and emotional issues, handled by Alabama mediator Lee Borden.

divorcenet.com
Legal questions answered state by state.

divorcesource.com
Finding professional legal help state by state.

divorcesupport.com
Articles, discussions, book recommendations, and links to 300 divorce sites.

divorcewizards.com
Helping with divorce solutions.

easy-divorce.com
Divorce kits and forms.

4divorce.4anything.com
Information, legal advice, and resources.

kidsturn.org
California-based organization helping children and families through divorce.

mediate.com
*Online mediation information center with articles on conflict resolution
  and family mediation*

newdayservices.org
Helping families through divorce, based in Texas.

qualitybooks.com
Do-it-yourself no-fault divorce kits.

secondwivesclub.com
Organization and newsletter for second wives and stepmoms.

sandcastlesprogram.com
Based in Florida, helping children of divorce recover.

smartdivorce.com
Practical solutions to divorce challenges.

split-up.com
Based in Illinois, offering divorce resources.

ufa.org
*United Fathers of America, based in Washington, D.C., offering national resources and
  legal advice for fathers.*

womenswire.com
Practical financial advice for women.

Acknowledgments

This book, conceived in love and tears, has been birthed with the help of hundreds of people.

To my mate, Thomas, thank you for your strength and self-lessness, for your support, and, most importantly, for your unwavering love.

To my former husband, J C M, the father of our children, for all the years together; thank you for helping me become the woman I am.

To my children, grandchildren, other family, and friends, a million kisses for your patience, your encouragement, and your loyalty.

To my mentors, Helen Jo Smith, Twilo Jones, Jim Coulter, and Judy Wardell-Halliday, my gratitude for your indomitable spirits.

To my agents, Anne Edelstein and Laura Williams at the Edelstein Literary Agency, blessings to you both for your faith in me and this book.

To my editor, Patty Gift, and all the staff at Three Rivers Press, my appreciation for your warmth, insight, and guidance.

Finally, to all those interviewed, and those whose books and lives have been my inspiration, my heartfelt thanks.

Index

For further information,
consultations, or seminars
you can contact
Susan Allison at:

Hidden Falls Center
P.O. Box 1570
Felton, CA 95018

Or by telephone at:
(866) 268-2121

If you enjoyed excerpts
of the author's poetry at the
beginning of each chapter,
you can call and order
her new book:

Breathing Room:
The Leaving of a Marriage—
Selected Poems.